Controversies in Management

As the role of the typical manager has become more diverse, the phenomenon of management has become increasingly puzzling. As demand for formal management training, theories and qualifications has increased, so our ability to think critically about management has lessened. And at a time of organizational and environmental turbulence, the question of effective management is more complex than ever.

Unpicking the puzzles faced by both the manager and the student of management, *Controversies in Management* is an introductory guide to the major issues of management, organization and knowledge, asking questions of our 'guru' culture and raising debates on so-called expert thinking. Written from the viewpoint that the most effective managers are those that can think for themselves and put aside the advice of the management 'guru', *Controversies in Management* is a topical, challenging and thought-provoking study.

Thoroughly revised and reorganized, this second edition features two completely new chapters that cover gender issues in management, debates on globalization, postmodernity and the future of management. Designed to bring readers into the debate, rather than simply providing a framework of answers, this new edition also includes an orientation questionnaire, discussion questions for each area covered and further reading suggestions.

Dr Alan Thomas is Senior Lecturer in Sociology and Organizational Behaviour at Manchester Business School, University of Manchester. He is widely published in the field of organizational behaviour and management studies.

D0081735

Controversies in Management

Issues, debates, answers

Second Edition

Alan Berkeley Thomas

Routledge
Taylor & Francis Group

LONDON AND NEW YORK

First edition published 1993 by Routledge

This edition published 2003 by Routledge
11 New Fetter Lane, London EC4P 4EE

Simultaneously published in the USA and Canada
by Routledge
29 West 35th Street, New York, NY 10001

Routledge is an imprint of the Taylor & Francis Group

© 1993, 2003 Alan Berkeley Thomas

Typeset in Times New Roman by
Florence Production Ltd, Stoodleigh, Devon
Printed and bound in Great Britain by
The Cromwell Press, Towbridge, Wiltshire

British Library Cataloguing in Publication Data
A catalogue record for this book is available from the British Library

Library of Congress Cataloguing in Publication Data
A catalog record for this book has been requested

ISBN 0–415–26900–8 (hbk)
ISBN 0–415–26901–6 (pbk)

For Brian Noel Lewis, 1929–1986

Contents

Illustrations

Preface

This book deals with a selection of controversial topics in the field of management studies. The aim of this second edition is the same as when the original appeared nearly ten years ago, namely to encourage critical thinking about management. This kind of thinking is, I believe, essential for success as a management student and as a management practitioner.

This revised and extended edition includes two entirely new chapters. One deals with the issue of gender and management and the other with the future of management in a globalizing, post-modern world. Both issues amply meet the criteria for controversy set out at the beginning of the book! Elsewhere new material has been introduced and references updated wherever possible. Questions for discussion and suggestions for further reading have also been added to each chapter to encourage readers to engage in controversy themselves. An 'orientation questionnaire' will be found at the end of Chapter 1 as an aid to getting started.

I would like to thank the following for their help at various times and in various ways: Peter Anthony, D.H. Burt, Ron 'Nobby' Clark, Lynn Dalton, Ardha Danieli, Mary Gorman, Gerard Hodgkinson, Paula Hyde, Mary Ann Kernan, Bob Lee, Omar Mughal, B.S. Pullan, Heather Spiro, Haridimos Tsoukas and Karin Winroth.

Special thanks to the anonymous reviewers for their helpful suggestions for revisions, to Kathy Kirby and the staff of the MBS Library and Information Service for their excellent support, and to my editor, Catriona King, and to Rachel Crookes for all their work behind the scenes.

Alan Thomas
Manchester Business School

Abbreviations

ASEAN	Association of South East Asian Nations
BAM	British Academy of Management
EU	European Union
HRM	Human Resource Management
ICT	Information and Communication Technology
MERCOSUR	Mercardo Comun del Sur (South American Common Market)
MNC	Multinational Corporation
TNC	Transnational Corporation
UN	United Nations
WTO	World Trade Organization

1 Controversies in management

A writer may try his best to draw a map of how things are, that will be equally valid for all; but all he can really do is to paint a picture of what he sees from the unique and transient viewpoint which is his alone.

Vickers (1970)

Our task is to look at the world and see it whole.

Schumacher (1995)

It's not easy being a manager today. There's a lot to do, a lot to understand, a lot to learn. And it doesn't seem to be getting any easier.

Once upon a time things were different. Management hardly existed, there were no management theories, no management books, no management gurus and no management qualifications to be earned through study. Life was a lot simpler – but also a lot shorter. Today, of course, all that has changed.

Modern management emerged as a decidedly indistinct occupation in nineteenth-century Britain. It grew remarkably in the twentieth century as industrialism spread around the world. In a relatively brief span of time, management was transformed from a barely acknowledged sideline in a world of rumbustious entrepreneurship (Pollard, 1965) into an occupation of vital importance. The greater diversity and technical sophistication of production processes and products stemming from developments in science and technology, and the emergence of very large, complex organizations have played an important part in increasing the demand for managers and the status of management. Yet the quest has not been simply for more managers but for better quality managers and the more effective management of people and organizations. Both experienced managers and those who aspire to become managers have been urged to bring more professionalism to their work, to rely less on gut feelings, intuition and experience and to pay more attention to the contribution which the management sciences can make to the practice of management. Thus as the scale and stature of management has grown so too has the volume of research and writing on management and management processes and the provisions for the transmission of this knowledge to managers.

Each year thousands of new books and articles are published on management and there can be few aspects of the field lacking their own substantial literature and even their own specialized journals. Within this growing literature of management it is not difficult to find considerable differences of view on its nature and purposes, its meaning and significance, on how it is done and how it should be done. Modern managers thus have to cope not only with a complex and rapidly changing world but also with increasingly diverse ways of thinking about that world, of understanding it and of managing it. Coping with diversity has thus become a central challenge for the modern manager, for in many ways, management, both as a practical activity and as a subject for study, is puzzling.

This book sets out to explore some of these puzzles. It deals with a number of key topics in the broadly defined field of management and organization that have been a focus of considerable debate and dispute over the years and which look likely to continue to be so in the foreseeable future. It aims to treat each of these topics as a controversial issue, laying out the main arguments and points of contention and then drawing some conclusions about the current state of each dispute.

When well-informed people disagree about important matters, we are faced with a number of ways of reacting. We can wait until the 'experts' have reached a consensus, we can ignore expert opinion altogether in favour of whatever variety of commonsense appeals to us, or we can attempt to invest our energies in coming to grips with the disputed issues in order to develop our own, well-considered conclusions. Partly because the world in which managers work has become more complex and less stable the first option, of waiting until the experts come up with the answers, is today less viable than it once might have been. There are too many 'experts' busily constructing widely differing maps of management for it to be reasonable to expect to find one that is 'equally valid for all'. Yet to rely solely on our own, personal maps, without regard for the efforts of the professional map-makers, means placing needless reliance on the inevitable narrowness of our unique experience. A more realistic if more difficult and demanding alternative is thus to recognize controversy where it exists and to engage with it fruitfully. Why this needs to be done and how this can be done will be explained in the rest of this chapter.

The messy world of management

Perhaps the most obvious question we can ask about managers is 'what do they do?' In the next two chapters we will be looking at some of the answers to this question in detail, but for the moment we can say that at the very least managers have to know what to do and how to do it and they then have to get it done. However they would like to see themselves, managers are not simply 'action men' (or women); like any normal human being they think as well as act using knowledge, in the broadest sense, as a basis for their actions. Getting to grips with management therefore involves, and has always involved, the acquisition of knowledge and skill together with the ability to apply them *in situ*. Current conditions have, however, made these processes much less straightforward than they once were. At this point I think it may be helpful to tell a little story.

Once upon a time, management was a simple affair. A manager's job was to get things done through people. Managers' goals were clear and were derived from the organization's goals which were few in number, explicitly stated and not in conflict with each other. Managers knew what had to be done to achieve these goals on the basis of their own and the organization's accumulated experience, and used the authority that was given to them by their position in the organization in order to get subordinates to do it. Subordinates were committed to the organization and respectful of managerial authority. There was plenty of time to think and plan and tasks were pursued within an explicit and consistent set of rules and procedures that were well understood and widely accepted by everyone. Conflicts were few and could readily be resolved by resort to higher authority. There was a fundamental consensus among employees that work organizations were dedicated to the betterment of themselves and society as a whole by means of the production and distribution of wealth. The organization and the wider world in which it operated were stable and well understood and the organization grew steadily, helping to advance the progress of society. At the heart of the organization were the managerial problem-solvers, smoothing the way to success and receiving due recognition for their efforts. The possibilities for personal and organizational growth seemed unlimited. And they all lived happily ever after.

Those were the days! At least they might have been but for the fact that they probably never existed. Yet the managerial world depicted in this story still holds a certain fascination for managers and particularly for those who are coming to management for the first time (Lawrence, 1986; Sayles, 1989). The trouble with it is that it represents an attractive but idealized view of the realities of management, one that drastically oversimplifies the complex world in which managers actually operate. That world is probably better described by such words as ambiguity, change, uncertainty, recalcitrance, improvisation, conflict and mess rather than stability, order, consensus, clarity and certainty. Indeed Ackoff (1979) has argued that managers do not so much solve problems in a well-ordered world as manage messes; and all the signs are that the world is getting messier by the minute.

Understandably, the prospect of being a manager of messes is not one that is easily accepted by aspiring managers and particularly not by those whose previous education and inclinations have led them to adopt an 'engineering' view of the nature of management. Such a view portrays management as a process of control in which the application of reliable techniques leads to the achievement of indisputably desirable ends, such as profit, lower unit costs, and economic growth, and so on. Managing an organization is seen as rather like piloting a flying-machine, albeit an unusually complicated one, whereby the manager sits at the control deck surrounded by an array of levers, switches and buttons which are manipulated according to sound engineering principles in order to navigate the craft to an agreed destination. Learning to be a manager, on this view, is to do with acquiring knowledge of the map which depicts the links between the control devices and the behaviour of the machine. The map itself portrays the findings of 'management science'. Time, I think, for another little story.

Once upon a time there were no managerial sciences. Managers managed according to commonsense based on their day-to-day experience. A few of these managers chose to set down the lessons of their experience on paper in the form of codes, principles and laws of management. They intended these to serve as guidelines or even mandatory instructions for future managers to follow. Then one day social scientists started to investigate managerial behaviour and organizations. As a result of their researches they concluded that the codes and principles were inadequate because they did not seem to hold up when subjected to rigorous logical and empirical scrutiny. The processes of effective management and organization looked to be much more complex and much more difficult to capture in the form of scientific laws and generalizations than the early management writers had thought. Some managers were dismayed and decided to ignore the social sciences for ever more. Some social scientists decided to press on with their research in the hope that better 'engineering' principles might be produced one day, but this tended to create even more complexity. Some management teachers decided that the best way to keep the social science baby in the managerial bath was by throwing out a good deal of the uncertainty surrounding managerial science. Result – no one lived happily ever after (except for a few management 'gurus' – some of whom we will be meeting later in this book).

Of course this story should not be taken too literally. It is only a story. But the point to emphasize is that the machine view of organizations and its associated engineering conception of management which is implicit in current conceptions of managerial science is not wholly invalid, but rather, that it is limited and incomplete. In fact, I would suggest that there are some aspects of management which are machine-like and which involve the implementation of predictable routines. But much of management and perhaps the most significant parts of managerial practice come much closer to the messiness referred to by Ackoff. As it was once put to me, managing an organization is like dealing with a very jellyish jellyfish – and one that is usually capable of stinging!

One implication of the idea that management is about coping with a messy world is that management in inherently controversial. A messy world is one in which the connections between means and ends are poorly understood so that there is ample room for significant disagreement over what to do and how to do it. Moreover, a messy world is one in which there is no consensus on values; even if we know how to achieve particular ends, we may still disagree about whether those ends are worth pursuing or about the priority that should be given to one end as against another. What it comes down to saying is that management is less like the process of controlling a machine than it is like seeking to influence events and processes under conditions of uncertainty and value conflict. It also means that when learning to manage, whether at the workplace or in the lecture theatre, managers are faced with controversy.

Critical thinking in management

There have been a number of attempts to specify the skills and competencies needed by managers if they are to be effective (Boyatzis, 1982; Burgoyne and Stuart, 1976; Jacobs, 1989; Kotter, 1982a) but critical thinking is one skill that is seldom given much prominence. No doubt this is partly because research on the identification of managerial skills has usually been based upon observations of managers at work, and while the products of thinking may be observed, thinking itself cannot be (Carroll and Gillen, 1987). The lack of attention given to critical thinking probably also reflects the values of a management culture in which thinking, pure and simple, is perhaps not quite proper and certainly not something that should be allowed to get in the way of the 'man of action'. Punch (1981) caught the flavour of this view when he referred to management as one of the 'non-thinking professions'.

There are some writers, however, who have drawn attention to the importance of critical thinking for effective management. Brookfield (1987) has summarized a number of these contributions and also provides a helpful analysis of the nature and uses of critical thought. He identifies four components of the critical thinking process.

1   *Identifying and challenging assumptions*: much of our thinking and behaviour is based on unexamined assumptions which we take for granted and of which we may hardly be aware. One aim of critical thinking is to unearth these hidden assumptions, to check their validity or plausibility, and to modify them if they are found wanting.
2   *Creating contextual awareness*: this involves becoming aware of how the social, political and historical circumstances of the times in which we live conditions our ideas and assumptions. The way we think and act is not simply a natural and inevitable given but is a product of historical and social circumstances.
3   *Identifying alternatives*: contextual awareness opens up the possibility of identifying or imagining different contexts in which things are done differently. Alternatives are examined to see if they can be adopted.

4   *Developing reflective scepticism*: awareness of alternatives encourages a sceptical attitude towards fixed and final beliefs, ultimate explanations and universal truths. Accepted ideas and practices are not regarded as inevitable, necessary or above questioning. Critical thinkers are unwilling to accept that authoritative pronouncements are automatically beyond rational justification and challenge. They believe, as Carr and Kemmis (1986) have put it, that someone who claims to know 'must convince us that their ideas survive critical examination: that they can be justified, that they can survive attempts to show them to be false, and that they are not incredible.'

When applied to management a critical approach might yield the sorts of inquiries shown in Box 1.1. In addition, Brookfield (1987) suggests that critical thinking is a key skill that needs to be brought to the management of such tasks as: strategic planning, which involves devising and evaluating alternative business scenarios and strategies; effective decision-making, which often requires critical questioning of assumptions and the ability to deal with fuzzy, non-quantifiable issues; creative problem-solving, in which conventional ways of thinking must be challenged; situational leadership, in which managers must be able to think out the links between alternative styles of leading and local circumstances; entrepreneurial risk-taking, which involves sceptical scrutiny of accepted ways of doing business; research and development activities, which depend for their success on unconventional ways of thinking; and organizational team-building, in which team members must be able to develop ways of coming to terms with views and outlooks which may be very different from their own. Brookfield concludes that critical thinking can in fact be seen 'as the central element in improving organizational performance'.

Critical thinking can be contrasted with its opposite, uncritical thinking. Uncritical thinking is the kind in which we accept commonsense assumptions at face value without systematically checking their validity, deny or ignore the significance of context for influencing beliefs and practices, fail to seek out and evaluate alternatives, and cling rigidly and unquestioningly to dogmas and authoritative pronouncements. Critical thinking is, then, not so much a step-by-step process as an attitude of mind, one which places emphasis on the need to ask 'why?'.

The value of critical thinking lies ultimately in its ability to enhance our freedom, even to increase our chances of survival. So long as our assumptions and habits of thought and action 'work' we can, if we choose, live out our lives in a mechanical, unreflective way. But in an unstable, fast-changing world, if our assumptions fail to keep up with reality we may find ourselves drawn into ever more destructive and self-defeating circles. By failing to recognize that the context of our lives is changing, by following 'tried-and-trusted' ways of thinking and acting as if what worked today has always worked and will always work, we may end up living in an unmanageable world of our own making.

Box 1.1 Critical thinking in management

1   Identifying and challenging assumptions about:
    - the nature of management, its tasks, skills and purposes
    - the nature of people and why they behave as they do
    - the nature of organizations
    - learning, knowing and acting
    - values, goals and ends.

2   Creating contextual awareness by understanding:
    - how management has developed historically
    - how management is conceived of in other societies
    - the implications of different industrial, organizational, economic, political and cultural contexts for management
    - the interrelation between organizations and society.

3   Identifying alternatives by:
    - becoming aware of the variety of ways in which managing and organizing can be undertaken
    - inventing and imagining new ways of managing and organizing
    - specifying new goals and priorities.

4   Developing reflective scepticism by:
    - adopting a questioning, quizzical attitude
    - recognizing the limitations of much that passes for knowledge in the management field
    - knowing how to evaluate knowledge claims
    - developing a resistance to dogma and propaganda
    - being able to distinguish systematic argument and reasoned judgement from sloppy thinking, simplistic formulae and sophistry.

To think critically is not, however, to adopt a posture of total scepticism, treating everything and everyone with suspicion and doubt. Nor should a critical attitude be equated with a negative one; positive commitment is a desirable outcome of critical thinking. As Brookfield (1987) says, 'We can commit ourselves wholeheartedly to an idea, social structure, or cause and still be critically aware. The point is that this commitment is informed; we have arrived at our convictions after a period of questioning, analysis, and reflection.' The kind of know-nothing scepticism which leads to amoral, relativistic nihilism in which anything goes and nothing really matters represents a critical approach taken to an absurd extreme and that is certainly not what is advocated here.

No one, of course, can think critically about everything. Life would become impossible if we had to scrutinize every assumption we make about the world so there is much that we have to take on trust. But when it comes to the most important aspects of our lives critical thinking comes into its own. This is particularly the case in our working lives when we face key decisions which are surrounded by considerable uncertainty. Under these conditions, which have become more prevalent in an era of rapid change, we are very likely to face complex issues whose resolution is open to dispute – that is to say we encounter controversies. And adequate handling of controversies, I suggest, demands critical thinking.

What are 'controversies'?

Since this book deals with controversies, it is important to examine what we mean by the term and why we think they are worthy of attention. We begin by considering the tricky matter of definitions.

In order to justify the designation of any topic as controversial we need to be able to show that it meets the appropriate definitional criteria. However, as Wellington (1986) has pointed out, this is problematic because the question of what are the defining criteria of a controversy is itself controversial! For example, a definition offered by Bailey (1975) has been disputed by Dearden (1981) whose own conclusions have themselves been challenged by Gardner (1984). Since it would not be helpful if we were to become bogged down in this 'controversy about controversy' and since there are no clearly agreed criteria to hand, we can best proceed by stating our own view on the matter as best we can.

We begin by noting that controversies can be considered both as issues and as processes. As processes, controversies are debates, arguments or disputes engaged in by at least two parties. They may thus be considered as a special kind of conflict which 'occurs when one person's ideas, opinions, conclusions, theories and information are incompatible with another's when they discuss problems and make decisions' (Tjosvold, 1985). Controversy in this sense is something *you do*. As issues, however, controversies are the objects of the process of controversy; they are what the controversy *is about*. The problem of definition mainly arises over the latter because although we may have no difficulty in agreeing on whether or not we are witnessing parties engaged in argument and dispute, we may find it much harder to do so when it comes to deciding whether a particular issue should be considered controversial.

Three criteria for designating an issue controversial are proposed here.

1   For something to be a controversial issue it must be an object of dispute. If everyone agrees about some matter it cannot be considered controversial. However, the criterion of being disputed is not sufficient to define a controversial issue.
2   For an issue to be controversial it must also be considered to be important. As Gardner (1984) has argued, to say that ' "It was controversial but no-one thought it to be of any importance" is a contradiction.'

When people debate unimportant matters we might say that they are not dealing with a controversial issue but with a mundane dispute.

3 To be considered controversial an issue must be a focus of dispute and be considered important but it must also be the focus of an actual debate. This means that simply because one party disputes some important matter this does not mean it can be regarded as a controversial issue. The matter must be accepted as being contentious by those who hold opposed views and must be actively debated. So, for example, there are those who still assert that the Earth is flat but this is not a controversial issue because those who disagree do not regard the matter as open to dispute and no active process of controversy takes place.

Clearly controversies arise in every field of thought and there is no way of knowing precisely what will become controversial. At one time, for example, it was not controversial to assert that the Earth was the centre of the Universe just as it is not controversial now to assert that it isn't. But we can see that controversies tend to differ in their significance irrespective of historical circumstances. What we might call 'private' controversies focus on issues of very limited scope. A dispute between two friends on whether synchronized swimming ought to be considered as an Olympic sport might be regarded as of this kind. At the other end of the scale be have 'public' controversies which engage national or even international debate; on the implications of global warming, on capital punishment and on political matters generally. Somewhere in between we can distinguish 'local' controversies which occur, for example, within specific fields of thought such as physics, history or philosophy and which tend to be open mainly to those actively engaged in those fields. It is this 'local' species of controversy with which we are dealing in this book when we refer to controversies in management.

Perhaps I have said enough to give a flavour of the way in which controversies have been conceived here. Our working definition of a management controversy is therefore that it is an important issue in the field of management that has been a focus of active debate. Such issues have not been of purely 'private' interest but seldom either of 'public' concern even if some of them perhaps should be. Rather, they are ones that have been considered important by management thinkers and theorists.

It is important to emphasize at this point that the issues discussed in later chapters are not ones I regard as being of concern only to scholars. I have no wish to embroil the reader in not simply 'another sterile academic controversy' (Lupton, 1971) but a whole series of them! The issues discussed here seem to me to be of practical significance to managers. I have therefore tried in each case to indicate the significance of the debate for the practice of management. Mention of this takes us to a further question – why bother with controversies?

Why bother with controversies?

> 'You see', one director explained, 'the Chairman and I went to the States one time. He went to Harvard and I went to MIT. He came back saying that you mustn't have wide spans of control, and I came back saying that you mustn't have long lines of command. So we looked at each other and said "To hell with it" and got on with our jobs.'
>
> (Klein, 1976)

By definition, controversies are matters of dispute and often of the kind in which contradictory positions are adopted in relation to the same issue. In the story recounted above the issue is to do with effective forms of organization structure, one view advocating narrow spans of control (a small number of subordinates to be responsible to any one superior) which implies many organizational levels, while the other advocates the opposite. Not surprisingly, such diametrically opposed views might well tempt us to react, as these managers did, by ignoring the whole business in the interests of getting on with the job. Is there any sense, then, in taking controversies seriously?

Needless to say, I think that there is. As a response to what we have called mundane disputes, 'to hell with it' might well be appropriate but when we are confronted by important issues this will hardly do. The behaviour of the director and chairman might have been different if the problem of span of control had been regarded as a life-and-death issue upon which the whole future of their firm and perhaps their own careers had depended. In that case they would have been obliged, as responsible managers, to have made the best resolution of the issues as they could. They would have needed to explore the problem, seeking out evidence and expert opinion, and to have debated and deliberated upon it before reaching a conclusion. By doing this they would be seeking to develop an informed basis for judgement which would enable them to justify whatever decision they eventually took and so discharge their obligation to make *responsible* decisions. In the end, they still have to make a decision one way or the other but this does not mean that the way in which the decision is reached is inconsequential, for justifiable decisions have to be well-considered ones and that requires careful analysis, critical thinking and systematic debate. In a court of law, for example, the outcome of a trial is either guilty or not guilty but no one would suggest that tossing a coin is a responsible way of deciding which it should be. The main reason for taking controversies seriously, then, is because if we don't bother with them they will very likely come to bother us.

As Tjosvold (1985) has indicated, many aspects of organizational management are controversial and the future is likely to see more controversy rather than less. This is because organizations and the environments in which they operate are becoming increasingly diverse and less stable which means that there are many more differences, of outlook, circumstance, culture and values around. The likelihood of competing views about such matters as strategy, structure and in general how to manage seems much greater than in more placid times. This being so, developing the skills for the successful management of controversies becomes increasingly important.

The controversies discussed in this book cannot, however, be those which confront my or your organization as it is now in all its real and rich complexity. Rather, we are dealing with controversies in management thought, that is in the body of thinking and theorizing (which go hand in hand as I shall argue in Chapter 4) which has implications for management practice. The rationale for troubling with controversies in these fields will be developed in a later section but at this point we can say that one reason for drawing attention to them is because if we do not do so we run the risk of misrepresenting those fields. As Dearden (1981) has put it:

> to teach a subject in a way that makes no reference to the controversial parts of it is to misrepresent it. This misrepresentation may arise simply through giving the impression that a subject is a monolithic block of certain knowledge which requires only that we turn to the appropriate authority in order for any problem concerning it to be solved. In this way the truth-criteria, critical standards and verification procedures appropriate to the subject may never themselves be mentioned. If, however, controversial matters are raised, then immediately there is an open invitation explicitly to consider how they might be settled.

Since just about every important topic dealt with by the management disciplines could well be regarded as controversial, this is an important consideration. To treat these fields as the embodiments of absolute truth might indeed be to seriously misrepresent the current state of management thought.

What then is the status of the management disciplines and most especially those that deal with behavioural and organizational affairs? Are they perhaps monolithic blocks of certain knowledge that can be absorbed by practitioners with confidence like a well-tested drug? If so, to dwell on their controversial aspects might be at best a luxury and at worst an irritating distraction.

Anderson, Hughes and Sharrock (1985) have distinguished between what they call 'knowledge subjects' and 'argument subjects'. Knowledge subjects are those like physics (and perhaps mathematics and engineering) in which 'there is a received body of information about the subject-matter of the discipline which is passed on to the incoming student'. Argument subjects, on the other hand, are those like philosophy which consist of 'dissenting points of view ... normally presented to the student through the presentation of the different ideas or schools of thought, often in the form of a history of the controversies which have brought the discipline to its present disagreements'. Most disciplines, of course, fall somewhere between these two extremes and none consists entirely of knowledge or entirely of argument. Modern physics is far from being free from controversy and even philosophers occasionally agree on something!

The management disciplines are often, even typically, presented as if they were more like knowledge subjects than argument subjects, more like physics than philosophy. In part that reflects a wish for these disciplines to be seen to be useful but in part also a reluctance to wash one's dirty intellectual linen in public. This is not to deny that they contain a good deal of 'knowledge' but, rather, to suggest that a balanced view of them is required, one that gives a proper place to argument alongside the transmission of 'facts'. Management as a discipline seems closer to history than it is to either physics or philosophy, just as management as an occupation seems more like that of an army officer or a politician than of an engineer or poet.

Why controversies in management?

As we have seen, controversies are essentially disputes about ideas, but disagreements about ideas are seldom far from disagreements about action. Even the well-known scholastic dispute about the number of angels that could stand of the head of a pin had implications for practical activity, if not for everyone at least for the theological scholars who were party to the dispute. In the eighteenth century, when what is now the famous Harvard University was a theological college, scholars worked hard and long on such seemingly bizarre topics as 'When Balaam's Ass Spoke, Was There Any Change in its Organs?' and 'When the Shadow Went back on the Sun-dial of Hezekiah, Did the Shadows Go Back on all Sun-dials?' (Sexton, 1967). I do not know whether these controversies were ever satisfactorily resolved but they were clearly important to theologians and had implications for theological practice.

The relationship between knowledge and action in management has been characterized by Lupton (1984) in terms of the link between 'fields of knowledge' and 'fields of action'. The fields of action are the organizational settings in which managers work and in which managerial tasks are pursued on an everyday basis. It is there that managers encounter the challenges, problems and difficulties of practical management and it is there that practical controversies emerge and are resolved. The fields of knowledge, on the other hand, consist of the management disciplines and the activities of research, writing and teaching that embody them. These fields are inhabited primarily by scholars and it is there that one encounters management theory and management science. There too one encounters controversy. Indeed, the fields of knowledge are, we might say, the home of the professional controversialist because scepticism and a willingness to question prevailing assumptions and habits of thought are part of the professional duty of the scholar.

The fields of knowledge which deal most directly with management, and particularly with the behaviour of people and organizations which is the focus of this book, are the fields of social science, and the kind of knowledge produced by social science is inherently open to dispute.

It is acknowledged by many philosophers of science today that all scientific knowledge, even of the most seemingly certain and final kind, is provisional and open to revision. But this is especially the case for the social sciences. Quite why this is so is itself a matter of considerable argument and debate, but four reasons can be suggested.

1   Scientists, whether natural or social, never have direct access to the phenomena they study. Scientists use theories, concepts and models in order to interpret experience so that our ideas about how the world works are heavily dependent on the initial assumptions we make. As Morgan (1997) has shown, if you think that organizations are rather like 'machines' instead of, say, 'organisms' or 'psychic prisons' the sorts of evidence you will look for to back up your claims will differ and the implications your findings have for action will differ too. Presumably you oil a machine, feed an organism and escape, if you can, from a psychic prison! Different interpretations of the world are always possible, yielding different 'maps' which will be more or less valid depending on your starting point.

2   Even when assumptions are agreed, the methodological difficulties of producing compelling evidence in support of specific theories are formidable. Scientists deal, for example, in generalizations; they want to know not only how this organization works now but how all organizations work, not what it is that motivates this person but what it is that motivates anyone. To do this they need to draw on evidence gathered from representative samples, yet studies based on such samples are the exception rather than the rule in the organizational sciences (Freeman, 1986). Even collecting valid and reliable data is a problematic process; questionnaires may be poorly understood, interviews may yield distorted information, observation may change the behaviour being observed, documents and records may be incomplete or inaccessible. By comparison the difficulties facing the chemist or physicist seem pallid.

3   Human systems are inherently open (Sayer, 1992). This means that their behaviour is affected by processes which occur outside them and these processes may be neither predictable nor intelligible. Although all systems are open, some of them can be sealed off and studied under controlled laboratory conditions. Apart from the difficulty of doing this with humans and the impossibility of doing so with organizations, even when this is done the system at hand is taken out of its context.

Watching how people behave in a sealed room may help us to understand some aspects of human behaviour but we must not expect them
to behave in the same ways when they are at work or at home. The
context makes a difference to what we are likely to observe.

4   The various contributors to management knowledge have different
goals and priorities. Thorngate (1976) has argued that it is desirable that
our 'knowledge maps', or theories, possess three main characteristics
– generality, simplicity and accuracy. A general theory explains the
behaviour of all the units of interest. So for example, a general theory
of motivation would explain what motivates anyone. A simple theory
employs the smallest possible number of factors in its explanation. A
simple theory of motivation might propose that people are motivated
entirely by just one factor such as greed. An accurate theory predicts
outcomes perfectly. In the case of our hypothetical motivation theory,
if we could measure 'greed' then once we know how greedy any individual is we could predict correctly their level of motivation! So theories with all three properties look to be very useful since they are
accurate, easy to understand and are of wide applicability.

But here's the bad news. Thorngate also proposes that social science theories can never possess all three properties at the same time. Because the
social world is so complex, it may be possible to attain any two but this
is always at the exclusion of the third. So, for example, if you want a
general and accurate theory, it will not be simple but complex. Similarly,
if you want a simple and general theory, it will be of only limited accuracy. And if you want an accurate and simple theory, it won't be general
but will apply only to a rather limited range of the things you're interested
in. That, says Thorngate, is simply the way it is; there's nothing that can
be done about it. Don't waste your time trying to create the perfect theory
that has all three characteristics. That is impossible.

Figure 1.1 represents these ideas by a triangle, each side representing a
commitment to the two characteristics it links, the characteristic on the
opposite apex being non-attainable. On each side I have placed a group
of contributors and users of management knowledge, the scientists, the
management 'gurus' and the managers. Each of these stakeholder groups
prioritizes two characteristics and thereby sacrifices the third. Scientists
are mainly interested in producing general, accurate theories. If they turn
out to be complicated, that's too bad. Gurus, on the other hand, are mainly
interested in general, simple theories. If they turn out to be inaccurate well,
they weren't expecting to win the Nobel Prize. Managers are mainly interested in simple, accurate theories that apply or work in their particular
circumstances.

It should not therefore be surprising to find that:

•   Managers tend to find 'academic' theories difficult to understand and
not obviously related to their specific problems.

- Managers tend to find gurus' theories easier to understand but often inaccurate – they don't necessarily produce the expected results.
- Scientists tend to be critical of gurus because the gurus' theories lack accuracy.
- Gurus tend to be critical of scientists because scientists' theories are too complicated and 'academic'.

If Thorngate's argument is correct (and I think it is at least plausible) it indicates that there will always be a gap between the maps presented by scientists and gurus and the world as it is perceived by managers. Managers must therefore expect to have to work to 'customize' these theories – to 'fit' them to their own situations. They cannot expect 'off-the-shelf' solutions to their problems, if, that is, they want solutions that stand a reasonable chance of working. Both scientists' and gurus' theories may help. But they will never be sufficient and must always be supplemented with managers' own theorizing. Managers must become map-makers for themselves.

Unfortunately, the understandable demand for useful knowledge among managers offers a powerful disincentive to acknowledge the uncomfortable fact that most of the products of the social sciences are controversial. As Shipman (1972) says:

> But in all social science there is a pressure to produce results and produce them in unambiguous form. Foundations, departments and businesses giving money for research expect results as a sign that their money has been well spent ... Yet certainty and clarity are often

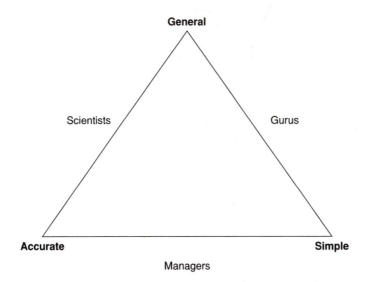

Figure 1.1 Choices and stakeholders in management theory

impossible in the messy arena of everyday life. The ambiguous results and imperfect methods are cleaned up for public consumption. In the research marketplace as elsewhere it is all things bright and beautiful that sell.

In the management world too it's bright and beautiful things that sell and there are plenty of 'behavioural entrepreneurs' (Watson, 1986) around to sell them. But we should not confuse form with substance; just because it looks good, that doesn't necessarily mean it's going to work.

Can controversies be resolved?

Our inclination to take controversies seriously might well hinge on whether we believe they are capable of resolution. Controversy can be fun but it has to be said that someone looking for kicks will find plenty of other ways of getting them. Unless we are willing to indulge in controversy for its own sake our primary motivation is likely to be because we need to resolve the controversy so that we can, like the managers mentioned earlier, get on with the job. What is the likelihood that controversies can be resolved?

We can distinguish two senses in which a controversy can be said to have been resolved. The first sense refers to our adopting a position on the controversy by satisfying ourselves as best we can as to which of the competing arguments is to be preferred or by formulating a position which goes beyond these arguments. In this case we reach a 'personal' resolution which enables us to move on but which acknowledges that the issue remains controversial. In this sense, all controversies can be resolved. In the second sense, we mean a situation in which the controversy is resolved to *everyone's* satisfaction. This is what we can call a 'public' resolution in which case the issue ceases to be controversial and sinks back into the grey realm of the accepted, the taken-for-granted and the obvious. Here there is no guarantee that all controversies can be resolved yet it is just this sort of resolution that we would most like to have; unresolved controversies force us to expend energy and effort to reach personal resolutions which are still open to dispute whereas public resolutions free us from the need to engage in controversy at all at least on the issue at hand.

We can identify three grounds which underlie controversial issues, each of which may occur simultaneously: facts, values and frameworks. As we move from facts to frameworks the chances of 'public' resolution become increasingly problematic. Factual controversies are resolvable in principle so long as there is agreement on which facts are relevant. Some examples would be:

- Who assassinated President Kennedy? The issue remains unresolved in the absence of certain key facts, but were these to be available the matter could be resolved.

- Was the man who committed suicide in Spandau Jail in 1987 Rudolf Hess or an impostor? As above.
- The Moon always presents the same face to observers on Earth. Is the hidden face cratered like the one we can see or not? With the advent of space satellites this issue has been resolved. The hidden face is much like the one we can see.
- Are corn circles hoaxes, natural phenomena or the work of alien beings? Unresolved but potentially open to resolution on factual grounds.

Clearly factual controversies are amenable to resolution and many have been resolved. But there is no guarantee of this and an issue may remain open indefinitely if the requisite evidence is unavailable. We may never know, for example, who murdered the Princes in the Tower.

Value controversies present a much more difficult problem. It is apparent, for example, that someone who believes that it is always wrong to kill another human being may never be able to agree with someone who advocates capital punishment. Although value disputes may be resolved by an appeal to facts which lead to a reappraisal of values (Meehan, 1969) this cannot be assured. As Mills (1970) has put it:

> when there are values so firmly and so consistently held by genuinely conflicting interests that the conflict cannot be resolved by logical analysis and factual investigation, then the role of reason in that human affair seems at an end . . . in the end we may be reduced to mere assertion and counter-assertion . . . In the end, if the end comes, we just have to beat those who disagree with us over the head; let us hope the end comes seldom. In the meantime, being as reasonable as we are able to be, we ought all to argue.

Some examples of value controversies might be:

- Is abortion justifiable?
- Should there be a free market in health care and education?
- Should medical experiments be permitted on human embryos?
- Should religious groups be allowed to set up their own schools?

In practice it may be difficult to distinguish clearly between factually based and value-based controversies, this distinction itself being a matter of considerable contention. In management such issues often tend to be fused despite a tendency to treat matters with value implications as if they were purely factual, technical issues. Debates about 'directive' as opposed to 'participative' styles of management, for example, are often treated as if they were simply to do with the relative technical effectiveness of each. But whether we decide to tell people what to do or encourage them to tell us what to do is more than a technical issue; it also involves matters of values concerning employees' and managerial rights and those are essentially moral problems.

The third and most problematic grounds for controversy is what Dearden (1981) calls 'frameworks of understanding' (or, more technically, 'paradigms'; see Chapter 4). In this case what is at issue is not simply facts and values but the very framework of concepts within which matters of fact and value may be discussed. What is disputed here is not only specific facts and explanations but what it is that is to count as a fact or explanation. The classic example of this type of controversy is that between theologians and scientists on the origins of the Universe; the only acceptable basis for explanation to the scientist, observational data, is regarded as inadequate by the theologian. In such cases we reach the outer limits of what might be considered a legitimate controversy. Because there are no overlapping or agreed grounds for the dispute it might well be called pseudo-controversy in which the parties are talking not to each other but past each other. These controversies seem to be the least promising in terms of the possibility of public resolution.

Some possible examples, depending on your point of view, are:

- Is the Shroud of Turin evidence of the divinity of Christ?
- Is analytical psychology (e.g. Freud's psychoanalysis) more valid than behaviourism ('rat psychology')?
- Are human beings any different from complex machines?
- Are ideas more real than things or the other way around?

In conclusion, it looks as if no controversy can be guaranteed to be open to public resolution. Factually based controversies hold out the best prospects, value-based controversies seem less promising although they certainly can be informed by factual evidence, while framework-based controversies offer little hope of resolution. Yet even if the choice of a framework is ultimately a matter of faith, faith need not be blind; for what kind of a faith is it that cannot justify itself?

In each case what we must hope for is public resolution. But few of us can wait for that in the pressing world of human affairs. What we are left with is the need for personal resolution and that is always possible, is often necessary, and is usually difficult. But this is to be expected for who said that dealing with controversies was easy?

Selection, structure and approach

The issues discussed in the rest of the book are ones that have been debated by writers and researchers in the fields of behavioural and organizational studies. These fields, which are sometimes brought together under the generic title of organizational behaviour, deal with the human aspects of organization and management but they are obviously not the only ones that do so. Disciplines such as economics, marketing, strategy and business policy, industrial relations, personnel management and so on might equally lay claim to offering controversial perspectives on management. The issues I have selected are not therefore intended to represent everything that might be taken to be controversial in the management field. Nor do I touch at all on the controversies surrounding the behaviour of some prominent managers and business figures which regularly feature in the business columns of the press. Instead I have chosen eight issues that I regard as meeting the criteria of the controversial discussed earlier and which also strike me as interesting and capable of reasonably concise exposition. These issues are briefly outlined below.

In the next two chapters we tackle the basic question of the nature of management in modern society. Chapter 2 explores the prevailing image of management as a 'rational profession' in which technically efficacious means are applied to socially agreed ends. This image is contrasted with the findings of studies of managerial work that have increasingly challenged the validity of this view. In Chapter 3 we examine more radical departures from the rational profession image drawing on exploitative, political and magico-religious conceptions of management and managerial behaviour.

In the next two chapters we focus upon the nature of the knowledge that underpins management practice. Chapter 4 tackles the key question of whether the social sciences are capable of producing knowledge that can be useful to managers. Can managers draw upon a managerial science akin to the medical and engineering sciences? Chapter 5 is concerned with the early 'classical' management theorists' attempts to produce valid principles of management and the subsequent history of this project in the light of research studies and critiques offered by social scientists.

Whatever the basis of managers' knowledge their ability to exert significant degrees of influence over organizations typically depends upon their securing high-level positions in organizational hierarchies. How that access is achieved is therefore of considerable interest. Chapter 6 examines organizational selection and promotion processes in an attempt to assess the reality of meritocracy in organizations. The following chapter deals specifically with gender relations in management, posing the question of why management and especially top management continues to be dominated by men. Chapter 8 complements these themes by asking whether who gets into positions of leadership and what they do when they get there actually matters. Is organizational leadership a myth?

The key focus of managerial practice, the organization and control of work, is the subject of the next chapter. Chapter 7 examines the debate on whether forms of work organization and styles of management can successfully be transposed between countries and whether industrialization is producing a convergence of national management systems. The case of

Japanese management and its appropriateness and applicability in the West is examined in detail.

Finally, we turn to the future of management. Management and organization, it has been widely claimed, are undergoing a radical transformation as the world experiences globalization and the arrival of post-modern society. How are we to distinguish the hypothetical from the hype?

One or two additional points need to be made before we leave this introduction. In presenting the issues it would have been possible simply to lay out the main strands of each debate and then stand aside, leaving readers to make up their own minds on how to interpret them. But this has seemed to me to be unsatisfactory because it might give an unwarranted impression of impartiality on my part and might also be taken as a sign that I am unwilling to take a stand on them myself. Each topic is therefore prefaced by a brief overview which provides a thumbnail sketch of the debate. This sketch is then developed in more depth in the main body of the chapter and towards the end I have presented a commentary which expresses my personal assessment of each issue. Needless to say, it would be contrary to the critical spirit of the book if these were to be regarded as definitive conclusions, but I have felt obliged to offer some conclusions despite the open-ended character of controversies.

Dealing adequately with even eight controversial issues in the space of a fairly short book is a daunting task. Any one of them could easily be made the subject of a separate volume and indeed many thousands of words have been written on each one. It is therefore as well to be aware at the outset of the limitations of this enterprise. It has been necessary to be selective in the choice of supporting materials and although I have tried to give prominence to the better-known contributions to each debate, specialists in any one of these areas will probably be aware of items that have been missed. Like many important controversies the ones discussed here are live issues still open to new evidence and additional arguments.

It also seems likely that the debates as presented here are (hopefully!) somewhat clearer and better defined than they have been in reality. As Anderson, Hughes and Sharrock (1987) comment, in the interests of clear exposition a dispute may be represented as 'an ongoing debate in which the pros and cons are clear, the sides well defined, and conducted in the civilised manner of a debating society'. If only that were so! In a messy world, of course, it is not – which is, I think, where we came in.

Where do you stand? Orientation questionnaire

Before going further, explore your views about management by indicating whether you agree or disagree with the following statements:

		Agree	Disagree
1	There is nothing controversial about management	☐	☐
2	Management is a profession	☐	☐
3	Politicians and managers have little in common	☐	☐
4	No one in their right minds can expect Karl Marx and his followers to have anything worthwhile to say about management	☐	☐
5	Managers work for the good of everyone	☐	☐
6	Management is a science	☐	☐
7	It is absurd to think that management has anything to do with magic and religion	☐	☐
8	The social sciences have little to offer practical managers	☐	☐
9	If you follow the laws of management you can't go wrong	☐	☐
10	Only the most able managers get promoted	☐	☐
11	I prefer to be told what to think: it's easier than thinking for myself	☐	☐
12	Managerial ability is genetic	☐	☐
13	We can't expect women to be effective managers	☐	☐
14	An organization's leaders have a decisive effect on its performance	☐	☐
15	Anything that has been written about management that is more than five years old is irrelevant to me	☐	☐
16	Effective management is the same the world over	☐	☐
17	It is certainly possible to control what people do at work	☐	☐
18	The future of management lies in virtual organizations	☐	☐
19	Globalization is largely a myth	☐	☐
20	Management is unlikely to change much	☐	☐

Now read on. Return to this questionnaire when you have finished the book. Have any of your views changed?

Questions for discussion

1   Compare the answers you gave to the questionnaire with those of your colleagues. Identify disagreements and explore the arguments supporting opposed points of view.
2   Select any one of the items on the questionnaire. Discuss arguments in favour of and against the position stated.
3   What is to be gained from debating controversies in management?
4   What does it mean to say that we are living in a 'messy' world?
5   Why do controversies arise in management?

Further reading

Ackoff, R. (1993) The Art and Science of Mess Management, in C. Mabey and B. Mayon-White (eds), *Managing Change*, London: Paul Chapman, pp. 47–54.

Phelan, P. and Reynolds, P. (1996) *Argument and Evidence: Critical Analysis for the Social Sciences*, London: Routledge.

Thomson, A. (1996) *Critical Reasoning: A Practical Introduction*, London: Routledge.

Thorngate, W. (1976) Possible Limits on a Science of Social Behaviour, in L.H. Strickland, F.E. Aboud and K.J. Gergen (eds), *Social Psychology in Transition*, New York and London: Plenum, pp. 121–30.

Udwadia, F.E. (1986), Management Situations and the Engineering Mindset, *Technological Forecasting and Social Change*, 29, pp. 387–97.

2 What is management?

A term in search of a meaning

To manage is to forecast and plan, to organise, to command, to co-ordinate and to control.

Fayol (1916)

If you ask a manager what he does, he will most likely tell you that he plans, organises, co-ordinates, controls. Then watch what he does. Don't be surprised if you can't relate what you see to those four words.

Mintzberg (1973)

The emergence of management from a position of obscurity to a promi-nent place in modern society was one of the more remarkable events of twentieth-century history. Little more than a hundred years ago manage-ment as we know it barely existed (Florence, 1961), yet today managers are numbered by the million. One survey estimated that in Britain alone there were 2.75 million people engaged in management with 90,000 persons entering the occupation each year (Constable and McCormick, 1987). Similarly, census data for the United States has shown that there were more than ten million managers working in that country in the early 1980s and an annual intake of over 500,000 students to basic courses in management (Carroll and Gillen, 1987). That management exists today can hardly be doubted, so it seems all the more curious to discover that the seemingly simple question, 'What is management?', continues to provoke considerable confusion and puzzlement. Like many simple questions, it is a lot easier to ask than it is to answer.

Management in the sense of the co-ordination and control of collective endeavour is, of course, an age-old activity, identifiable in the work of the pyramid-builders and empire-builders of ancient times. But the origins of modern management lie in the great social and economic upheavals of the eighteenth and nineteenth centuries, which we now know as the Industrial Revolution. Even then, systematic reflection on the nature of management was largely absent. In the 1850s, when Britain was at the height of its industrial supremacy, organizations were generally small, managers were few in number and their tasks were relatively unsophisticated (Pollard,

1965). Above all, industry as a whole was largely successful. So there was little reason to pay much attention to the nature of management. From an early date, industrial management in Britain was endowed with an aura of gritty pragmatism that militated against attempts to provide a systematic account of its nature and functions or to root it in rigorously constructed theory (Wiener, 1981). But with the spread of industrialism around the world and the growth of competition, the increasing size and technical complexity of economic organizations, the consequent expansion and specialization of management, and the emergence of management education on a large scale, the need to understand management in an abstract way has become more pressing. If the nineteenth-century entrepreneur had little need to develop a reflective appreciation of management, the twenty-first-century manager can hardly avoid it. Important decisions about the organization and control of work and the selection, promotion, training and development of managers have to be based on some kind of answer to the question, 'What is management?'

The controversy in brief

The what-is-management debate is closely tied up with post-war developments in the social sciences and the growth of management education. Although provisions for 'high-level' management education have existed in the United States for nearly a century, it was only in the 1960s that similar provisions were made on any scale in Britain (Thomas, 1980). The establishment of courses and curricula for managers necessarily raised questions about the nature of management for even if it could be accepted that management was something that could be taught it was less easy to be clear on what should be taught. If educational courses were now to be offered to managers, much as they were for doctors, lawyers or engineers, there was a need to establish the subject-matter of management. And for management education to be relevant to the practice of management, assumptions had to be made about the tasks and characteristics of management itself.

The earliest attempts to provide a systematic analysis of modern management were made chiefly by practising managers writing during the early decades of the twentieth century, and this body of work proved highly influential in structuring the subject-matter taught through management courses. But with the growing involvement of the social sciences in the study of management these early 'classical' writings became increasingly subject to attack. In particular, the conception of management offered by the 'founding fathers' of management thought, such as Henri Fayol, Lyndall Urwick and others, was presented with a substantial challenge by professional social scientists who developed alternative views of the nature of management.

These alternatives were derived both from the varying theoretical perspectives which different social scientists brought to the topic of management and from a difference in approach to the task of understanding it. On the one hand, the classicists were criticized for their narrow, unsophisticated and managerially biased attempts at management theorizing, and on the other for basing their views more on beliefs derived from experience than on careful study and observation of managerial work. Reaction against the classical writers has thus taken two main forms, theoretical and empirical. The theoretical reaction has been evidenced by a proliferation of different 'schools' of management theory (Koontz, 1961, 1980) and 'analytical perspectives' (Reed, 1989), each tending to claim superiority for its conception of management, while the empirical reaction has produced a substantial number of research studies of managers at work.

One upshot of these developments is that the what-is-management question is today a much more contentious issue than it was when the only systematic answer available was that provided by the classicists. The inquisitive reader seeking an answer to this question will find not only differences of view but complete contradictions and may well be inclined to beat a hasty retreat from the confusion to the safe haven of commonsense. Yet confusion about what management is 'really' about seems likely to have important consequences. Although I think it is overstating the case to say, as Scott and Rochester (1984) do, that 'most of the troubles in our organizations start from misunderstandings about what "managing" means and from failures to think out what abilities it needs', it does seem reasonable to suggest that misconceptions about managing and management can hardly be helpful to the practising manager. Commonsense may be comforting but may do little more than give us an ultimately false sense of security. What is needed is some way of getting to grips with the diversity of approaches to understanding management, so before taking up the strands of the debate the next section outlines a basic framework within which we can locate different ways of answering the question 'What is management?'

A framework for analysis

Writers on management, like managers themselves, base their understanding of management practice on certain fundamental assumptions. Whether explicitly stated or held implicitly these assumptions define the parameters within which accounts of the nature of management practice are developed. Different assumptions therefore give rise to different 'theories' of management, although these theories are often more like loosely defined metaphors or images (Morgan, 1997) than the rigorously constructed conceptual schemes which we sometimes think of as scientific theories. Nonetheless, these theories can have important implications for management practice. To the extent that they define both the ends and means of management they serve to clarify both what management does and how it does it.

We suggest that there are two fundamental issues which underlay most attempts to grapple with the problem of understanding management. Our starting point is to consider management as a social practice in which various means are deployed to achieve various ends. In that sense it is no different from many other social practices, such as teaching or medicine, or from many everyday activities in which actors attempt to realize particular outcomes by behaving in particular ways. Management then is concerned with trying to attain certain states of affairs, usually in the context of work organizations, by implementing various courses of action. Analytically this draws attention to two facets of management practice, the means of management and the ends of management, and it is to these facets that basic differences in assumption apply.

The key issue with regard to means is that of *rationality*. What we are proposing is that theories of management tend to differ according to the assumptions they make about the rationality of the means adopted by management to achieve given ends. We will explore the difficult concept of 'rationality' in more depth in a moment, but for now we can say that while some management theories assume that management is, or could be, largely a rational process, others emphasize the partially rational character of management action.

The key issue with regard to ends is that of *sectionalism*. Theories of management can be seen to differ according to whether they assume that management is concerned with the pursuit of unitary ends or with the advancement of sectional interests. Thus while some theories take it for granted that management involves the pursuit of goals which embody the interests of all an organization's stakeholders, and ultimately of society at large, others depict management as the pursuit of 'one-sided' interests whether those of specific groups within an organization or of broader social groups.

By combining the assumptions made about each of these fundamental issues, rationality and sectionalism, we can define a conceptual space within which different theories of management can be located (Figure 2.1). At best this framework amounts to no more than a sketch-map of the terrain, and one which necessarily leaves out the fine detail, but at this stage a sketch-map will probably serve us better than an atlas. Its value lies less in its capacity to accurately depict everything that has been said about management than in its helping us to get our bearings in a confused field.

This framework identifies four major ways of understanding management: as a rational professional practice, as an exploitative practice, as a magico-religious practice, and as a political practice. We will be looking at each of these conceptions in more depth later, but before we do so we must explore further the basic dimensions of rationality and sectionalism that frame these views.

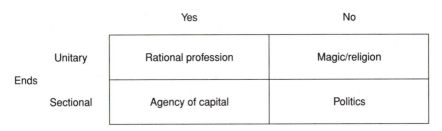

Figure 2.1 An analytical framework for management

Rationality in management

Perhaps the most basic source of controversy over the nature of management is the question of its rationality. 'Rationality' is one of the most important concepts that has been used to analyse the nature of human conduct but it is one that has itself been the subject of considerable controversy (Benn and Mortimer, 1976). For our purposes we are concerned with rationality as an attribute of the means managers use to implement given ends, that is, as an attribute of managerial techniques.

Following Brubaker's (1984) interpretation of Max Weber's writings on rationality, we can distinguish between the objective and the subjective rationality of actions intended to bring about a given end. Such action is objectively rational when the connection between the actions and the intended results can be shown to hold objectively. Since the reality of these connections can be most reliably demonstrated via the application of scientific procedures, objectively rational action in its purest form involves action in which 'the techniques for achieving ends are determined in accordance with scientific knowledge' (Brubaker, 1984).

While not all action is objectively rational, all action self-consciously orientated to some end is subjectively rational. Insofar as it is based upon a set of beliefs about how means are related to ends, action is subjectively rational. It makes sense and appears reasonable to the actor. It may or may not be objectively rational. So, for example, someone may believe that by drinking five glasses of water a day they will lose weight, even though a scientist, having carried out rigorous studies of the effects of drinking water on weight loss, can show that doing so has no effect. In terms of the slimmer's beliefs their action is subjectively rational but it is objectively irrational. To draw attention to the subjectively rational character of management action is not, therefore, to depict managers as lunatics or as unreasonable. Rather, it is to highlight their limited capacity to act in objectively rational ways.

Weber also identifies some actions as 'non-rational'. Such actions are not orientated to the deliberate and self-conscious pursuit of ends and do not, therefore, involve the selection of means. They therefore cannot be distinguished according to notions of objective and subjective rationality. A trivial example might be that of singing to oneself while out walking. Although managers, like everyone else, undoubtedly engage in forms of non-rational conduct, these fall outside the scope of the means–ends scheme which we see as inherent to the concept of management. For this reason we see assumptions about the rationality of management as differing chiefly in terms of the emphasis placed upon its objective rationality or upon its objective irrationality. Whatever position is adopted, management is usually assumed to be at least subjectively rational.

Assumptions about rationality tend to be related to assumptions about science. To assert the objective rationality of management practice tends also to involve the assertion of its scientific basis. As we will see later, although there are few who would claim that management is based on the application of scientific knowledge, there are many who have argued that it could and should be so based. On the other hand, there are others who are deeply sceptical of the possibility of there being an applied science of management for reasons that are partly bound up with controversies surrounding the nature of science, and especially social science itself. These issues will be taken up in Chapter 4.

Before leaving our discussion of rationality, it is important to realize that assumptions about rationality do not fall neatly into either the objectively rational or objectively irrational categories. We are dealing with a continuum so that various intermediate positions may be adopted. For example, the concept of 'bounded rationality' (March and Simon, 1958) falls somewhere between the poles of objective rationality and objective irrationality. Furthermore, we are not claiming that any view adopts one or other polar position but that different views reflect differences of emphasis leaning in one direction or the other.

Sectionalism in management

The second major issue underlying controversies about the nature of management concerns not the means but the ends of management practice. We suggest that a key division among management theories is between those that depict management as orientated to 'unitary' ends and those which see management as orientated to 'sectional' ends.

Since management is a collective practice which impinges on the behaviour of a multiplicity of individuals and groups in an organizational setting, the issue of whose ends are to be made the object of management always arises. Theories of management making 'unitary' assumptions about ends depict management as the pursuit of a set of organizational goals which are held to embody the interests of all the organization's stakeholders. Although management may be directed towards multiple goals, it is assumed that these goals are regarded as legitimate by all parties. Management is thus seen to be the neutral means whereby widely shared ends are achieved. In contrast, assumptions of 'sectionalism' depict management as merely one among several groups with a capacity to influence organizational outcomes. Managers are held to possess distinct interests which conflict with those of other stakeholders. Management practice is therefore depicted as essentially self-interested; the notion of 'organizational goals' is regarded as a myth in which the ends of one group, such as higher management, are portrayed as 'everyone's goals' the better to mobilize collective effort on the group's behalf.

Four approaches to management

At this point we can briefly outline the 'images' of management that can be derived by combining different assumptions about the character of the means and ends of management practice.

Objectively rational means, unitary ends

This view depicts management as the rational administration of unitary organizations. Organizations are assumed to be social technologies, or 'tools', systematically designed in order to attain specific goals. Management is thus seen as a process focused upon the construction, selection, evaluation and implementation of courses of action which are judged according to organizational criteria, especially of efficiency and effectiveness, and which are intended as means to the realization of widely shared ends. These courses of action are based on systematic calculation of the relationship between alternative means, and ideally are, or should be, derived from rigorously established scientific knowledge. The manager acts as a kind of applied scientist or as a technician whose chief task is to take appropriate steps, in the light of established knowledge, to achieve non-controversial ends.

In Britain in particular, the combination of devotion to 'the public good' with practice rooted in a scientific or objectively established body of knowledge has come to be closely identified with the notion of 'professionalism'. Professional practice is often held to be based upon both systematic expertise and a 'service ethic'. The idea of professionalism is therefore closely linked with a concept of practice as the application of rational means to unitary ends. Not surprisingly then, management and especially modern management has often been characterized as a profession although not with any notable degree of success (Thomas and Anthony, 1996). Even so we can sum up the image of management portrayed by this approach as that of the rational profession, and that of managers as rational professionals.

This image has been the most widely promulgated characterization of management and represents the established view of what management is and should be about. Its origins can be traced to the early writings of the 'classical' school of management thought, a tradition which continues to be influential today. It is assumed by much of the 'technical' literature on management and underlies a good deal of management education. Whilst it is not necessarily the case that managers themselves subscribe to it, or are even particularly aware of it, there is little doubt that they have been increasingly encouraged to accept it. Managers may not believe that management is a rational profession, but they are nonetheless expected to believe it, to base their behaviour on its precepts and to justify that behaviour in its terms. Any substantial questioning of this view is therefore likely to provoke discomfort and controversy.

Objectively rational means, sectional ends

The second approach shares with the rational professional view the assumption that managers are concerned with the application of efficacious techniques in order to realize particular ends. It diverges from this view most significantly on the matter of ends.

Originating in Marx's analysis of competitive capitalism, this view depicts the process of production, or the 'labour process', as set in the wider context of capitalist society. In such a society, the means of production are owned by the capitalist class, while the bulk of the population are dispossessed of the means to secure their livelihoods. As such they are forced to sell their labour power to the owners who systematically exploit this to achieve maximum output at minimum cost. Because the system is geared to the creation of profit, and because this can only be achieved by returning to the workforce less in wages than it actually produces, with the surplus being expropriated by the owners, capitalism is based on the exploitation of one social class by another.

Such a system poses a dual problem for management. On the one hand, managers must continually seek to develop and implement more efficient production processes that will enable the organization to survive in the competitive struggle. On the other, it must continually secure the compliance of a workforce that is 'alienated' from the system. To achieve both these ends, management draws increasingly on systematically derived knowledge of production processes and organizational methods of employee control. Managers come to act as technicians but not as neutral technicians. Rather they serve as witting or unwitting allies of the capitalist class.

The image of management yielded by this view is thus one of the exploitation of alienated labour with managers cast in the role of 'agents of capital'. To achieve this exploitation, managers deploy objectively rational means.

Subjectively rational means, unitary ends

The third approach shares, often tacitly, with the rational professional view the idea that management is geared to the attainment of widely shared ends. But it emphasizes the partial and limited rationality of the means that managers deploy to realize these ends. It thus draws attention to the divergence between the subjective rationality of managerial action and its objective irrationality: much managerial behaviour appears to be objectively rational, but in fact it is not.

It is important to recall that objectively irrational conduct is not to be understood as unreasonable or insane behaviour. What is being emphasized here is that managers operate in a complex environment in which the elements with which they have to deal (people, markets, governments, and so on) are interrelated in intricate and poorly understood ways. For this reason, managers are faced with substantial uncertainties about what to do to achieve given ends. While they may use anything from intuitive guesswork to the most rigorous findings of science to enable them to reach decisions on what to do, the element of uncertainty always remains substantial. In the extreme, to talk of management 'control' is a misnomer; managers are seen to exert influence in a complex system but this influence is liable to produce unexpected effects. Thus while managers may seek out objectively rational courses of action, and may justify what they do on the grounds of objective rationality, managerial behaviour seldom reaches the rational ideal. Management has more to do with magic and religion than it has to do with science.

By aspiring to behave in an objectively rational manner, this view proposes that managers nonetheless promote the unitary ends of the organization. The extent that belief in the value of rational conduct is shared by the organization's members, participation in 'rational rituals' helps to integrate them. This view therefore makes two assumptions about ends. First, that organizations are geared to the realization of shared ends, and, second, that although the organization's capacity to attain these ends is fraught with uncertainty, acting as if certainty can be attained serves to unify the organization and so increases the likelihood that ends will be attained.

From this point of view, the key task of management is that of coping with uncertainty. Unlike rationalist views, which assume that uncertainty can be substantially curbed, here it is assumed that managers encounter ineradicable uncertainties at the very heart of their practice. Since these cannot be eliminated by objectively rational means, managers are forced to fall back on purely subjective rationality, much as 'primitive' shamans do when faced with a drought or a disease or a priest may do when making offerings to appease the gods. The image of management derived from this view is therefore that of uncertainty reduction, and of the manager as a magician-cum-priest.

Subjectively rational means, sectional ends

Finally we come to our fourth approach, which departs most radically from the rational professional view of management. On this view, not only are there no overriding, agreed goals towards which managers steer organizations but managerial capacity to exert influence in pursuit of even their own ends is seen to be heavily circumscribed.

In common with the exploitation view, this approach denies the existence of neutral goals as the ends of managerial conduct. But unlike the exploitation view, management is not seen as an 'agent of capital' driven by the logic of capitalism to implement strategies and procedures which serve to maintain the capitalist system as a going concern. Property-owners and shareholders are seen as one among many sets of interest groups, each in possession of a variety of resources, which interact through micro-political processes to produce organizational outcomes. Because these processes are complex and essentially indeterminate, management acts rather like a player in a multidimensional game of chess. Moves are made in pursuit of ends which are not given by the game itself but which are constructed by the players as they play. Furthermore, players lack complete information, or even any information, on other players' intentions, resources, capabilities and so on. The outcome of the game at any particular point in time is thus the result of the interplay of all the interacting elements and forces that are currently in play.

On this political view, management is itself not a unitary entity. In any organization managers or groups of managers may adopt conflicting conceptions of the organization's priorities and problems and of the appropriate means of dealing with them. The goals pursued at any time are those to which resources are devoted as a result of the outcome of processes of bargaining and conflict among managerial groups and other influential parties. Although managers may pursue the interests of capital, this is by no means guaranteed and depends on the overall balance of forces operating within the system.

Like the magico-religious view of management, this political approach emphasizes the bounded rationality of managerial behaviour. Indeed, on this view, bounded rationality is inevitable because the complexity of organizations means that complete scientific knowledge of organizational systems is impossible to attain. Managers must therefore always work with high levels of uncertainty so that the outcomes of managerial actions cannot be guaranteed. Rather, the likelihood is that those actions will produce unintended and unanticipated consequences which feed back into the managerial process. In the management game unexpected surprises are to be expected!

Management, then, is depicted from this perspective as essentially bound up with politics, with the exercise of influence in pursuit of contentious and contended goals. The game-like character of this process implies that the dominant form of behaviour is subjectively rational. Management is centrally an activity of satisficing and troubleshooting since, as Collins (1982) has suggested:

> The complexity of an organization is simply greater than the human capacity to process information. Human cognitive limits do not allow the social world to work like a machine. Instead, we must adapt to our limitations by following a more defensive strategy, which lets many things be partially out of control in return for allowing us to keep things for the most part within acceptable bounds.

Now that we have outlined these four approaches to understanding management we can pursue the issues they raise in more depth. In the rest of this chapter, we will examine the rational professional view of management as presented by some of the early writers on management together with the critiques which have been offered by later writers and researchers. In the following chapter we will take up the three contrasting points of view before presenting a general commentary on the 'what-is-management?' debate.

Management: the rational profession

Perhaps the most widely canvassed though not necessarily the most widely accepted approach to understanding management is one which depicts it as a rational profession. It brings together and asserts the ideas that management is a practice rooted in knowledge, especially scientific knowledge, and that it serves the ends of society rather than of sectional interests.

The essence of the rational professional model of management can be found in the writings of the 'founding father' of modern management thought, Henri Fayol (1841–1925). Born into a lower middle-class family, Fayol trained as a mining engineer and spent his entire career with the French metallurgical and mining company, Commentry–Fourchambault. For thirty years he held the post of managing director during which time he is reputed to have rescued the firm from near bankruptcy. Although he published a number of technical papers on mining engineering he is chiefly remembered for his only book, *Administration industrielle et générale* (1916, 1949). In this book, Fayol provided an analysis of the role of management in organizations and a definition of management which continues to be highly influential (Box 2.1). Many management textbooks, for example, have been organized around his ideas (Carroll and Gillen, 1987). He also proposed a set of general principles of management which we will be examining in Chapter 5.

To understand Fayol's ideas it is important to set them in context. Fayol was centrally concerned to establish something which is much more obvious today than it was in his time, namely that management is a definite

---

Box 2.1 **Henri Fayol's concept of management**

'All activities to which industrial undertakings give rise can be divided into the following six groups:

1 Technical activities (production, manufacture, adaptation)
2 Commercial activities (buying, selling, exchange)
3 Financial activities (search for and optimum use of capital)
4 Security activities (protection of property and persons)
5 Accounting activities (stocktaking, balance sheet, costs, statistics)
6 Managerial activities (planning, organizing, command, co-ordination, control).'

'To manage is to forecast and plan, to organise, to command, to co-ordinate and to control. To foresee and provide means examining the future and drawing up the plan of action. To organise means building up the dual structure, material and human, of the undertaking. To command means maintaining activity among the personnel. To co-ordinate means binding together, unifying and harmonising all activity and efforts. To control means seeing that everything occurs in conformity with established rule and expressed command.

'Management, thus understood, is neither an exclusive privilege nor a particular responsibility of the head or senior members of the business; it is an activity spread, like all other activities, between head and members of the body corporate. The managerial function is quite distinct from the other five essential functions.'

Source: H. Fayol, *General and Industrial Management*, trans. C. Storrs, London: Pitman, 1949.

---

and distinct activity in its own right which has an independent contribution to make to the effective operation of organizations. He believed that this contribution was insufficiently recognized, management generally being regarded as something rather vague and insignificant. In particular he wanted to offset the tendency for management to be overshadowed by the more widely acknowledged and more prestigious engineering activities which tended to dominate the conduct of French industrial concerns. Thus he wrote:

> The number, variety and importance of technical activities, the fact that products of every kind (material, intellectual, moral) originate with technical men, the almost exclusively vocational teaching of our technical schools, the openings available to technical men – all these contribute to make the technical function, and in consequence technical ability, stand out from and overshadow other abilities that are

just as necessary for, and sometimes more conducive to, the progress and prosperity of business. Nevertheless the technical function is not always the most important.

This tendency for 'technical men' – they no doubt were male – to dominate business affairs was due partly to the prestige that they derived from their education, itself based on the existence of established bodies of knowledge, and partly to the fact that management was not a well-defined activity and had no place in the education system. In other words, within organizations, management tended to be placed in a subservient position even though, Fayol argued, it was a 'very important function at least as worthy as the technical one of attracting and holding public attention'.

To escape from this situation, and so give management its proper place in organizations, Fayol argued that three developments had to take place. First, it was necessary to isolate the main types of activity, or 'functions', which had to be carried out in any undertaking, management being one of them. Second, it was necessary to identify the elements or tasks that constituted the management function. Third, and in some ways most important of all, it was necessary to establish a body of knowledge or theory which would guide the practice of the management function. Only with the latter would it be possible to go beyond the commonsense level of managing, based as much on personal whim as sound technique, and it would only be possible to incorporate the teaching of management into the education system if this body of knowledge had been created.

For Fayol there could be no doubt about the importance of management. Management could be practised well or badly, but however it was practised, it made a difference. Management unquestionably mattered. It was, or had the potential to be, a rational activity in the sense that it was possible to provide clear grounds for its existence, tasks and necessity, and to suggest definite principles connecting managerial behaviour to outcomes. It also seems clear that Fayol believed that these principles could be established on a scientific basis, or at least that management could be approached 'in a spirit of scientific inquiry' (Brodie, 1967). Finally, Fayol was dedicated to the notion of professionalism in the sense that management was something to be taken seriously, to be based on established knowledge, to be capable of transmission partly by means of education and training, and to be dedicated to the realization of general rather than sectional interests. For Fayol, then, management could and should be a rational profession.

Fayol's writings on management were not, therefore, simply the reflections of an old man (he was in his mid-seventies at the time of publication) on his lifetime's experience as a manager. His book was as much a manifesto for management and management education as it was a cold description and analysis of its elements, inspired by a conviction about its importance and the possibility of improving it.

Although Fayol's book first appeared in 1916 it did not become widely available in English translation until 1949. Prior to this date the dissemination of his ideas in the English-speaking world largely depended upon the activities of those who both knew of his work and supported his aims. One of the most influential of these was Lyndall Urwick who had been a lieutenant colonel in the British Army during World War One and who later became the director of the International Management Institute at Geneva and the head of the management consultancy firm, Urwick Orr. In his book, *The Elements of Administration* (1943), Urwick restated and extended many of Fayol's ideas and views on management, together with those of a number of other advocates of management 'professionalism'. In particular he emphasized the notions of rationality, science, and professionalism with renewed force.

Urwick wrote that 'the art and science of administering the social groups, large and small, which are increasingly characteristic of our civilisation, has emerged during the past quarter of a century as a technical skill'. He went on to refer to 'the underlying sciences on which the art of administration rests' and to 'a body of professional knowledge without which those who attempt to manage other people appear increasingly amateurish'. Administration was not a wholly scientific activity, but it was increasingly becoming so as science and its associated techniques came to underpin it with a body of professional knowledge. He also emphasized the importance of the social role of administration:

> social organization, on whatever scale, can only prove successful in so far as it is social. That is to say, the aim which is pursued by all concerned in the administration of each group is an objective enlisting the interest of the group as a whole, and consistent with the interest of all larger groups of which it is a part, not some extraneous purpose desired by certain individuals in that group, either as individuals or as members of some other professional or social grouping.

Here then Urwick is arguing for the importance of common interests that stand above personal, professional and class interests as a condition for successful administration.

That Urwick's book referred not to the elements of management but to those of administration was no accident. In a foreword to *General and Industrial Management* (1949), the English edition of Fayol's *Administration industrielle et générale*, Urwick noted some of the difficulties of translating Fayol's ideas into English without changing their meaning. The translation of the French term 'administration' as 'management' was, he suggested, unfortunate. This was partly because the word 'management' retained an association in English with deceit and trickery and this was unlikely to enhance 'the dignity of the subject or of those who practise the activity'. In other words, the English term 'management' had connotations that were at odds with those of professionalism, a notion which both Fayol and he himself wished to promote.

Urwick noted other ways in which the accepted meanings of 'management' were unhelpful to understanding Fayol's concept of 'administration'. For Fayol 'administration' was a function that was carried out, in varying degrees, by employees at all levels in an undertaking. Although those at the top of the organization dealt almost exclusively with 'administration', every job in the undertaking was concerned with it to some degree. Even the shopfloor worker played some part in the 'administration' of the enterprise. In Britain, however, 'management' tended to be seen as the exclusive province of 'the management', a specific group within the organization, rather than as an organization-wide function exercised in part by everyone. To identify the function of 'administration' with a group of employees called 'managers' was contrary to the spirit of Fayol's ideas, and Urwick thought that the likelihood of misunderstanding had been increased by substituting the English 'management' for the French 'administration' in the English edition of the book.

Finally Urwick noted that by translating 'administration' as 'management' it was implied that Fayol's ideas were only relevant to industrial organizations. In fact, Urwick pointed out, Fayol had been committed to a belief in a general science of administration that was equally applicable to both public and private enterprises.

Through the publications and proselytizing activities of Urwick and other management intellectuals, the idea of management as a rational profession gained some acceptance in Britain. While this conception attracted increasing support in government and educational circles in the decades immediately following the Second World War, whether it has ever been generally accepted by Britain's managers, other than as a comforting symbol of respectability, is doubtful. As Handy has pointed out, British management 'has traditionally been more to do with pragmatism than professionalism' (Handy, 1987) so it is perhaps not surprising to find that the ideas of those like Fayol and Urwick were often treated sceptically: they did not fit easily with the prevailing ethos of management.

But there was more to it than that. If managers themselves have not been persuaded by the rational professional conception of management they have not been alone, for many scientists, and especially those who have turned their hands to the study of managerial work, have been equally sceptical of this view. Perhaps, then, Fayol and his followers were simply wrong.

The practice of management

If we want to develop a better understanding of management then one obvious line of attack is to study the activities of those who spend their working lives managing. This seems likely to take us much closer to the reality of management than any abstract theory is able to do because if anyone knows what management is all about it surely must be managers. If, as Lupton (1983) declared, 'management is what managers do during their working hours' then close observation of what they do seems indispensable to the development of any satisfactory account of management.

Reasoning of this kind, motivated partly by doubts about the validity of the image of management portrayed by the writers of the 'classical' school, has underpinned a good deal of the research effort which has been devoted to the study of managerial work. Evidence on what managers actually do has accumulated in a series of studies in both the United States and Europe since the 1970s. Among the best known of these are Mintzberg's (1973) study of American chief executives, Kotter's (1982b) study of American general managers and a set of studies by Stewart (1967, 1976, 1982) of British managers and administrators. In general these investigators have drawn a sharp contrast between the 'traditional' view of management portrayed by the classical writers and the 'reality' as revealed by direct study of managers at work.

In *The Nature of Managerial Work* (1973), Mintzberg began by suggesting that most previous writing on management had failed to pay much attention to what managers actually do. Thus he wrote that he 'felt that there were too many misconceptions in the field, that managers had had enough of the fact-free wisdom of the armchair and that they were ready for a new look at their job, substantiated by systematic research'. Mintzberg's own researches began in the late 1960s when, as a student, he carried out an observational study of the work of five chief executives. The results of this study were subsequently integrated with those of other studies of managers to yield a general analysis of managerial work.

In his review of contemporary views of the manager's job Mintzberg was highly critical of the classical school. This school, originating in the work of Fayol, described managerial work in terms of 'composite functions' which, he argued, did not refer to the actual work of managers but to 'certain vague objectives of managerial work'. As such they had, he believed, 'served to label our areas of ignorance' and so block attempts to achieve a deeper understanding. He therefore found 'little use in the writings of the classical school'.

Mintzberg drew attention to an important distinction among the observations that could be made of managerial work. By recording such features as how long managers worked, where they worked, and with whom, it was possible to describe the characteristics of managerial work. But these observations said nothing about the content of managerial work, about what was done and why. The latter had to be described in terms of functions or roles. Mintzberg therefore presented his findings in terms of both characteristics and roles and these are summarized in Box 2.2.

Drawing mainly on earlier studies, Mintzberg identified six characteristics which, he claimed, are common to managerial work at all levels from

---

Box 2.2 **The characteristics and content of managerial work**

Characteristics: the manager at work

- Performs a great quantity of work at an unrelenting pace
- Undertakes activities marked by variety, brevity and fragmentation
- Has a preference for issues that are current, specific and non-routine
- Prefers verbal rather than written means of communication
- Acts within a web of internal and external contacts
- Is subject to heavy constraints but can exert some control over his work.

Content: the manager's work roles

> Interpersonal roles
>> Figurehead: representing the organization/unit to outsiders
>> Leader: motivating subordinates, unifying effort
>> Liaiser: maintaining lateral contacts
>
> Informational roles
>> Monitor: of information flows
>> Disseminator: of information to subordinates
>> Spokesman: transmission of information to outsiders
>
> Decisional roles
>> Entrepreneur: initiator and designer of change
>> Disturbance handler: handling non-routine events
>> Resource allocator: deciding who gets what and who will do what
>> Negotiator: negotiating

All managerial work encompasses these roles, but the prominence of each role varies in different managerial jobs.

Source: H. Mintzberg, *The Nature of Managerial Work*, New York: Harper and Row, 1973.

---

the foreman to the chief executive. The resulting image of the work of the manager is less that of the captain of industry, coolly commanding from the bridge, than of the honey-bee flitting noisily from bloom to bloom. So, for example, Mintzberg found that few of his chief executives spent much time in general planning, one of the mainstays of the classical view of management. Hence he commented that 'the classic view of the manager as a planner is not in accord with reality'.

In general, Mintzberg presented the results of his analysis in a way that suggested that the reality of managerial work was seriously at odds with the classical view. Furthermore, managerial work, as it could be observed in practice, did not even square with managers' own beliefs about it. Whilst they seemed to subscribe to the classical view, their behaviour belied its validity, so that: 'If you ask a manager what he does, he will most likely tell you that he plans, organizes, co-ordinates, controls. Then watch what he does. Don't be surprised if you can't relate what you see to those four words.' Managers seemed to have been sold an erroneous view of management which could not be reconciled with what they actually did.

Mintzberg's scepticism about the 'traditional' view of management was substantially reinforced by Kotter's (1982b) study of the work of fifteen general managers. In particular, Kotter explicitly refuted the notion of the 'professional manager'. According to Kotter, if this notion implied that managers tended to rely on universally applicable principles and skills when managing rather than upon a detailed knowledge of the business they were managing then none of the managers in his sample could be regarded as 'professional managers'. Formal concepts and tools were important to their work but were not sufficient in themselves to yield effective management. Managerial expertise was best understood as a product of certain personal characteristics and experiences and was developed in specialized form in local contexts. His general managers relied less on formal processes of planning, organizing, motivating and controlling than upon the pursuit of broad-ranging and informally specified agendas of problems and issues which were pursued through extensive networks of organizational contacts rather than through the formal organization structure. Management appeared to be a seat-of-the-pants activity in much the same way as it had been popularly conceived and not a rational analytical process. Yet this 'unprofessional' approach nevertheless seemed to work because it fitted the objective demands of the general managers' jobs as well as their own preferred management style.

The critical attitude to the classical view of management which was evident in the studies of Mintzbeg and Kotter was echoed in the studies of Stewart. Drawing together the research evidence on managerial behaviour, Stewart (1983) contrasted these findings with the 'traditional picture' of management. That picture had, she proposed, emphasized rationality, planning and the pursuit of organizational goals as central to management at all levels. But studies of managerial behaviour showed something very different. For example, the pattern of managers' daily work had been shown to be typically episodic: managers tended to work for only brief periods on any one activity and rarely had much time for uninterrupted thinking or planning. In her study of 160 middle and senior managers (Stewart, 1967) she had found that over a period of four weeks the 'average' manager experienced only nine uninterrupted periods of at least half-an-hour. Similarly, Mintzberg (1973) had noted that his chief executives spent an average of ten minutes on any one task apart from formal meetings. The brevity, variety, and fragmentation of managerial work did not square with the idea of the manager as a reflective planner nor as a cool, logical decision-maker.

Managers actually existed in a 'whirl of activity', spent most of their time talking to other people, and were located in a web of relationships, with peers, bosses, and subordinates, in which they were often as much a dependent party as someone upon whom others depended. For this reason they had to pay a lot of attention to interpersonal relationships and to organizational politics.

Drawing on Dalton's (1959) observational study of American managers, Stewart contrasted the reality of management as a political activity with the traditional concept of 'organization man':

> The traditional picture of the manager was, and often still is, of someone who helps to set organizational goals, or even if not involved in doing so, is committed to them. This conflicts with Dalton's and other descriptions of the manager as someone who has individual and sectional interests which may conflict with organizational goals and policies, and who may pursue them by lobbying, concealment or misrepresentation of information.

Watson's (2001) ethnographic study of managers at ZTC Ryland, a telecommunications plant, also questioned the extent to which managers' behaviour could be adequately understood in terms of the classical precepts. Watson refers to the 'human angst, insecurity, doubt, and frailty' of the managers he observed. ZTC's managers seemed embroiled in an all too human struggle to keep the organizational show on the road and themselves intact in the face of uncertainty and incipient chaos.

These studies of managerial work seem, then, to pose a serious challenge to the views of the classical school. If management is supposed to be about planning, organizing, commanding, co-ordinating and controlling there appears to be precious little evidence that this is what managers actually do. Nor do they appear to make much use of 'scientific knowledge' in their work. And rather than pursuing agreed goals in a context of harmony and consensus, managers seem to have interests of their own which they may pursue irrespective of official organizational goals. In terms of both functions, processes and interests, management appears to depart significantly from the classical view. The classical image of management thus seems to be little more than an idealized conception of what it ought to be rather than a valid account of what it is. As such it would appear to contribute little to an understanding of the realities of management.

Back to the classics

A common conclusion of studies of managerial work is that the 'reality' of management is very different from the 'image' of it that has been presented by classical writers. The latter has therefore tended to be relegated to the status of folklore (Mintzberg, 1975) or dismissed altogether as misleading, unhelpful and inadequate. But some recent reviews of research on managerial work have suggested that such conclusions are themselves highly questionable. There are good reasons for believing that the criticisms of the classical writers' views of management that have been derived from studies of managerial work have in fact been attacks on a straw man.

In a review of more than twenty-five studies of managerial work conducted since the early 1950s, Hales (1986) offered some telling criticisms of the conclusions they typically draw about management. One major problem is that these studies have tended to start out from the position that the nature of management can be inferred from the observable activities of employees who carry the title 'manager'. What tends to be missing from these descriptions, however, is an interpretation of their meaning in terms of the functions of management, something which requires a prior theoretical framework in which management is located and defined in an organizational context.

For this reason it is difficult to distinguish between the things people called 'managers' do which contribute to the management of the organization (such as co-ordination and control) and those which anyone does anywhere (such as talking to other people). The latter, for example, is certainly part of what managers do but the extent to which it can be seen to be managerial work appears to depend on what the talk is intended to achieve.

The writings of the classical school provided just such a theoretical framework. Fayol's analysis of 'administration', for example, was an attempt to identify the tasks and processes which had to be carried out in any undertaking; certain functions were inherent in the administration of any organization. But how these functions were allocated across the organization's personnel was a different matter. As we saw earlier, Fayol certainly did not assume that administration was something undertaken in its entirety by a chief executive or by a group of people called 'managers'. Nor was it assumed that every 'manager's' job dealt exclusively with the managerial functions. His list of functions was not to be taken as a job description for managers but as a set of general requirements which had to be dealt with in any organization. If, therefore, the observable behaviour of individual managers does not appear to square with Fayol's categories, this is less a reflection on the adequacy of his analysis than a consequence of the failure of researchers to relate their observations to his, or indeed any, theory of the nature of management.

When the findings of studies of managerial behaviour are recast in terms of the categories defined by classical writers, their much maligned analysis turns out to be surprisingly robust. Summarizing the findings on the activities 'typically' pursued by managers, Hales (1986) commented that they show 'striking parallels with the supposedly outdated "classical principles of management" '. However, Hales also argued that the studies of managerial behaviour he reviewed did not provide an adequate basis for evaluating the classical view because they had simply not asked what managerial function the observed behaviour of individual managers implied. By focusing on the surface features of managers' behaviour at work they failed to consider the non-observable functions and responsibilities which lay behind it and which give it meaning. Managers may behave in typical ways, but this does not of itself explain why they behave like this.

Hales has returned to these issues in his more recent review of studies of managerial work (Hales, 1999). There, however, he largely abandons management functions as a basis for explaining why managers do what they do. Instead he sees managerial behaviour as shaped by the rules and resources of environing systems which serve to constitute, define and legitimize it. But in a reappraisal of the value of the classical functions as a way of describing managerial work, Carroll and Gillen (1987) have drawn on evidence from largely American research which shows not only that managerial activities can be described in terms of the classical categories, but also that managers who devote more of their time to them and who display more skill in carrying them out tend to produce better unit and organizational results.

For example, a study by Mahoney *et al.* (1963) sampled the observable activities of twenty-one managers over a two-week period. The managers were asked to describe what they were doing, why they were doing it, and to what basic management function they were contributing when they did it. The results of this and similar studies showed that managers did tend to spend time on the types of function identified by Fayol and other classical writers. How much emphasis was placed on the functions varied from case to case, but this is consistent with Fayol's view that jobs in organizations consisted of a variety of different activities only some of which were managerial. The fact that managers do not spend all their time executing managerial functions does not mean that Fayol was wrong about management. It only seems wrong if he is thought to be saying that every 'real' manager must be someone who spends all his or her working time carrying out all the management functions. Or to put it the other way around, if observations of managerial behaviour were to show that managers spend a lot of time on activities which are unrelated to management functions, this is not a ground for saying that everything they do must 'really' be management. To do so is to equate the sum total of someone's work activities with a theoretically defined concept of management. This would be rather like concluding from the observation of doctors at work that because they spend significant amounts of time 'keeping the books' on their practice that accounting is 'really' part of medicine.

Like Hales, Carroll and Gillen acknowledge the useful contribution made by studies of managers' behaviour to our understanding of managers and their work. The weakness of these studies, however, arises from their failure to distinguish among observable activities in terms of their contribution or otherwise to those managerial functions which must be undertaken if an organization is to survive. In that sense, while they tell us a lot about what 'managers' do and how they do it, they do not tell us whether what they do is management. To answer that question some prior conception of the nature of management is required and it is this that has been provided by the classical 'school'. Carroll and Gillen (1987) thus conclude that:

> the classical functions still represent the most useful way of concep-tualising the manager's job, especially for management education, and perhaps this is why it is still the most favoured description of manage-rial work in current management textbooks.

Commentary

On the face of it, studies of managers at work present a very different view of management to that offered by the proponents of rational profes-sionalism. Managers, and even senior managers, seem to rely little on scientific knowledge, formal principles or theories in the conduct of their work so that to depict management as a practice based upon objective rationality is problematic. Similarly, the recognition that managers may pursue personal and sectional goals rather than social ones questions the idea that management is concerned with overriding unitary ends. On both counts the image of management as a rational profession seems flawed.

The contrast between the classical and empirical depictions of manage-ment must not, however, be drawn too strongly for they are far from wholly incompatible. Whatever the doubts about managers' reliance on scientific knowledge as a base for management, few students of managers at work doubt its rationality. Managers may not often act as organizational or behavioural scientists applying universal laws or principles, but they do operate with local rationalities based upon means–ends relations in specific contexts much as Fayol (1949) envisaged when he stated that 'there is nothing absolute or rigid in management affairs' and that 'allowance must be made for different changing circumstances'. Moreover, the seeming gulf between what managers can be observed to do and the classical functions of management turns out to be little more than a case of mistaken iden-tity; these functions can be seen to be reflected in managers' work, provided one looks for them. The classical and empirical accounts of the means of management begin to look not so different after all.

But what about the ends of management? Some classical writers were well aware of the contentious nature of organized production in the soci-eties in which they lived, Fayol (1949), for example, making reference to the 'conflict between Capital and Labour'. The notion of 'unitary goals' was therefore something they advocated as necessary or desirable rather than something that could be treated as an extant fact. Studies of managerial work, however, have tended to assume that management is a neutral, technical activity whose ends are unproblematic, and this assumption has seldom been treated as contentious in studies of this kind. Although Dalton's (1959) observations of the reality of managerial micro-politics did point to some cracks in the 'traditional picture' (Stewart, 1983), their implications for an understanding of management have not made much impact on later studies of managers at work. In that respect Mintzberg's (1994) analytical 'rounding out' of the manager's job, for example, does not go much beyond the view of managerial work he put forward two decades previously. On the matter of ends, empirical studies of managerial work have generally offered little by way of challenge to the idea that management functions within a unitary framework. They have thus implied that what the classicists believed ought to be the case actually is the case, so reinforcing the rational professional management view's claim to acceptability.

That view has continued to appeal strongly to many management writers and educators and has been enshrined both in 'popular' management books (Willmott, 1984) and in the more formal textbooks mentioned by Carroll and Gillen (1987). It can still be regarded as the established answer to the question 'What is management?' Research on managerial work appears to have substantially questioned its validity yet I have argued that this is by no means obviously so, for although the traditional picture of management has been changed by studies of managers at work it remains pretty much the same. For some rather different images we need to turn to approaches to answering our question which adopt alternative perspectives, such as those which see management in terms of Marx, magic and politics. It is these possibilities that will occupy us in our next chapter.

Questions for discussion

1   In what sense is management a profession?
2   Is Fayol's view of management of any worth to today's managers?
3   If managers do not behave as the classical writers envisaged, does that simply make them bad managers?
4   Which of the four ways of understanding management depicted in Figure 2.1 is likely to be of most help to the management practitioner and why?
5   Is the term 'management' too vague to be of any value?

Further reading

Fayol, H. (1949) *General and Industrial Management*, trans. Constance Storrs, London: Pitman.

Hales, C. (1999) Why Do Managers Do What They Do? Reconciling Evidence and Theory in Accounts of Managerial Work, *British Journal of Management*, 10, pp. 335–50.

Mintzberg, H. (1994) Rounding Out the Manager's Job, *Sloan Management Review*, 36 (1) pp. 11–26.

Watson, T.J. (2001) *In Search of Management*, London: Thomson.

3 What is management? Exploitation, politics and magic

An industrial army of workmen, under the command of a capitalist, requires, like a real army, officers (managers), and sergeants (foremen, overlookers), who exercise authority on behalf of the capitalist during the labour process. The work of supervision becomes their established and exclusive function.

Marx (1867)

Business *is* a political process.

Hague (1971)

I speak of faith in McDonald's as if it were a religion. I believe in God, family and McDonald's – and in the office that order is reversed.

Ray Kroc, McDonald's founder, quoted in Thompson (1986)

As we have seen, the technocratic model of management as a rational profession has been challenged in two important ways. First, the results of studies of managerial work have frequently been contrasted with the image of management portrayed by classical writers such as Fayol in order to show that the reality of management is very different from its image. Real managerial work, it is often argued, does not have much to do with the classical functions, with planning and organizing, with issuing commands or working through the formal structure of the organization, with the use of formal techniques or with the application of scientific knowledge.

Second, it has been proposed that managers do not necessarily act as the disinterested trustees of all-embracing organizational interests seeking to maximize the performance of their organizations and to promote the welfare of all. Rather, they bring personal and sectional interests to the workplace which they pursue in the context of the 'micro-politics' of the organization by unofficial and informal means.

The rational professional model is thus found wanting in terms of its assumptions about both means and ends; management does not necessarily act in a unified way in the pursuit of enhanced organizational performance for the benefit of everyone, nor does it make much use of general precepts derived from scientifically established bodies of knowledge. Management practice seems to be much more haphazard than the rational professional view implies drawing on localized knowledge and prior experience in order to pursue personalized and functionally based agendas rather than abstract general knowledge to further consensual organizational goals.

Yet these qualifications, important though they are, offer only a limited challenge to the rational professional view of management. Competition for influence within organizations, for example, can be seen largely as disputes over which means should be adopted to maximize organizational performance such as whether the firm should be market or production oriented. Intra-managerial conflicts can thus be seen as ones over the best way to meet the legitimate interests of the organization's stakeholders. In that sense the broad assumption of the rational professional model that management serves socially agreed ends is not seriously challenged; managers may disagree over how best to serve society but the notion that the organizations they manage are dedicated to this end is not questioned. Similarly, if managers do not make much use of 'science' when managing, their behaviour is no less rational for that. Managers, or at least successful managers, use rich, contextual knowledge as a basis for their actions and this works in spite of, or even because of, its 'unscientific' character. Hence although management may be seen not to fully live up to its rational professional image, that image remains valid as a reasonable characterization of management in contemporary society.

There are, however, at least three alternatives to this revised version of rational professionalism. The first of these, derived from Karl Marx's analysis of capitalism as a social system, explicitly rejects the idea that management in capitalist societies serves to promote the interests of all whilst not denying that managers act in a calculative quasi-scientific manner when carrying out their tasks. On this view, managers, aided by a panoply of social science techniques for manipulating human behaviour, do control organizations but they do so in the interests of a narrow propertied class. The second alternative also rejects the notion that organizations are run in the interests of all but also questions the capacity of managers to exert significant control; management is seen as essentially a political process in which outcomes depend on the prevailing balance of forces at any given time. Finally a third magico-religious view questions the rationality of much managerial behaviour without having much to say about the ends to which managerial behaviour is directed. In each case insights into the nature of management are offered which yield a sharp contrast with those embodied in the rational professional view.

Management: the exploitation of labour

The task of understanding management can be approached in a variety of ways. One is by observing managers at work, tackling the problem at the ground level and working up. By examining the bricks and mortar of management, how managers spend their working time, what they do and why they do it, an appreciation of the architecture of the managerial edifice as a whole might be gained. Alternatively, one might try to understand management by exploring the phenomenon of organization, locating management practice within the context of the formally organized character of work in modern society as the 'classical' theorists tried to do. But another approach insists that in order to understand management one must start not with observations of managers nor with the study of organizations but with an analysis of the society in which managers work and in which organizations are constructed. To understand the parts one must understand the whole and the whole on this view is that form of social organization known as capitalism.

This way of interpreting the nature of management is rooted in the works of Karl Marx (1818–1883) whose wide-ranging analyses of social and economic organization have given rise to a flourishing tradition of research and scholarship on the contemporary nature of capitalism and its management. In particular the publication of Braverman's *Labor and Monopoly Capital* (1974) generated a renewed interest in the nature of management among both those who are sympathetic to Marx's basic conceptual framework and those who are critical of it.

In this section we begin by reviewing Marx's own comments on management, drawing on Bottomore and Rubel's (1963) selections from his voluminous writings. Although Marx has relatively little to say about the role of management in the capitalist mode of production much of the basic framework of ideas developed by subsequent writers is present in his original works. We then introduce Braverman's updating of Marxist theory with its applications to developments in the twentieth century. Finally we explore some of the reactions to Braverman's ideas insofar as they bear on the issue of the nature of management today.

Marx on management

According to Marx, management emerges as a distinct activity in society as a result of the growth in scale of co-operative enterprise. Marx observed that whenever a number of people come together to share in a production process a 'directing will' is required to co-ordinate and unify their actions. The role of this agent is akin to that of the conductor of an orchestra enabling the players to make music successfully; the co-ordination of the separate elements that go to make up the whole production process is a necessary task when people work not as isolated individuals but as parts of a collective entity. 'Management' in that sense is essential to collective acts of production. But, Marx argued, this function assumes a special form when production takes place within a capitalist system. Management is not to be understood as a task or occupation that can be considered in the abstract as something outside specific historical conditions. The nature of management is closely bound up with the nature of the mode of production that prevails in a society in a given historical period. Management in a capitalist society is therefore something very different to management under other conditions.

The capitalist mode of production is one in which the essential elements of production, capital and labour, are possessed by distinct social groups. Capitalists possess the instruments of production; tools, machines, factories, materials and so on. Workers, on the other hand, possess only their labour power which, since they are deprived of direct access to the instruments of production, they are forced to sell to employers. Inequality of power is thus an inherent feature of the capitalist mode of production for, in principle, capitalists may employ the instruments of production to secure their own livelihood without the co-operation of labour. Labour, however, cannot subsist by applying labour power alone since this power is neutered without access to the instruments of production.

In a capitalist society production is geared to the maximization of profit and this objective alone dictates the behaviour of the capitalist. In order to realize profit capitalists seek to exploit labour in a double sense. Exploitation occurs by putting labour to its most productive uses and this requires the employer to organize and control work, or the 'labour process', in a way that yields the maximum output from the workers. In addition labour is exploited by being deprived of a full return for its efforts. According to the theory of surplus value, labour receives in return for its efforts only a portion of the product it creates, at the bare minimum enough to keep the worker alive and capable of further labour. The excess is expropriated by the capitalist both as personal income and as investment capital for the further development of the enterprise. It is in this manner that the capitalist extracts profit. Moreover, competition between capitalists forces each enterprise to constantly seek out ways of increasing the output of labour while reducing its return to a minimum. Ultimately, Marx believed, workers would be driven into poverty and revolt.

The capitalist system is therefore one in which the relationship between employers and employees is fundamentally antagonistic. This is both because the workers' labour 'always remains essentially forced labour' and because work has to be organized and controlled in a way that reduces each worker to 'a crippled monstrosity'. Efforts to cheapen labour by, for example, the use of machines and the narrow specialization of jobs, rob workers of their skills and their dignity and expose them to degrading and dehumanizing conditions. Work is organized purely according to criteria of efficiency without regard to the well-being of the worker. Such a system inevitably generates resistance to the demands of capital and hostility between employer and employee, and although this conflict may not necessarily be openly expressed or explicitly recognized, the potential for industrial and social warfare is ever present, lurking beneath the surface of everyday life.

In the early stages of the development of the capitalist system enterprises are small and are managed by the capitalist owners. But as capitalist enterprises grow the task of the supervision and control of labour passes out of the hands of owners to 'a special kind of wage labourer', the manager or supervisor. These agents are not capitalists since they do not own the enterprise but they 'exercise authority on behalf of the capitalist during the labour process' and their exclusive function is that of supervision. Managers thus act according to capitalist priorities and objectives seeking to exploit labour to the full. Increasingly management becomes separated from ownership and owners cease to be involved in the day-to-day management of the firm. With the emergence of the joint-stock company and the growth of banking and the credit system, the individual capitalist disappears from the site of production leaving managers in charge. At this point managers cease to be agents of identifiable individual owners and instead become the agents of a more diffuse entity, the capitalist class. Managers can then be seen to act not so much as the agents of capitalists as of the capitalist system.

In the capitalist system, the principal function of management is to exploit labour power to the maximum in order to secure profits for the owners of capital. Management therefore involves more than the co-ordinating and unifying activities required by any production process engaging the efforts of many people; it also involves managing the antagonistic relations which arise when production is organized on capitalist lines. As Salaman (1981) has put it:

> At work this conflict relationship between expropriating employer/capitalist and expropriated employee gives rise to a number of necessary features of work under capitalism; the need for management to direct and organise the labour power that is purchased, and to control and discipline potentially recalcitrant employees whose commitment is always unreliable and who may at any moment demonstrate their hostility to their work, their product and their employer.

Management is not, then, a neutral administrative function executed for the benefit of all those who co-operate in productive activity but a repressive and exploitative one deeply concerned with keeping the lid on a fundamentally unstable and potentially explosive system. Whether they know it or not, managers are engaged in the maintenance not only of organizational systems but also of the system of power and advantage inherent to the structure of capitalist society. Management under capitalism is not simply the co-ordination of labour in the interests of society but the exploitation of labour for the benefit of the owning class.

Braverman and beyond

Marx's original analysis of the functions of management in capitalist society has been given considerable prominence by the work of Braverman (1974) who developed and applied Marx's original ideas in the context of twentieth-century industrialism. Following Marx, Braverman argued that the nature of human labour, which is 'infinitely malleable', offers both prospects and problems for the employer. Unlike animals, the capacities of humans for labour are not fixed by biological instincts but can be directed and developed in many ways. This offers the employer the possibility of changing workers' behaviour in a manner that best serves the employer's interest in securing maximum output. Workers can be trained to take on new tasks and to carry out old tasks in new ways. But humans also possess the capacity to resist the influence of employers and to behave in ways that are not necessarily in accord with the employer's wishes. For this reason 'it is essential for the capitalist that control over the labour process pass from the hands of the worker into his own' and this gives rise to 'the essential functions of management in industrial capitalism, control of the labour process'.

Braverman states that the role of management in industrial capitalism is control which 'is indeed the central concept of all management systems as has been recognised implicitly or explicitly by all theoreticians of management'. With regard to the labour process, control has been sought by many means, initially by concentrating labour under one roof where it can be subject to constant supervision and by the institution of elaborate systems of factory rules, but latterly by the systematic separation of conception from execution. This means that the traditional production process, in which a worker both conceives the product and then produces it, much as a craftsman or artist might do, has been fragmented so that one group conceives and plans and another puts the conception or plan into effect. Conception becomes the special province of management whereas execution is left to the workers. In order to gain full control of workers, management takes over all responsibility for deciding not only what work is to be done but also how it is to be done; managers do the planning and organizing (conception) and workers do as they are told (execution)!

In the twentieth century the handmaiden of the extension of managerial control over the labour process was F.W. Taylor's scientific management. Taylor's ideas, Braverman suggests, can be represented by three principles: work study, to discover the most efficient ways of carrying out work tasks, the concentration of the resulting knowledge in the hands of management, and the application of this knowledge to the total specification of workers' behaviour. 'Modern management', Braverman declares, 'came into being on the basis of these principles', the separation of conception and execution providing a clear functional rationale for the existence of management and a potent means for subordinating labour to managerial control.

Among the consequences of this process are the destruction of craft skills and the creation within the social organization of production of a division between 'white-collar' managers and 'blue-collar' workers who are related to each other in an antagonistic fashion. Yet, as Marx himself pointed out, the exploitative nature of the capitalist system, which tends to turn the worker into 'a mere appendage of the machine' and which robs workers of the full value of their labour, cannot be maintained by sheer force. This is an unsubtle and inefficient mode of control. Rather, workers are encouraged to accept capitalism by having it portrayed to them as natural and inevitable, that is, by the perpetuation of an ideology which 'mystifies' capitalism and hides its true nature from those, whether worker or manager, who are subject to its demands.

The twentieth century saw the emergence of the large corporation which increasingly came to dominate productive activity. This development created new forms of labour and new challenges for management. In the large modern corporation the individual owner is now replaced by a mass of shareholders most of whom play no part in controlling the firm. Increasingly day-to-day control passes into the hands of 'professional' managers although at top management level these are often drawn from the ranks of the capitalist class or acquire shares which serve to ally their interests with those of owners. Management itself becomes specialized with the emergence of departments dealing exclusively with such functions as finance, marketing, production and personnel and, like the shopfloor production process, the activities carried out within these departments become subject to the same logic of division, specialization and control. Thus 'management has become administration, which is a labour process conducted for the purpose of control within the corporation'. As managers control they are themselves controlled.

How do managers in modern society fit into the polarized class structure envisaged by Marx? Braverman argues that whilst top managers are 'part of the class that personifies capital and employs labour', middle and junior managers are in a more ambiguous position. Fitting these managers into the Marxist system is problematic. Indeed the problem of the class location of such managers has been a matter of considerable debate within Marxist circles (see Reed, 1989). Braverman argues that they stand in effect as part workers, in Marx's words 'a special kind of wage labourer' dispossessed of the instruments of production just as is the blue-collar worker, and part capitalist, acting as the agents of owning interests. As such they are in a highly ambivalent position being at one and the same time part employer and part employee.

Braverman's work has provoked considerable discussion and debate, in particular on the nature of managerial strategies of control. An important criticism of his analysis focuses on the central role he gives to Taylorist forms of work organization as the means to managerial control of labour. Subsequently this notion has been found too limiting and attention has shifted to the identification of different types of control strategy albeit still implemented within the overall constraints of the capitalist system. Thus Friedman (1977) has argued that Taylorist scientific management is but one type of control strategy that may be implemented by management in order to secure workers' compliance with capitalist objectives. Such a direct-control strategy can be contrasted with the strategy of responsible autonomy whereby workers are allowed a degree of discretion over the conduct of their work, not because this is desirable in itself but because under certain circumstances this is the best way of reducing resistance. Similarly Edwards (1979) identified simple, technical and bureaucratic control strategies as alternatives which had been adopted in American industry during different periods of economic development and which represent the outcomes of efforts by managements to secure control under different conditions.

Much writing on management in the Marxist tradition emphasizes the conflictual nature of work relationships but it has been suggested that this tends to downplay the extent of day-to-day co-operation between workers and management. Since for much of the time work proceeds without overt conflict it might appear that what really needs to be explained is the acquiescence of labour to the working conditions imposed by capitalism rather than resistance to them. Why is it that workers co-operate with an exploitative system and so help to perpetuate it?

Littler and Salaman (1984) point to a number of factors including the adoption by management of control strategies, such as responsible autonomy, which are intended to secure commitment. But another key factor is the promulgation of ideologies which structure the basic assumptions which employees are expected to bring into the workplace and which define the ground rules within which employment relationships are supposed to be played out. A central element of these ideologies is their exclusiveness for they tacitly rule out alternative conceptions of the nature and purpose of production and disqualify any fundamental questioning of the legitimacy of capitalism as a social system. These authors propose that the characteristic general assumptions of these 'work-legitimating' ideologies are that capitalism is inevitable and unchangeable, that 'rational' technocratic forms of management and work organization are both neutral and necessary, and that private ownership of the means of production is legitimate.

In addition to these general themes, managerial ideologies serve to legitimize management by defining it as important and necessary and seek to justify the existence of distinct managerial occupations and their associated rewards by reference to notions of specialized managerial expertise and skills. 'The establishment of management', Littler and Salaman argue, 'as a separate function distinct from shopfloor workers, with unique expertise and responsibilities, and with major and critical claims to authority over the shop floor upon which the efficiency of the whole enterprise depends . . . is a crucial first step in the establishment of control over the workforce.' This is because once this role for management becomes taken for granted the workers have largely accepted 'the normality of their subordination'. Henceforth if the workforce wishes to argue then this is mainly about the details of decisions that have been made by management. So by acquiescing to managerial definitions of the respective roles of capital and labour the workers sustain the system in which they are exploited.

From a Marxist perspective, then, the fundamental antagonisms that are inherent to capitalist forms of work organization are constrained partly through the dissemination of ideas which mask its real character. These ideas are formulated and passed on in many ways but, in the case of managerial ideologies, management education supported by a growing body of social science knowledge has been of growing importance. Business schools, for example, have been described by Westergaard and Resler (1975) as functioning 'in part to polish the public face of capitalism without questioning its profit drive'.

Despite the many extensions and elaborations of Marx's original ideas on management the basic insights he offered have continued to be fundamental to Marxist thinking. In keeping with Marx's historical orientation, management, is seen as a product of a particular social system and is to be understood within the overall framework of capitalist society. Management as we encounter it today is 'management under capitalism' and it is the nature of the capitalist system that defines its meaning and significance. Alternative interpretations should, on this view, be seen as little more than bourgeois mystifications which obscure rather than reveal, much as claims that capitalism is inevitable and necessary stand as 'ideological fig leaves to hide the naked self-interest of a tiny minority' (Sweezy in Braverman, 1974).

Management: the politics of organization

From the point of view of those who emphasize the 'logic of capitalism' as the key to understanding management, managerial work is by its very nature political. Managers are not seen as neutral technicians deploying the most effective and efficient means available in order to realize consensual goals but as agents of the most powerful group in society, the capitalist class. As such, and whether they realize this themselves or not, managers have taken sides in the class war and are active parties in a fundamental dispute about how and in whose interests collective production should be organized. The role of management is to maintain and develop efficient methods of production but with the proviso that this must ensure that the basic structure of power inherent to capitalism is maintained despite resistance by recalcitrant employees. Politics is therefore seen to be a central fact of organizational life in a capitalist society.

However, the centrality of politics to management has also been highlighted by writers who do not work within a Marxist frame of analysis.

Focusing largely upon management in organizations, often with little reference to the wider societal context, the 'political perspective' adopts a pluralist view in which managers and managerial subgroups are seen to use the tactics of power and influence in order both to define the ends to which organizational resources should be devoted and the means to be used to achieve them. The political perspective, as Reed (1989) has put it:

> reconceptualises management as consisting of a plurality of competing groups or coalitions that often come into conflict over decisions concerning the choice of organizational designs and temporarily resolves this disagreement through the exercise of power in one form or another ... political analyses of managerial decision-making over organizational design concentrate on the continually shifting balance of interests and power within management (particularly top management or the 'dominant coalition') and its impact on the way in which the agenda for decision-making is constructed.

On this view, the goals of an organization are not depicted as fixed parameters, established by some overriding logic of the economic system, but as issues to be resolved and as matters open to an important degree to choice. Similarly, the ways in which any particular set of goals are to be pursued is also open to decision and choice. Since organizations are taken to be made up of a variety of interest groups, each with their own priorities and preferences, managers are seen to be engaged in a more or less permanent process of dialogue, bargaining and conflict-management which seeks to resolve issues of means and ends if only on a temporary basis. Rather than running a grand machine, whether dedicated to promoting the well-being of all or to maintaining the privileges of an owning class, managers are seen to be embroiled in webs of uncertainty within which they must negotiate their way forward in a precarious and sometimes fitful manner.

This view has been well expressed by Bacharach and Lawler (1980) who argue that:

> Organizations are neither the rational, harmonious entities celebrated in managerial theory nor the arenas of apocalyptic class conflict projected by Marxists. Rather it may be argued, a more suitable notion lies somewhere between those two – a concept of organizations as politically negotiated orders.

The term 'politically negotiated orders' refers to the idea that organizational structures and outcomes are the products of negotiation and bargaining between differentially advantaged groups. Organizations are what they are because of the 'conscious political decisions of particular actors and interest groups'.

Bacharach and Lawler identify five assumptions which underlie their political theory of organizations:

1 Organizations are best conceptualized as political bargaining systems.
2 Specific decision-making spheres are the primary arenas for bargaining and conflict in organizations.
3 Within the decision spheres, most organizational politics involves the efforts of actors to mobilize interest groups and coalitions for the sake of influencing decisions of those in authority.
4 On the basis of collective objectives, interest groups merge into coalitions and select tactics to achieve their common objectives.
5 The formation of coalitions and coalition alliances will depend on the nature of the organizational structure and on the distribution and control of organizational resources.

The key units in organizations are interest groups and coalitions and the key process is that of bargaining. Interest groups consist of those members who share common goals beyond those formally defined for them by the organization. Interest group membership does not therefore necessarily coincide with membership of organizational units such as departments although it may do so in relation to some issues. Coalitions are sets of interest groups which form in order to advance a common goal and which stand outside the formal organization structure. Coalitions attempt to exert influence on those who hold formal authority in the organization by engaging in bargaining processes. These processes may be undertaken overtly or be hidden from view.

From this perspective, managers occupy a double role in organizations. On the one hand, they occupy positions of formal authority and as such are likely to be exposed to the influence attempts of various coalitions. On the other, they are likely themselves to be members of a variety of coalitions according to the issues that are dominant at any particular time. This does not necessarily mean, however, that all coalitions are equally influential nor that the outcomes of coalition bargaining will be in line with coalition goals.

Two useful ideas which can be used to illuminate this political view of management are those of the 'dominant coalition' (Cyert and March, 1963) and 'bounded rationality' (March and Simon, 1958). The former depicts the structure within which organizational decisions are reached, while the latter offers an account of the processes of organizational decision-making.

The dominant coalition

Cyert and March (1963) argued that firms are faced by a seeming paradox. On the one hand, if they are to be organized in an efficient and effective way they seem to need agreed goals against which alternative decisions can be evaluated. Yet individual employees and groups of employees tend to have goals of their own which may be in conflict with each other. Different managers, for example, may have different views on the priority to be given to different products and markets, on how resources should be allocated between departments, and on who should be promoted to a particular job. Managers may differ both in terms of organizational and personal objectives, and even if they did agree with each other, other employee groups may not agree with them. Under these conditions it would seem that firms are permanently at war with themselves and so unable to secure co-ordinated and concerted action.

These authors suggest, however, that firms do define something akin to agreed goals and that this is achieved through processes of bargaining between members of the firm's dominant coalition. This coalition brings together parties with different objectives and priorities who attempt to reach a consensus on business objectives. This consensus is, however, likely to be reached only on rather vague, high-level aims such as 'to remain a leader in the industry' or 'to give high quality to our customers' but so long as this agreement is sufficient to give the coalition members a sense of unity it provides the grounds for co-operation. On more specific policy matters, members of the dominant coalition tend to achieve compromises which satisfy the parties to some minimal degree. The resulting policies may not be fully consistent, but this is the price which has to be paid for imperfect information and for the continuation of the coalition. If some members are denied any acceptance of their objectives they may withdraw from or be forced to leave the coalition, an outcome which is likely to be avoided because the coalition may be weakened to the point at which it ceases to be viable. From the individual member's point of view, exclusion means loss of influence and relegation to a passive role, dependent on whatever decisions the remaining coalition members reach, so the incentive to compromise is strong.

Decisions about ends are thus reached as a result of argument, debate and conflict in much the same way as a political party achieves a consensus on policy issues. Party members may rarely agree with everything that appears in the party's manifesto, and may strongly disagree with some policy proposals, but compromise involves being willing to support proposals with which one disagrees in order to increase the likelihood of seeing those one does support put into effect. In management as in national politics, individuals are engaged in a collective enterprise which demands bargains be struck, alliances be formed, and common interests identified.

The concept of the dominant coalition is treated by different writers in somewhat different ways. In some formulations, the coalition is depicted as including representatives of interest outside the organization, such as major shareholders, in others as being formed among the members of senior management, and in still others as consisting of any set of individuals who are able to muster sufficient resources to enable them to exert decisive influence over organizational decisions. The common thread in these views is nonetheless that the capacity to influence organizational decisions is not fixed by the formal organization structure (although this capacity will be influenced by the structure) and may shift as coalitions are formed and reformed. It is assumed then that some coalition or other will usually be in a position of dominant influence but that its membership and hence the interests which are brought to bear will vary over time.

Bounded rationality

The concept of bounded rationality takes issue explicitly with that of objective rationality. Objective rationality is not possible because, according to Simon (1947):

> Objective rationality . . . would imply that the behaving subject moulds all his behaviour into an integrated pattern by (a) viewing the behaviour alternatives prior to a decision in panoramic fashion, (b) considering the whole complex of consequences that would follow on each choice, and (c) with a system of values as criterion singling out one from the whole set of alternatives.

In reality all the alternative courses of action confronting an actor cannot be known nor can all the consequences of any one of them be reliably ascertained. Similarly it is impossible to estimate the value or utility which will accrue from each alternative. The possibilities of rational choice are therefore constrained or limited and managers have to work with simplified models of what is in fact a much more complex reality. Managers will thus tend to seek acceptable solutions to problems (satisficing) rather than search for the best solution (optimizing). They will also establish routines for handling recurrent decision situations and will not seek novel alternatives unless the existing routines fail.

Because objective rationality is impossible to achieve, bounded rationality inevitably characterizes everyday behaviour. We all have to work with simplified models of the world which screen out much of its complexity so that we can at least do something! One consequence of this is that our actions often have unexpected effects which may react back on us in problematic ways.

The following example, from Thomas (1996), provides a good illustration. During the American Skylab space missions the ground controllers tried to manage the astronaut crews' behaviour by issuing highly detailed plans, instructions and minute-by-minute work schedules. Unfortunately this centralized way of managing tacitly assumed that the conditions on the spacecraft would enable these instructions to be carried out to the letter. In fact the astronauts faced many unanticipated problems. Equipment could not be found or did not operate as expected, sleeping was difficult, rest-breaks were inadequate, and so on. The third crew to inhabit Skylab fell progressively behind schedule but the response from the ground was to push them even harder. In part as a response to what they perceived to be this unsympathetic treatment, the crew staged a twenty-four hour work stoppage and so achieved the world's first strike in space!

Of course some of these events might have been foreseen, but no one could have known for sure what was to happen. The ground controllers' decisions were inevitably a product of bounded rationality. And as the issues become more complex and uncertain, as they tend to do at the highest levels of organizational decision-making, the likelihood of decisions yielding unexpected effects is all the greater.

Taken together, the ideas of dominant coalitions and bounded rationality draw attention to the essentially political nature of management. Ends are not consensually agreed by all participants in the organization nor are they imposed by a single class of owners. Rather, they are established on temporary and shifting ground according to the balance of forces within the organization which create the bases for the formation of 'winning' coalitions. How and whether such coalitions are formed is not determined 'in advance' but is heavily dependent upon the activities of managers as well as other parties.

When it comes to proposing specific policies or courses of action, the notion of bounded rationality suggests that the capacity to demonstrate unequivocally that specific consequences will follow and that specific values will accrue will often be limited, the more so as the complexity of the decision grows and the longer the lag between implementation and expected payoff. For this reason securing support for some proposed course of action will require advocacy, argument and persuasion. Also, because of the likelihood of unintended consequences, even when intended courses of action are implemented they may generate unanticipated results which change the balance of forces between current and potential coalition participants.

Since management is at the very least concerned with influencing organizational events and processes, and since participation in coalition politics will often be a necessary condition for the successful exercise of influence, political awareness and political skills are seen, on this view, to be central to any notion of management.

Politics at work

The necessity of organizational politics arises, it is argued, from the fact that organizations are not well-integrated, harmonious units, but rather loose assemblages of diverse people and resources. Organizations are not unitary wholes but pluralistic entities in which multiple groups with differing interests, resources, skills and aims engage in both co-operative *and* conflictual activities. Politics in the broadest sense, far from being an abnormal or unusual aspect of managerial life, is better thought of as inherent to the task of managing (Stephenson, 1985).

Management involvement in political activities occurs most visibly at the top levels of large firms where organizational politics intermesh with national political institutions. Studies of the behaviour of dominant coalitions at the higher levels of business firms and their impact on internal affairs are, however, scarce, in part because research access to the 'higher circles' of big business is problematic, but accounts of power struggles between top executives are somewhat easier to come by and give some support to the political conception of management at the highest level.

Take, for example, the case of Lee Iacocca. The son of an Italian immigrant to the United States, Iacocca started work as a management trainee with the Ford motor company in 1946. Ten years later, he became Ford's marketing manager, and was appointed head of the car division soon after. In 1970 he had reached the top as president of the Ford Motor Company, but following a disagreement with Henry Ford over policy he was demoted and then fired. According to Iacocca, he was dismissed not because the firm was failing but because Henry Ford simply didn't like him (Davis, 1987). Martin and Siehl's (1983) account of John De Lorean's struggle to establish himself at General Motors gives another graphic insight into organizational politics at the topmost level; respecting authority, fitting in and being loyal were the core values at GM and woe betide anyone who refused to conform to them.

But a political view of management emphasizes that politics is not the special province of top managers and directors as they deal with governments, shareholders and other external parties. Rather, day-to-day management is seen to proceed very much within a political context with conflict, bargaining, and coalition building the essential means to achieving change, keeping things under control or simply getting by (Murray and Gandz, 1980; Zaleznik, 1970).

From the very start of their careers managers encounter the politics of organization for, as Izraeli (1977) has shown, the business of 'settling in' or 'getting one's feet under the table' is largely a political process. Izraeli's study examined the efforts of a newly recruited manager to 'settle in' to his job with an electrical goods manufacturer. In order to convert his formal authority into real power he had to replace subordinates who were loyal to the 'old guard', win the support of neutrals, and secure the backing of the higher levels of management, doing all this with meagre resources. Only after he had successfully managed the political process of 'settling in' was he able to exercise the prerogatives that were formally his.

Managers typically hold positions of formal authority in organizations but this does not necessarily mean that they can actually get anything done. Managerial authority may be subverted by the capacity of subordinates and colleagues to use their discretion in ways that make life difficult or impossible for those 'in charge'. Managers therefore need to develop political sensitivity and not place exclusive reliance on their official authority if they are to survive.

One form of political sensitivity is to appreciate the extent of one's dependence on those over whom formal authority is exercised. Once this is realized, the importance of 'looking after your own people' becomes clear. As Lawrence (1986) has noted, the effective manager needs not only to be able to solve problems for higher management but also to do so for subordinates by acquiring valued resources for them and protecting them from outside interference, unreasonable demands and unwarranted pressures. Nor need the problems managers seek to solve for their subordinates be strictly work related. Lawrence recounts the story of a divisional manager in a German precision-engineering company who claimed that his reputation with the shopfloor rested not upon his outstanding technical achievements but upon his ability to re-line motor-car clutches!

Dalton's (1959) classic study provides an excellent illustration of the way middle managers engage in political activities at the workplace. In one firm, managers in the production department recognized that their ability to control production costs was seen by higher management as a key indicator of their performance and worthiness for future promotion. Because they valued promotion prospects highly, they had a strong interest in keeping production costs down, but the factors influencing these costs were not entirely within their control. One problem, as they saw it, was the behaviour of the maintenance department, which could significantly affect the production department's costs according to how quickly it repaired breakdowns in the equipment. The production managers therefore developed a coalition with the maintenance managers which served both parties' interests, using both the offer of rewards and the threat of sanctions to persuade the maintenance people to co-operate. The rewards included the willingness of the production department to support maintenance when the time came to put its case to higher management for increased resources, while the threats included ceasing to cover-up for maintenance when they made errors. Maintenance, in return, would clandestinely give the production staff advance notice of snap inspections of the production facility so that potentially embarrassing revelations could be prevented. In these ways departmental managers were able to retain control over their preferred ways of doing things, irrespective of the formal requirements of the organization, and to secure what they saw as their best interests.

Promotions and the more general allocation of personnel provide another important focus for political behaviour (Ferris and King, 1991). In the game of politics those who can bring highly valued resources to the bargaining process stand a better chance of winning than those who cannot, and since promotion has traditionally been one of the most valued rewards sought by managers, anyone who can significantly influence promotion chances is in a strong position to exert influence. Moreover, by securing promotions for one's friends and denying it to one's enemies the process of coalition building is greatly enhanced. As we will see in Chapter 6, appraisal and promotion processes can be the focus of intense political manoeuvring despite the 'rational' selection systems and procedures that are frequently established in the hope of achieving objective selection on merit.

Management, magic and religion

On the face of it, it may seem baffling or even facetious to consider modern management, and especially business management, as closely involved with magical and religious practices. Because, for many westerners, religion has a medieval, otherworldly air about it while magic is associated with the superstitious outlook of the pre-scientific age, both seem to be marked-off sharply from the rational, technological ethos of the business world. What we can call the 'magico-religious' interpretation of management suggests, however, that this demarcation is much less clear than has generally been believed.

This approach is rooted in the discipline of social anthropology, which takes as its central theme the understanding of the cultures of human societies. Social anthropology has been strongly identified with the study of 'primitive' peoples in simple, pre-industrial societies, where magic and religion were closely linked and often central features of the society's culture. Modern anthropologists have, however, expanded the scope of the discipline to cover contemporary peasant and urban societies while retaining much of the conceptual and theoretical framework developed during the analysis of simpler cultures.

One element of this framework proposes that human beings and human societies face certain fundamental common problems which give rise to the emergence of a variety of social practices which serve to cope with them. The precise form these practices take varies from culture to culture, but they can be classified together because they are oriented to dealing with the same underlying problems. The notion of 'functional equivalence' suggests that a given problem may be coped with in different ways, so that seemingly disparate practices may be seen to be simply alternative ways of achieving the same end. For example, the Chiricahua Apache's girls' puberty rite and a US presidential inauguration ceremony may be seen as alternative ways of enhancing social integration, bringing together the members of each society to celebrate important social ideals and values. Using this reasoning, much management practice can be seen to be magical or religious in character because it serves similar ends in modern society as magic and religion does among 'primitive' peoples.

The nature of magic and religion

In practice, magic and religion are often closely related, but for analytical purposes it is helpful to treat them separately. Although there is some disagreement among scholars as to how these terms should be defined, it is broadly agreed that magic and religion serve partly to cope with fundamental problems of uncertainty in human life.

Beals and Hoijer (1971) describe magic as 'a body of techniques and methods for controlling the universe, based on the assumption that if certain procedures are followed minutely, certain results are inevitable'. As such, magic may be thought of as analogous to western science where, it is often assumed, the careful application of certain formulae guarantees the production of certain outcomes. What distinguishes magic from science is not so much the form of their respective practices as that magical procedures are validated by those who practise them by means other than those associated with scientific method. Whereas scientific knowledge is thought to be self-correcting, on the basis of rigorous experiment and test of carefully defined hypotheses, magic is largely closed to disconfirmation. Failures in magic can thus be explained away on such grounds as the incorrect application of the required procedures, the countervailing influences of other magicians, or the absence of propitious circumstances. Magic can thus be seen as directed at achieving certain ends in the material world, but to be based essentially on faith (Cleverley, 1971). Like science, however, it is a means of reducing uncertainty about the way the world works, and hence valuable to society's members.

Religion is a broader concept than magic, but it also deals with uncertainty. Gods, for example, when conceived of as all-knowing and all-powerful, may be seen as the ultimate uncertainty reducers! Yet belief in gods and the supernatural is not a defining characteristic of religion. As Giddens (2001) has pointed out, belief in gods is not found in the religions of Buddhism, Confucianism and Taoism. Nor does religion necessarily involve moral prescriptions of human behaviour. What characterizes religion is a set of revered symbols linked to the performance of rituals and ceremonies which are practised by a community of believers.

These symbols may be of many kinds such as special words, objects, books, buildings, places, spirits and gods. Religious symbols are regarded as sacred, as supremely important and perhaps dangerous (Collins, 1982), and must therefore be treated in a special way. Believers engage in rituals which may be linked together to form ceremonies during which reverence for the symbols is expressed. Such ceremonies may be conducted under the guidance of priests who act as guardians of the purity of ritual acts.

Religion, in this sense, may be seen as a set of beliefs and practices which provide an overarching meaning to human existence. Through participation in rituals and ceremonies, believers come to share in and to pass on this meaning and also experience heightened emotional identification with fellow celebrants.

This view of religion remains close to everyday ideas of what is meant by the term, but some scholars have treated religion as simply one example of systems of beliefs which are used by people to make sense of the world in which they live (Berger, 1967; Berger and Luckmann, 1963, 1967). This approach encourages us to see the similarities between what appear to be very different belief systems. For example, religion and science can both be seen as belief systems, underpinned by different bodies of knowledge, different ways of acquiring this knowledge and different standards of 'truth'. Both religion and science have recourse to experts whose role is to define authoritative beliefs and distinguish them from error. Most importantly, both are concerned to develop explanations, predictions and understandings of the perplexity of experience and so transform a potentially threatening and ineffable world into one that is orderly, predictable and knowable (Thompson, 1986). Science is thus seen not to be radically distinct from religion; both are self-contained systems of belief which rest, ultimately, on certain basic articles of faith.

Magic in management

Both magic and religion are closely associated with managing life's uncertainties, but magical practices tend to have a narrower, more technical character than the more overarching sets of beliefs associated with religions. Magic is used to attain specific ends, such as the curing of a sick person or the bringing of rain, and is often drawn on to deal with situations that are believed to be important and dangerous. Thus Malinowski (1982) noted that among the Trobriand islanders, those who fished from the open sea with its attendant dangers performed various magical rites before setting out; but islanders who were able to fish in the calmer inshore waters of the Trobriand archipelago did not do so. Magic, then, is particularly likely to occur when people try to achieve ends which are highly important to them but which are surrounded by uncertainty.

Do managers engage in magic? If they do, then we would expect to find them doing so in those areas of management that are believed to be of great importance and that present the greatest uncertainty. This points to two major foci for magic in management, the management of people and the management of strategy; the former because people are believed to be the key source of uncertainty in organizations, and the latter because it deals with the greatest uncertainty of all, the future.

The magic of personnel techniques

The popular adage that 'management is getting things done through people' points to the central role of people in the management of organizations.

Yet people also present high levels of uncertainty to those whose task it is to manage them. Human beings cannot necessarily be manipulated with certainty, like machines, nor conditioned to respond like performing animals, despite the best efforts of some managers to do so. For, as Watson (1986) points out:

> The human animal is to be distinguished from other species by its ability to reason, its ability to evaluate and its capacity to think constantly in terms of alternatives. There is always the likelihood that humans will ask 'why should this be?' or 'cannot things be otherwise?'. This means that those managing the work efforts of others cannot expect every instruction given and every procedure laid down to be happily and willingly followed by every individual on every occasion.

Yet managers are given precisely this responsibility for getting things done through people despite their capacity for going their own way and for resisting or evading even the most carefully constructed systems of control.

As we saw earlier, the dominant image of the manager is that of the rational professional. The modern manager's professional identity is therefore closely bound up with the notion that managers are experts in the application of techniques. In the area of 'man management' such techniques have increasingly been devised by behaviourial scientists thus providing a 'scientific' basis for coping with the uncertainties of employee behaviour. Management by objectives, 3D management, grid training, one-minute management, transformational leadership are but examples of the host of personnel techniques that have been offered to managers to help them deal with people problems. But, as we shall see in more detail later during our examination of leadership and of managerial selection and promotion practices, these 'techniques' are themselves frequently fraught with uncertainty. Their roots in the social sciences are often shallow and insecure and these sciences tend to be drawn on selectively to support them. The social sciences thus become embroiled in sorcery (Andreski, 1974).

Like magic, personnel techniques require the careful application of arcane procedures in the belief that certain desired outcomes will follow; motivation will improve, conflict will be avoided, assent will be secured or the right person for the job will be selected. So, for example, job evaluation can be seen as an institutional myth, a sacred narrative which expresses deeply held beliefs which are beyond objective testing (Quaid, 1993). Even a 'hard' approach to structural change like business process reengineering can be seen as a magical search for salvation (Fincham, 1996). Like magic, such procedures have little direct bearing on the outcomes. What they do provide, however, is a sense of security to those who face the task of 'getting results'; by using the 'best available techniques', fears of accusations of irrationality or bias can be successfully warded off.

From a magico-religious point of view, such techniques are best seen not as rational means of controlling employees' behaviour but as magical rites which take a rational form. Furthermore, managerial faith in the possibility of the control of the uncertainty presented by human involvement in organizations reflects reverence for the sacred symbols of rationality and professionalism.

Strategic magic

An organization's strategy consists of the plans and objectives it has adopted in order to realize its goals. Strategy formulation is concerned with establishing these goals and identifying the means to be used to achieve them. Strategy-making is therefore inherently forward-looking because it involves predicting how an organization and the environment to which it relates are likely to develop over time. These predictions or forecasts provide the basis for here-and-now decisions about how to manage and structure the organization in order to achieve these future goals. Since strategy aims to determine both the structure and performance of the organization, it typically assumes overriding importance in the eyes of at least higher management.

Yet strategy-making is also surrounded by considerable uncertainty. At base, this stems from its concern with the future which cannot be known with any certainty. Indeed, it cannot be known at all (Kumar, 1978); at best we can surmise that the future will be much like the present but this is always an assumption rather than a provable fact. Quite apart from these fundamental difficulties, under current conditions of environmental turbulence and change, fathoming the future has become highly problematic.

Since strategy-making requires predictions and forecasts it is no surprise to find that many corporations expend considerable effort and expense to obtain them. On the face of it, this seems perfectly rational. But is it?

Why, ask Gimpl and Dakin (1984), do managers continue to seek forecasts when conditions are highly uncertain and unpredictable? It is not, they argue, because modern forecasting techniques are actually capable of producing reliable forecasts because there is considerable evidence to indicate that they are not. Hence they contend that 'management's enchantment with the magical rites of long-range planning, forecasting, and several other future-oriented techniques is a manifestation of anxiety-relieving superstitious behaviour, and that forecasting and planning have the same functions that magical rites have'.

Forecasting the future, they point out, is a very ancient human activity and one that has become increasingly popular in management in recent years. But evaluations of modern statistical forecasting techniques show them to be no better, and sometimes worse, than commonsense methods. Hence 'the difference between modern economic forecasters and the shaman predicting and inducing rain may be more in their appearance than in the substance of their predictions'. Similarly, long-range strategic planning, which aims to mitigate future uncertainties, is long on analysis and prediction but short on implementation and evaluation. It serves less as a basis for action and decision than as a comforting ritual whereby managers signal to themselves and others that they are behaving rationally and that 'everything is under control'. 'Is there', ask Gimpl and Dakin, 'any difference between a chief executive asking his strategic planners for scenarios for the future, and a Babylonian monarch making similar demands of his astrologer?' They suspect not. Although some statisticians, such as Makridakis (1996), believe that the impotence of business forecasting can be remedied by the adoption of appropriate assumptions and techniques, significant doubts about its role in business strategy and in planning remain.

Management: a 'secular' religion?

The magico-religious view of management has been most fully developed by Cleverley (1971) who draws telling comparisons between the behaviour of modern managers and that of 'primitive' tribesmen. Management, he suggests, incorporates a set of magico-religious beliefs akin to those found in simple societies. The management world is one in which supernatural forces are at work, and sometimes these operate in capricious and threatening ways. But these forces can be influenced by acting out suitable rituals.

Supernatural entities include the Shareholders, the Company (or Organization) and the Market. The Company, for example, is personified and is imputed with possessing goals, purposes or missions. It is seen as a sacred object commanding reverence through obedience, loyalty and dedication. These gods are threatening and must be propitiated. So, for example, the Shareholders are placated at the ceremonial of the Annual General Meeting. Moral prescriptions, indicating proper ways of behaving, are also in evidence. Foremost among these is 'Thou shalt seek profits', to which we might add 'And thou shalt seek promotion'.

The religion of management, Cleverley continues, is administered by a priesthood, the Accountants, and attended by magicians, the Consultants. Its belief system is developed and passed on partly by Behaviourial Scientists, and it embraces a set of rites; rites of passage, invoked during processes of managerial recruitment and promotion, and funerary rites, attendant upon retirement, resignation and dismissal. The belief system also defines certain taboo objects which are to be shunned. Women, for example, are to be avoided for fear of contamination.

Cleverley concludes that people are simply not rational creatures. A more fruitful view, however, might be that rationality is always relative to a belief system. For someone who believes himself to be Napoleon, it is perfectly rational to inquire after the health of Josephine. Rationality is therefore partly dependent on our perspective. In modern society, and particularly in modern management, the perspective which people are expected to adopt as a basis for their conduct is that of instrumental rationality, especially in employment settings. Managers are expected to act calculatively, estimating the most effective means to realize given ends and then implementing them, preferably on the basis of well-validated scientific knowledge. They are expected to behave in effect as everyday scientists for to do otherwise is to lay oneself open to charges of incompetence and irrationality. But because the capacity of the sciences, and especially the social sciences, to reduce uncertainty is limited, the knowledge required to realize this instrumental ideal is always insufficient. The appearance of instrumental rationality must nonetheless be maintained and takes the form of 'ceremonial conformity' (Meyer and Rowan, 1977) to the rational ideal. Many management techniques can thus be seen as symbols denoting adherence to the values of instrumental rationality enshrined in the wider society.

In that sense, management can be seen as a 'secular' religion (Collins, 1982) and business as a quasi-religious enterprise (Frank, 2000). Work organizations have come to replace churches as the major source of meanings in people's lives. Prominent among these meanings is the Myth of Management (Bowles, 1989, 1997). While overt belief in supernatural forces is generally eschewed in managerial belief systems, the rituals and symbols remain. Indeed the need to pay explicit attention to such matters as rites, ceremonials, myths, stories, symbols and legends has increasingly been emphasized in recent writings on corporate culture (see Brown, 1998). But the translation of culture into the perspective of instrumental rationality, by treating it, for example, as a 'tool' of top management, produces a very curious result. At one level, culture becomes demystified, but at another 'culture' becomes the latest addition to the set of symbols of the secular religion of management.

Commentary

In this and the preceding chapter we have set out four broad ways of understanding management. It will hopefully be evident that none of these frameworks is patently absurd and that each offers valuable insights into the nature of management derived both from the theoretical assumptions they bring to the topic and research evidence on managerial behaviour. We are now in a position to take stock and to consider the extent to which we have been able to answer the question 'what is management?'.

The first and most obvious conclusion we can draw from our exploration is that there is no one answer that is likely to satisfy everyone. As we saw in our discussion of the nature of controversies, the likelihood of resolving them depends partly on whether they are rooted in disputes over facts, differences of values or assumptions embodied in alternative frameworks of interpretation. When it comes to interpretations of the nature of management we appear to be dealing very much with the latter, with frame-work disputes, and these are of a kind that offer the least prospect of resolution. Although factual evidence is far from irrelevant here it can nonetheless play only a limited role in adjudicating between these positions.

Fortunately we do not need to treat these frameworks as mutually exclu-sive alternatives, and they are seldom presented as such by their proponents. Rather, it is possible to regard each view as having captured an important aspect of management. At this point we can best proceed by reconsidering the dimensions of sectionalism and rationality which we used as the basis for our organizing framework and then examine the possibility of recon-ciliation between the different approaches.

We have suggested that a major difference in approaches to the under-standing of management is in terms of the ends which management serves. Is management practice devoted to the realization of the interests of 'society' or is it more narrowly dedicated to advancing those of capital-ists or of managers themselves?

You do not have to be a Marxist to appreciate that capitalist forms of economic organization have become dominant in much of contemporary society. Management, in Britain, the United States, Japan, Germany and elsewhere is exercised within the framework of capitalism in which private ownership, the profit motive, a free market for labour and a set of supportive social, economic and political institutions constitute the basic context of management practice. Despite the growth of very large corporations and the development of a substantial management stratum divorced to a consid-erable degree from owning interests, managers show few signs of deserting the capitalist ethic. Commenting on the research into managerial orienta-tions, Eldridge *et al.* (1991) note that 'What stands out is how managers tend to behave as if they owned the enterprises that employ them; as if they were themselves owner-capitalists.' Even so, it can be argued that by doing so managers serve the interests of society, or at least the interests of those who must work within the confines of the assumptions of capi-talism. For in the competitive market, efficiency translates not only into profits and shareholder dividends, but also into affordable products, higher wages, secure employment and adequate pensions, none of which, it might be claimed, accrue to economies organized on a different basis. If this brings with it autocratic management styles, unemployment, meaningless work experiences, and perennial organizational instability and technolog-ical change, that is simply a price worth paying. Thus it can be claimed that even if managerial capitalism is a very inadequate method of organiz-ing the production process, it nonetheless yields more benefits to more people than any of the alternatives.

Irrespective of whether management is seen to be dedicated to furthering the interests of a narrow band of property owners or to the interests of society as a whole, there is evidence to show that those ends may be inter-twined with the more parochial goals of individual managers and groups of managers. The acquisition of wealth, status and power is an age-old human aspiration so it is not surprising to find that this continues to figure prominently on managers' agendas. Yet it does not follow that managers can pursue their own concerns without regard to the interests of others. In particular, managers may enter into vigorous disputes over how the organizational game should be played but they are not necessarily willing or able to change the objectives of the game itself.

The issue of sectionalism is therefore far from being clear-cut. One person's 'bourgeois ideology' is another's 'ethic of capitalism'. And even if managers do sometimes pursue parochial ends, this does not necessarily shield them from competing interests.

Turning to the matter of rationality, it seems clear that the idea that managers run organizations as if they were fully transparent machines where levers are pulled and buttons are pressed with highly predictable results is highly implausible. The social and organizational context of management is too complex and too fraught with uncertainty to allow this. Rather, managers appear to be caught up in a welter of conflicting pressures, contradictory alternatives and ambiguous situations which seldom permit calculated control or reliable predictions of outcomes. Despite this, management tasks have become more fragmented and specialized and associated with a growing body of techniques. While some of these tend to be acted out in a ritualized manner, the pursuit of technical rationality as a basis for management practice seems inevitable and central to any adequate conception of modern management.

The rational professional image of management can be seen as an idealization, an expression of belief in what management ought to be rather than a description of what it is. But, as Child (in Parker *et al.,* 1977) has suggested, this stereotypical view 'of formally defined functions, executed in a spirit of service by men who are conscious of belonging to an identifiable professional corps', though incomplete, nonetheless does have a degree of validity. The classical management functions do stand as a meaningful account of the major activities of management although this does not imply that all managers engage in all these activities all of the time. Yet it does seem that the work of at least some managers is oriented to these functions and it is difficult to see how an adequate account of management could dispense with them.

But there is more to the reality of management than the pursuit of formally defined functions. Forecasting and planning, organizing, co-ordinating, commanding and controlling are key management processes, but to understand management we need to take into account the contexts in which those processes occur. The political framework reminds us of the diversity of the interests which people bring to organizations and so offsets a tendency to depict management in too omniscient and omnipotent terms. What is to be planned, organized, co-ordinated, commanded and controlled is not given, clearly understood and accepted by all. Rather, the ends to which management processes are to be directed have to be worked out and rendered legitimate through political processes, processes that are attended by considerable uncertainty and ambiguity. The political framework therefore points to the significance of constraints on managerial control and the quasi-rational character of much managerial behaviour, a point further emphasized by the magico-religious framework.

It seems to me that the Marxist insistence that one cannot hope to understand management, or indeed any other institutionalized social practice, other than in its historical and societal context is correct. Management can be institutionalized in different forms according to differences in social structure, culture, and organizational context. But this applies within capitalist societies as well as to differences between capitalist and other societal forms. In countries such as Germany, Sweden and Japan, for example, the social meaning of management is somewhat different to that which has become established in Britain, as are the institutions with which management interacts. This suggests, then, that any general answer to the question 'what is management?' is likely to be of only limited value. To put it another way, there are only a few general characteristics of management and much that remains specific to different locales and contexts (Hickson and Pugh, 2001).

In this brief discussion, we have not been able to offer more than a few remarks on how the frameworks we have identified might be reconciled. More extensive presentations of theoretical approaches to management and organizations have been provided by, for example, Jackson and Carter (2000), Knights and Willmott (2002), Reed (1989), Thompson and McHugh (2002) and Watson (2002). Ultimately, we are left with the impression that management as a practice and as an object of knowledge is both complex, ambiguous and contentious. What managers do, how they do it, why they do it, in whose interests they do it and what kind of theoretical framework can best illuminate those issues, remain very much open questions.

Questions for discussion

1   In what sense are employees 'exploited' at work and why do they accept their exploitation?
2   Are organizational politics inevitable?
3   Can management ever be a fully rational process?
4   Can management be both a science and a religion?
5   Which view of management – rational profession, exploitation, politics or magic – seems most convincing to you, and why?

Further reading

Bowles, M. (1997) The Myth of Management: Direction and Failure in Contemporary Organizations, *Human Relations*, 50 (7), pp. 779–803.

Cleverley, G. (1971) *Managers and Magic*, London: Longman.

Jackson, N. and Carter, P. (2000) *Rethinking Organizational Behaviour*, Harlow: Pearson.

Knights, D. and Willmott, H. (2002) *Organizational Analysis: A Critical Text*, London: Thomson.

Watson, T.J. (2002) *Organizing and Managing Work: Organizational, Managerial and Strategic Behaviour in Theory and Practice*, Harlow: Pearson.

4 The social sciences

Can they help managers?

There's nothing so practical as a good theory.

Lewin (1946)

Practitioners and researchers tend increasingly to live in different worlds, pursue different enterprises, and have little to say to one another.

Schon (1983)

He that increaseth knowledge increaseth sorrow.

Ecclesiastes (*c.* 250–25 BC)

The purposeful organization of human labour on a large scale has a long history, but the idea that the organization and management of work could be based on science is relatively new. To have spoken of a science of management let alone to have suggested that scientific understanding was indispensable to effective management would have seemed absurd to the entrepreneurs who fashioned the Industrial Revolution. But with the emergence of the social sciences in the nineteenth and twentieth centuries and the widespread adoption of scientific rationality in the advanced industrial societies, it no longer seems ridiculous to claim that management practice would be much improved if it were based less on intuition and experience and more on sound scientific knowledge. On the face of it, and as the dramatic achievements of the physical sciences demonstrate, the best and perhaps the only way to bring order to the chaos of experience, and so increase the possibility of human control over the environment, is via the appliance of science.

In modern societies there are many occupations that have little to do with the application of science, but there are some which do make a more or less explicit claim to base their practice in scientific knowledge. In the Anglo-Saxon countries these occupations have frequently been institutionalized in the form of 'professions' in which an important claim to professionalism derives from training in the appropriate sciences. A good example is medicine which typifies the notion of a science-based profession. Thus medical practitioners undergo lengthy theoretical and practical training, learning about the biological sciences (biochemistry, physiology, anatomy, pharmacology, pathology and so on) in order to be able to diagnose diseases and apply treatments. Whatever its failings, modern medicine does a spectacularly better job today than it did before the development of the medical sciences. The application of science to the improvement of at least this kind of practice is clearly possible and desirable.

If the work of the doctor has been made much more effective by developments in the medical sciences and their incorporation into medical training, might not the work of the manager also be made more effective through the development and application of a management science, based not on biology but on the science of human behaviour? And if this were possible, might not the same advances in the capacity of doctors to cure patients find their counterpart in the ability of managers to deal with the 'diseases' of work behaviour and organization – absenteeism, job dissatisfaction, resistance to change and so on? Management might not seem as important to most people as medicine, but it is far from being a trivial affair. The development and application of a management science therefore seems not only desirable but essential if organizations and those who work in them are to be managed to good effect. But despite its obvious appeal, this idea, that management practice should be based like other professions on the sound knowledge of science, continues to be a focus of considerable scepticism and debate.

The controversy in brief

This controversy revolves around the problematic relationship between knowledge and action, theory and practice, the social sciences and management, and social scientists and managers. It carries us into some difficult and deep conceptual waters partly because the nature and status of science has been subjected to substantial scrutiny in recent years by philosophers of science. In addition, the nature of social science has been similarly examined not only by philosophers but also by practising social scientists. Whether it is science per se or the social sciences in particular that are at issue, little has emerged by way of a consensus on what are, in fact, highly complex and intractable problems. Even so, we can approach this controversy by organizing our thoughts around two broad views of the relationship between the social sciences and management practice.

The first and the oldest view depicts management as essentially an art. As such, management practice is unamenable to codification in the form of rules, procedures or principles of a kind which might be derived from rigorous theorization and experimental research. Effective managers, on this view, are those who possess the necessary innate qualities which enable them to 'get results' at the workplace. Because these innate qualities are difficult to describe and impossible to measure, literally beyond comprehension, management practice is mysterious. It is simply not possible to discover how effective managers get results, and even if it were, the way they practise reflects innate abilities so that there is little or no way of transferring their skills to others. While it is possible to learn by observing the 'mastercraftsmen', and through experience at the workplace, this knowledge is particular and localized and cannot be translated into general form. Hence it cannot be subjected to rigorous evaluation or experimental testing of a kind which might yield general knowledge. Nor can it be made the subject of formal instruction and examination. Managerial knowledge is therefore acquired chiefly by experience at work and effective managers emerge in the course of a Darwinian process of natural selection whereby only the fittest survive.

This management-as-art view denies, in effect, even the possibility of a management science. To the extent that science involves a commitment to generalized knowledge, in the extreme, universally valid knowledge, the art view declares this to be an unrealizable aim. Therefore, on the question of whether the social sciences can help managers it answers: no, because it is impossible to generalize about management, adding perhaps that the so-called social sciences are in any case anything but sciences. Similarly, the idea that management could be a 'profession' is equally unfounded because it can find no basis for its practice in science.

Against this view is the idea of management-as-science. Here management is seen as a deliberate and purposefully organized practice not unlike medicine, teaching, engineering and the law. Although it deals centrally with social entities, with human behaviour, rather than with biological or mechanical ones, it nonetheless involves the rational selection and implementation of means in order to achieve defined ends. Engineers build bridges, doctors make sick people well, and managers run profitable organizations, and just as a training in the appropriate sciences is essential for competent engineering and medical practice, so it is for management. And just as the natural sciences have created the knowledge which underlies the techniques of engineering and medicine, so the social sciences can, or could in time, play the same role in relation to management. The social sciences may have had greater difficulty in advancing with the degree of success of the natural sciences, but this is because of their relative immaturity and because there are special difficulties in applying scientific method to the social realm. Controlled experiments, for example, are difficult to conduct in the social sciences for both practical and ethical reasons. But in principle there is good reason to believe that the same kinds of knowledge will be forthcoming from the social sciences as from the natural sciences, and that such knowledge is as vital to effective management practice as it has been to competent engineering or medicine. Indeed, applied social science knowledge is already available and is taught widely through business schools.

Far from denying the possibility of management science, the management-as-science view sees it as not only possible but already in existence albeit in incomplete form. Can the social sciences help managers? The answer from this perspective is a resounding 'yes'.

Although I have caricatured these alternative views here, a debate along the lines of art versus science in management has been in progress ever since F.W. Taylor advocated his system of 'scientific management' in the early years of this century. And it is a debate with important practical implications. If the science view is sound, any neglect of the social sciences in management training seems perverse and likely to leave management in a similar situation to that of medicine before the rise of medical science, dominated by quackery and failure. If, however, the art view is correct, then the inclusion of contributions from the social sciences in management courses seems misplaced. To know about the social sciences might be interesting but essentially ornamental and irrelevant to the conduct of managerial work. It might even encourage managers to adopt wholly inappropriate policies and practices on the basis that they are derived from 'science' when in fact there is no science to speak of.

What we can be sure of is that many managers remain sceptical of the value of the social sciences to management. This could be a case of none being so blind as those who will not see, or it may be that managerial doubts about the usefulness of what passes for management science are in some sense justified. Can the social sciences really be of help to managers and if so how?

The idea of management science

The term 'management science' has come to be associated with a highly quantified discipline within the general field of management studies closely associated with operational research or OR. But for the purposes of the present discussion we are concerned with a much broader view of management science, one which conveys the general idea that management can be understood, and hence practised, in a scientific way.

As Chalmers (1996) has pointed out, science is a highly esteemed activity in modern society partly because scientists have been successful in establishing a particular image of the nature of science. Despite a growing unwillingness to accept that science is necessarily 'a good thing', scientific expertise still carries considerable prestige. To invoke science as a basis for one's pronouncements and actions is to claim a special kind of authority for them, one rooted in notions of fact, certainty and truth. When scientific knowledge comes to be seen as the only kind of knowledge worthy of the name, the alternatives, whether based on personal experience, religious authority, aesthetic insight or poetic vision, tend to be relegated to an inferior position or banished altogether from the realm of rational discourse. As scientific knowledge comes to be seen as high-quality knowledge, so practice based on this knowledge comes to be seen as high-quality, 'professional' practice. The link between knowledge and practice thus tends to crystallize in professional occupations, where practitioners bridge the everyday world of problems and the arcane world of science by means of their capacity to apply the latter to the former. Professional practice stands, as it were, in the shop-window of the scientific establishment, visibly demonstrating the relevance of science to everyday life. Science can then be seen not to be concerned simply with knowledge for its own sake, but to be an indispensable foundation for civilized living in a modern society. At least this is how citizens have been encouraged to see it.

This image of science, as both mysterious and otherworldly yet practical and accessible, is most closely associated with the natural sciences – physics, chemistry, biology and so on. The social sciences by comparison have failed to achieve anything like the same degree of public acceptance. Yet when the social sciences emerged as distinct disciplines in the eighteenth and nineteenth centuries, they too aspired to scientific status and to a practical role in the conduct of human affairs.

These aspirations are well expressed in the writings of one of the early 'founding fathers' of social science, Saint-Simon (1760–1825). He envisaged the development of a 'science of society' akin to the sciences of the natural world and this science would be used as the basis for the regulation and control of human affairs. Politics would therefore be supplanted by scientific administration or what we would now call management. Interestingly, Saint-Simon derived his model for the administration of society from what he took to be appropriate for the management of large industrial concerns (Kumar, 1978), a science of society being in effect a scaled-up version of a science of industrial management.

The natural science model of social science has come to be associated with the term 'positivism'. Although itself a focus of considerable debate, this approach to the study of the social world assumes that the key task of science is to identify causal relations between the facts of experience. These facts are accumulated by means of careful observation and measurement, and hypotheses about the relationships between these facts are tested by experimental methods. These methods aim to isolate the phenomena under investigation from outside influences so that causal relations can be disentangled. By a process of elimination only those relationships which have been found to withstand experimental testing by different scientists under different conditions are admitted to the corpus of scientific knowledge, so that in the long run a body of knowledge is established which shows how the world 'works'. In essence, the aim is to generate a set of scientific laws of the kind 'whenever A occurs, then B occurs' (Thomas, 2003).

Clearly, the existence of scientific laws of this kind could be extremely useful. Insofar as we are faced with the problem of achieving end B, then to know that A is a cause of B implies that if we wish to achieve B we should bring about A. But there is no guarantee that such laws will be useful, partly because the task of science, on this view, is to find out how the world works not how human beings could manipulate the world. So, for example, scientists may be able to tell us with considerable precision what the effects on the motion of the tides would be if the Moon were only half as far away from the Earth as it is. But because we are not in a position to move the Moon, it is not in that sense useful knowledge. If, on the other hand, we could establish laws that related causes to effects where the causes were open to human influence and the effects were ends we wished to achieve, then we would seem to have come close to a useful science. From basic science we could derive usable techniques. The link between this positivist view of science and action is therefore through the notion of technique.

Today there are few social scientists who would make the kind of revolutionary claims for social science put forward by Saint-Simon. On the contrary, social scientists have become increasingly aware of the limitations of social science, of its inability to provide conclusive answers to important social questions, and of its tendency to meet demands for greater certainty with greater uncertainty (Shipman, 1976, 1997). When social scientists tackle the problems of everyday life they usually turn out to be much more complex than they at first appear.

This has led to considerable debate on the status of social science as an activity capable of generating 'real knowledge'. Social scientists themselves have sometimes doubted whether they 'know' anything at all, let alone anything that could be used by practical actors (Phillips, 1971). As Cuff, Sharrock and Francis (1998) have put it for sociology:

> Once again there is a sense of crisis in sociology, and realisation of the grand ambition that it should contribute to (if not play the key role in) a rational reconstruction of society for the benefit of all humanity now seems further away than ever. At the present time, there are even suspicions that the discipline has virtually put itself into liquidation.

Similarly, Hudson (1972) has commented that psychology:

> is a subject, or series of subjects, in which one research fashion succeeds another, leaving surprisingly little behind it as a residue of re-usable knowledge. In this respect, even the most experimental forms of psychology resemble much more closely an art form, modern painting for instance, than they do an established science.

The dream of a science of 'man' in society has largely lost credibility among social scientists to the extent that the whole endeavour has been labelled an 'impossible science' (Turner and Turner, 1990). In the face of this fundamental scepticism from within, claims for the possibility of a science of management have come to look increasingly thin.

This long-standing debate about the nature of social science has been extended of late by growing interest in the notion of paradigms. The term 'paradigm' was first brought to prominence by Kuhn (1962) and has subsequently been applied extensively to the field of organization by Burrell and Morgan (1979). Broadly speaking, a paradigm consists of a framework of concepts and assumptions which serves to define alternative ways of interpreting, understanding and acquiring knowledge of the world. Paradigms are comprehensive 'ways of seeing', sets of conceptual spectacles through which we can and must come to terms with the experience which presents itself to us. On this view, the scientist is not a neutral observer who simply records the facts of experience and discovers relations between them. Rather, the scientist brings a set of presuppositions about the world to bear on the investigative process which define both what is to be taken as fact and how knowledge of these facts can be obtained.

The key implication of this paradigmatic view of science is that scientific findings have a relative rather than an absolute status. The image of science as an activity which reveals the truth about the world is replaced by one which depicts scientific knowledge as relative to the paradigmatic frameworks within which scientists work. If scientists adopt mutually exclusive assumptions about the world they are studying, then each may produce findings which are consistent with their alternative paradigms but which are otherwise incompatible. Furthermore, there may be no obvious way of deciding which of a set of paradigms is to be preferred against others. It is somewhat like two observers trying to make sense of a game they see being played on a sports field. One assumes that they are engaged in a game of soccer and the other that they are playing rugby. Foul play to one is legitimate to the other. But in the case of science, we do not know what game is really being played and there is no referee on hand to tell us. The conclusions we reach are strongly influenced by the conceptual spectacles that are available to us at any particular time.

Burrell and Morgan (1979) have identified four major paradigms which have underlain most attempts at systematic organizational analysis. These are briefly summarized in Box 4.1. Each paradigm combines different sets of assumptions about first the nature of social science and second the nature of society.

Scientific assumptions fall into two broad classes. Either social science is conceived in terms of a natural science model, in which case social reality is depicted as having a hard, external quality which can be understood in terms of a causal analysis of relationships between phenomena. Or social science is conceived as fundamentally different to natural science because the social world is held to be constituted by the subjective meanings which human beings create in their day-to-day lives. Rather than seeing the social world as a given fact, as a kind of grand machine whose workings can be unravelled by the traditional methods of natural science, this view emphasizes the unique, personalized and localized character of social life. This world cannot be understood in the same way or by the same means as the natural world, and the outputs of social science are

---

Box 4.1 **Four paradigms of organizational analysis**

Functionalist

Organizations are viewed as entities analogous to machines or biological organisms. Their characteristics can be observed and measured objectively to yield knowledge about how they work. Organizations are assumed to be unitary wholes characterized by order and consensus and the analytical problem is how to explain this unity so that it can be maintained.

Radical structuralist

Organizations are viewed as having an objective, thing-like character which can be analysed, described and measured. But they are assumed to be inherently unstable, fragmented entities which reflect the fundamental conflictual nature of the wider society. The analytical problem is to explain change in terms of the interplay of conflicting forces so that emancipating, radical change can be promoted.

Interpretive

Organizations are viewed not as things with an existence independent of their members but as sets of shared meanings which constitute organizational reality. The stable, repetitive, organized pattern of human behaviour is maintained by the subjective enactment of a meaningful organizational reality. The analytical task is to reveal how people maintain this reality in the course of their everyday lives.

Radical humanist

Organizations are viewed as stable patterns of interaction based on shared meanings. But in modern society these meanings are held to constrict human consciousness in a way that separates human beings from their potential for fulfilment. The analytical task is to identify how dominant ways of thinking and being can be overturned in a way which releases people from their alienated existence.

Source: Adapted from G. Burrell and G. Morgan, *Sociological Paradigms and Organizational Analysis,* Aldershot: Gower, 1979.

---

closer to those of history and ethnography than they are to the laws and universal generalizations of natural science.

Assumptions about the nature of society differ according to whether they depict society (or at a lower level of analysis, organizations) as a cohesive, consensual unity or as a fragmented, conflictual diversity. The former 'regulative' view leads to a concern with describing and explaining this well-ordered world and with making predictions about its workings. The latter 'radical change' view, by contrast, points to a concern with under-standing radical change, deep-seated conflicts, repressive processes and forms of domination. On this view, society is seen to be inherently unstable, fundamentally problematic and capable of radical transformation rather than as a self-maintaining system of smoothly meshed structures and processes.

According to these authors, each paradigm denies some key assump-tions of the others so that each is self-contained. Debate between paradigms is therefore largely fruitless because such a debate requires agreement on basic premises. For example, we are unlikely to get very far in a discus-sion over game tactics if you think the game is soccer while I think it is rugby. If we could agree on which game it is, of course, things would be very different. But in the case of science there is no guarantee that we can. It would seem then that we are faced with choices between paradigms but with no compelling criteria which will enable us to choose.

We must remember, however, that scientists and managers are likely to approach this problem from different points of view. Quite how scientists choose between alternative paradigms is unclear. But however this is done it is presumably in the light of their own occupational interests, to advance knowledge, develop their scientific careers, and so on. Managers will, in principle, be similarly guided by occupational concerns and these are likely to focus strongly on utility. Social science paradigms are therefore likely to prove attractive only if they are believed to yield useful, managerial knowledge. So when Burrell and Morgan declare that 'organization theo-rists face a wide range of choices with regard to the nature of the assumptions which underwrite their point of view' we must not lose sight of the fact that managers are organization theorists of a particular kind. As managers they are practical organization theorists operating in a utili-tarian context, and this constrains the paradigmatic options they face. All paradigms may be scientifically valid, but this does not necessarily mean that they are all equally useful to the practising manager. This is because management, as an occupation, is itself constituted upon certain paradig-matic assumptions. To the extent that social science paradigms deny these assumptions, their usefulness is called into question.

To explore this contention, we can usefully draw on Gowler and Legge's (1986) discussion of paradigms and personnel management. Drawing on the four major paradigms identified by Burrell and Morgan (1979), they note that each of these can be used to give a different image of the role of personnel management. These images might be adopted by personnel managers themselves in order to make sense of their practice under the changed conditions which now prevail. The adoption of the radical struc-turalist paradigm, for example, might lead personnel managers to see their role chiefly in conflict terms, aggressively asserting the rights of capital against labour. The interpretive paradigm, however, might encourage a focus on generating shared meanings at the workplace or on cultural engineering, while the adoption of the radical humanist paradigm might encourage attention to improving employees' job satisfaction or opportunities for self-actualization. But the paradigm which Gowler and Legge see as most likely to be adopted is some version of functionalism.

The functionalist paradigm combines a natural science model of social science with a regulative view of the social world. It therefore assumes that 'the social world is composed of relatively concrete empirical artifacts and relationships which can be identified, studied and measured through approaches derived from the natural sciences' (Burrell and Morgan, 1979) and that the key task of social science is to understand how society is and can be regulated and controlled. As such, it has had an obvious appeal to applied scientists and to the agents of regulation and control in society, be they politicians, administrators or managers, whom they address.

The attractiveness of functionalism stems from two related factors. One is that functionalism has been 'the dominant paradigm of prescriptive management studies and practice' (Gowler and Legge, 1986). The social science paradigm which has been most congruent with the implicit assumptions of management as an occupation has been functionalist. Furthermore, in the case of personnel management, under current conditions of challenge and change functionalist assumptions provide a powerful means of justifying the maintenance of personnel's power. By depicting itself as a management function concerned with adapting entities called 'organizations' to external 'environments', personnel management trades on a set of assumptions about management that are widely shared both by scientists and fellow managers. In terms of the occupational interests of personnel managers, the functionalist paradigm looks to be very helpful indeed.

If social science within the functionalist paradigm holds out most appeal to the manager, it is not difficult to see why. At the technical level it has a practical cast. As Burrell and Morgan (1979) put it:

> In its overall approach it seeks to provide essentially rational explanations of social affairs. It is a perspective which is highly pragmatic in orientation, concerned to understand society in a way which generates knowledge which can be put to use. It is often problem-orientated in approach, concerned to provide practical solutions to practical problems.

And at a value level, this perspective has often been associated with a conservative, rather than a radical, viewpoint seeing management as the neutral administration of human affairs in the interests of all. Functionalism thus holds out not only the prospect of more effective management but also more effective management with a clear conscience. What could be more helpful than that?

The dominance of the functionalist paradigm does not mean that managers have nothing to gain from alternative perspectives. As Morgan (1997) has argued, managers can fruitfully enhance their capacity to understand organizational and managerial situations by expanding the range of metaphors, or of ways of seeing and thinking, that they use to make sense of organizational life. But I think we have to acknowledge that there are limits to this. For example, a paradigm which denied the possibility of management as a rational activity or which excluded the possibility that organizations have some kind of reality seems an unlikely basis for managerial practice. This is not to say, of course, that such paradigms are invalid but simply that they constitute management in a way that is highly problematic from a practical point of view.

The case for social science

Our discussion of paradigms shows that while social science can be conceived of in a number of different and contradictory ways, only some of these are congruent with the interests of management as it is constituted in contemporary society. If we are interested in whether the social sciences can help managers, then it is to work within the functionalist paradigm that we must largely turn for an answer. But even if it appears that this perspective is potentially most relevant to managerial concerns, this does not necessarily mean that functionalist social science has been able to generate applicable managerial knowledge. Whether it has done so and is capable of doing so is a matter of some dispute. We will therefore now examine some contending views on this matter, beginning with one of the leading functionalist writers on management, Tom Lupton (1918–2000).

Lupton, a former professor of Organizational Behaviour and Director of the Manchester Business School, was a consistent and persuasive advocate of the value of the social sciences to management. This is nowhere more evident than in the three editions of his book *Management and the Social Sciences* (Lupton, 1966, 1971, 1983) where he aimed to dispel the considerable doubts which have prevailed in management circles about the relevance of social science. For Lupton, knowledge of the social sciences is not only relevant to managers but essential.

Lupton advances his case by means of a discussion of the nature of social science and the nature of managerial work. The justification for the relevance of social science to management lies in the overlap between the problems and methods adopted by social scientists to study human behaviour and the skills and ideas needed by managers if they are to carry out their tasks effectively.

He defines social sciences as 'all activities which are concerned systematically to investigate and to explain aspects of the relation between the individual and the society of which he is a part' (Lupton, 1983). These activities have traditionally been organized into disciplines, such as economics, social psychology, sociology, social anthropology and political science, each of which specializes in some specific aspect of social life. What unites them, however, is a shared assumption that there are patterns in human behaviour which can be observed and which can be causally explained. Since managers are themselves faced with problems of understanding and influencing human behaviour, there is a clear prima facie case for the relevance of social science to management. But there are some snags.

One of these is that social scientists have typically been concerned with problems held to be interesting, and hence worthy of study, by the scientific community. Any link between these and the problems faced by managers has therefore tended to be indirect, managers having to make do, as it were, with knowledge not specifically geared to their own purposes and interests. In addition, Lupton suggests that the endeavours of social scientists have a different 'logical structure' to those of managers. Social scientists have mainly been concerned with explaining narrowly defined phenomena, whereas managers are concerned with taking action in complex situations where reality has to be dealt with 'all of a piece'. Like the blind men and the elephant, each social science specialism provides partial insights into reality, grasping some part of it which it understands on its own terms, whereas the manager confronts the whole elephant. In the absence of an integrated social science of management, frustration on the part of the practising manager is therefore inevitable.

How might social scientists and managers respond to this awkward state of affairs? Lupton (1983) sees two alternatives:

> Either we give up trying to understand and explain and rely exclusively and riskily on practical personal flair, or we seek better ways to understand and explain, and to make our understandings and explanations available for practical men to use. This latter activity is, as I see it, the social role of social science.

The task for social scientists, Lupton proposes, is to work towards a comprehensive, integrated body of knowledge about management and organization. Managers, on the other hand, should be exposed to social science thinking early in their careers and must be encouraged to interest themselves in the practical utility of social science theories and methods. Both parties need to work to achieve a meeting of minds by supplementing the traditional arm's length relationship between the social scientist and the manager with more collaborative ones. These might foster a greater understanding among managers of what the social sciences can offer, and a greater understanding among social scientists of managers' problems.

At base, Lupton sees lack of integration as the key obstacle to the wider application of the social sciences in management. This lack of integration is, I suggest, manifested in three ways. First, there is the lack of integration between the various social science disciplines; psychologists, sociologists and economists, for example, deploy their own very different disciplinary languages, theories and methods of research, and often find it difficult to communicate across disciplinary boundaries (Hakim, 2000). Second, there is a lack of fit between the problems addressed by these disciplines and the problems encountered by management practitioners; the puzzles which social scientists set out to solve are not necessarily those which puzzle managers. Third, there is a lack of social integration between social scientists and managers; social scientists are often located in the academic world where their careers and interests are moulded by academic preferences and criteria, whereas managers are located in the world of industry, commerce and administration where they must respond to a different set of pressures and considerations (Warmington, 1980).

Despite these difficulties, which Lupton is particularly careful to acknowledge, his conclusion on the role of the social sciences is tentatively optimistic. Practical procedures for the management of organizations have, he argues, been increasingly derivable from social science theory and research. And there is more to come:

> I predict that when we learn better how to derive these procedures, and when managers accustom themselves to the ideas that lie behind them, much that now remains in the sphere of ideology and guess-work will be raised to the level of scientific discourse and technological know-how, and human relationships in industry will be the better for it, not to speak of economic efficiency.

On this view, then, while it is accepted that the actual relevance of the social sciences to management is currently limited, this is likely to increase as social scientists come to concern themselves more with managerial problems and as managers become more aware of the potential of social science. The gulf between 'theory and practice' is potentially bridgeable and the aspirations of the classical management theorists, such as Fayol, for the development of an applied science of management therefore remain valid even though there is still much to be done.

The case against social science

You do not have to be a social scientist to realize that there is something problematic about the relationship between the kinds of knowledge dispensed through courses and textbooks and the way we tackle problems in our personal and professional lives. As Lupton himself (in Buchanan and Huczynski, 1985) has observed, even social scientists seem to behave in much the same ways as other people do, if not when doing science then at least for much of the rest of the time. If there is a gap between the 'fields of knowledge' and the 'fields of action' might this not be because the knowledge produced by social scientists is of a kind which not only is not but *cannot* be used by people like you and me in everyday life? If this were so, it might be unrealistic to expect to look to social science as a basis for managerial practice. Rather, one might focus attention not on the social sciences and their implications for practice but on practice and its implications for social science.

It is from this point of view that Schon (1983) develops an incisive critique of the role of the social sciences in relation to 'professional' practice. What his analysis proposes is that the dominant project of the social sciences as they have developed in the twentieth century has been inherently biased towards a conception of knowledge, an 'epistemology', which is increasingly unable to relate to practice. This dominant epistemology, which is rooted in a positivist conception of social science, defines the link between knowledge and action in terms of technical rationality.

As we have seen, positivism sees knowledge as consisting of statements about causal relations derived from systematic observation and experiment. When causally related entities are amenable to manipulation, this knowledge offers the possibility of the construction of techniques. These techniques are programmes for behaviour in that they specify what must be done under given conditions in order to achieve a given end. So, for example, if you want to manufacture hydrogen, add sodium to water. Uncertainty about how to attain the end state is eliminated and alternative techniques, based on hunch, intuition or established authority, are relegated to pre-scientific status. Behaviour based on scientific knowledge thus becomes technically rational, amounting to the application of the 'one best way' and perhaps the only way to achieve the given end.

The implication of technical rationality for professional practice is the widespread adoption of the view that 'professional activity consists in instrumental problem-solving made rigorous by the application of scientific theory and technique' (Schon, 1983). Professional practice is thus seen to be a matter of applying established techniques to recurrent problems. A doctor, for example, dispenses a particular drug with known effects in order to cure a particular disease. A further consequence of the adoption of the model of technical rationality as a basis for professional practice is that anyone who pursues their practice without reference to science ceases to be regarded as a fully legitimate professional. Technical rationality therefore carries with it a moral imperative that practitioners *ought* to rely on scientifically established techniques. To do otherwise is to be at best an 'amateur' and at worst a mere charlatan.

Schon argues that this model of professional practice is inadequate and is one that devalues those forms of professional competence which undoubtedly exist but which cannot be accounted for on its terms. To understand and thus improve practice there is a need to study the ways in which skilful practitioners behave, to identify the common, underlying structure of their behaviour and so produce an 'epistemology of practice' which reveals 'the kinds of knowing in which competent practitioners engage'. Although technical rationality is not wholly irrelevant to practice, it is radically incomplete as a model for it. This is because it makes certain assumptions about the relationship between knowledge and action that can seldom be met under current conditions.

Technical rationality assumes that the practitioner's task is one of problem-solving, where the problem to be solved is given and the need is to find a solution to it. Specific problems are taken to be instances of a general class of problems for which science provides a solution. The practitioner's task is to locate the specific problem in the appropriate class and then read off the prescribed solution. In practice, however, the practitioner is faced with unique problems and these cannot be handled by the application of standard theories and techniques. The practitioner has to identify or create a framework within which the problem at hand can be understood and made amenable to solution, so that identifying the problem as well as solving it is a key skill of professional practice. Furthermore, in many fields there is not just one framework that can be applied but a number of alternative frameworks. In management, for example, the manager is confronted with advocates of a variety of different 'management styles' which could be used as a basis for practice, but none is demonstrably superior. Practitioners therefore have to choose between alternative frameworks using 'a kind of inquiry which falls outside the model of Technical Rationality'.

The competent practitioner operates not according to the model of technical rationality but in the mode of 'reflection in action'. Each case or problem is treated as unique and this prompts reflection in order to make sense of it. Previous experience and general knowledge is drawn on in this sense-making process, but this is not allowed to swamp out the particular features of the current situation. There is little concern with finding standard solutions. Rather, there is a concern with finding solutions that work in this particular situation, with this particular person, under these particular conditions.

In finding such solutions the reflective practitioner engages in experimentation. But this takes a less restrictive form than the classical controlled experiment which is often thought to be at the heart of the scientific method. For Schon, experimentation is at base concerned with acting in order to see what happens. In the positivist model of science the key concern is with testing hypotheses concerning causal connections between variables and this requires the adoption of particularly rigorous controls. Ideally, the variables under study must be isolated from external influences so that only the variables of interest are observed and manipulated. In practical situations this is not possible. Indeed, this is one reason for the separation of knowledge from action; only scientists can carry out controlled experiments and practitioners are expected to depend on them to provide the

knowledge for their practice. Nonetheless, practitioners do engage in experimentation. On the basis of their framing of a problem they act in various
ways in order to see whether this yields solutions that are both practically
and morally adequate. And they remain open to the possibility that their
expectations (or hypotheses) will be disconfirmed, just as the scientist does.
Rather than acting as a technician, applying prepackaged scientific knowledge, the reflective practitioner is a kind of 'scientist-in-action' who
assumes that practice itself is a kind of research, that means and ends are
intertwined, and that knowing and doing are inseparable.

What then can the social sciences offer to the reflective practitioner?
Insofar as they model themselves on positivism and so adopt a technical
view of practice, the answer would appear to be very little. Although some
practitioners in some professions can act as technical experts, drawing
on the findings of science, they can often do so only in relation to the less
significant, less controversial aspects of their practice. In the case of
management the proliferation of technical 'knowledge' of almost all management functions is belied by a widespread unwillingness to acknowledge
its relevance to practice. This is partly because growing uncertainty and
change have reduced the generality of managerial environments and increased their uniqueness. General knowledge thus comes to fit less and
less well with the diversity which managers actually encounter. In addition,
managers continue to recognize the importance of non-rational, intuitive
artistry for their practice and remain unresponsive to the technical imperative of positivism. So while positivist social science can prescribe
techniques for some parts of professional practice, a large part of it cannot
be embraced by the model of technical rationality.

It should not be thought, however, that Schon is arguing against science
itself. His critique is directed at a particular conception of science, one
that he sees as unhelpful to practice. Science is needed, but this must be
in the form of an 'action science' that 'would concern itself with situations of uniqueness, uncertainty and instability which do not lend
themselves to the application of theories and techniques derived from
science in the mode of technical rationality' and that would 'aim at the
development of themes from which, in these sorts of situations, practitioners may construct theories and methods of their own'.

Action research: a middle way?

Both Lupton and Schon believe that reducing the knowledge–practice gap
requires a recasting of the relationship between researchers and practitioners with much greater emphasis on collaboration. One prominent
approach to the promotion of collaborative relationships between managers
and social scientists has become known as 'action research', a term coined
in 1944 by Kurt Lewin. Action research is difficult to define precisely
because Lewin himself wrote relatively little about it, and as interest in

action research has grown, so have the length of the definitions! (cf. Rapoport, 1970; Hult and Lennung, 1980). According to Rapoport's (1970) well-known definition, 'Action Research aims to contribute both to the practical concerns of people in an immediate problematic situation and to the goals of social science by joint collaboration within a mutually acceptable ethical framework.' Action research therefore makes explicit the need to bring researchers and practitioners into close contact with each other.

As a social psychologist with a deep concern to bring social science to bear on practical social problems, Lewin believed that it was possible to develop general laws of social life and apply them to specific issues (Peters and Robinson, 1984). Both the development of these laws and their application depended on taking action in real situations in order to promote change. In the course of acting it was possible both to use the insights of established social science to promote desired outcomes and to develop and correct those insights. The imperfect knowledge yielded by the social sciences could thus be improved in the process of applying it; by observing the effects of actions taken in the light of social scientific knowledge, that knowledge would be improved together with the chances of improving practice. Effective practice and valid social science therefore went hand in hand, each developing through an interplay with the other so that the goals of social science, for valid general knowledge of human behaviour, and the practical concerns of people, for effective solutions to problems, could be met simultaneously.

Something very similar to action research has recently been advocated as the 'way forward' for management research in the UK (Tranfield and Starkey, 1998). Oddly no specific reference to the action research literature is made by these authors. But in their discussion of 'modes of knowledge production' it is clear that much of their argument can be found in earlier attempts to solve the theory–practice problem by action researchers. For example, Tranfield and Starkey's proposition that 'the problems addressed by management research should grow out of the interaction between the world of practice and the world of theory, rather than out of either one alone' could readily have come from Lewin's pen half a century ago. So much for progress!

In general, action research can be seen as a 'middle way' between the extremes of seeing the social scientist as expert dispensing technical knowledge to the lay manager or of seeing the manager as a kind of noble savage practising the managerial arts behind the back of a community of impotent scientists. But awkward questions remain. If general laws of management could be formulated, albeit of a contingent rather than a universal kind, there would be a clear role for the expert and the in situ investigation and experimentation advocated by action researchers would amount to an unnecessary and wasteful perpetual reinvention of the wheel. On the other hand, if, in the absence of general knowledge, every manager must act as an everyday commonsense social scientist, what role does this leave for the professional social scientist? These questions, which have been fruitfully brought to the surface by the phenomenon of action research, touch on deeper issues concerning social knowledge and science. We will therefore return to them later in this chapter.

The manager as a practical theorist

Cuff and Payne (1979) suggest that there are two distinctive features of the scientific approach to understanding the world. One is that scientific claims to knowledge are of a kind that can be verified or checked out by reference to those aspects of reality to which they refer. Scientific statements are not to be judged, for example, simply by reference to the authority of the person who makes them. It is for this reason that pronouncements by captains of industry on how to manage and run organizations are often treated sceptically by social scientists. Although such offerings may be valuable, and are perfectly legitimate on their own terms, the fact that they are made by experienced industrialists is not sufficient in itself to give them scientific status. They require some kind of rigorous test which relates them to the phenomena they predicate. Following from this, the second distinguishing feature of science is that it involves the systematic application of clear procedures of investigation of a kind which can be applied by others, and in principle by anyone, to check the knowledge claims of any particular scientist. Scientific knowledge is above all public knowledge open to checking by others.

These are, so to speak, the ground rules of science which apply irrespective of whether the concern is with the natural or social worlds and regardless of the paradigm adopted within any specific field. Pseudo-science fails to adopt these rules by making knowledge claims which cannot be checked or by adopting vague and unsystematic procedures of inquiry whilst still claiming scientific status for its endeavours.

A further distinguishing feature of science is, I believe, its commitment to theory. Theory has a bad image in the eyes of many managers, smacking of the abstruse and the irrelevant, but a well-founded adage has it that 'there's nothing so practical as a good theory'.

Although the term theory means different things to different people, a useful way of thinking about a theory is to see it as a kind of map. Maps are clearly very useful things, particularly if you want to get somewhere and don't know which way to go. They tell us what is there (roads, hills, buildings, rivers) and where these things are in relation to each other (the station is north of the river). Like geographical maps, scientific theories attempt to represent a terrain and so help us to manoeuvre within it. But unlike the road map, a theory consists of concepts, findings and relations. A social science theory posits the existence of certain entities, defines ways of identifying instances of them, and specifies relationships between them. So, for example, an organization theory may refer to the concept of

between it and formal theory. Social science can play a part, and even an essential part, but its potential contribution to the formation of practical theories should not be overestimated.

The second point is the recognition given in this model to the role of values. Practical theories include ethical or moral elements which interact with technical ones to form a techno-moral framework for action. Managers have to decide not only what can be done but also what ought to be done, to make simultaneously both technical and moral decisions, and while social science can inform those decisions it cannot dictate them. In the area where we perhaps need it most, the social sciences cannot help us. On these matters we have to turn to other sources of insight, to history, philosophy and religion.

Commentary

Our exploration of the question of whether the social sciences can help managers has taken us into some difficult terrain, and it is clear that this is a much more complex issue than it might at first appear. As we have seen, much depends on the fundamental assumptions we make about the nature of the social sciences and social life and the way in which we understand the position of the practical manager attempting to act within a turbulent and ambiguous world.

The rise of paradigmatic pluralism in the social sciences has made this difficult issue even more problematic (Thomas, 1997). Alternative paradigms have different implications for practice and although some may be more 'useful' than others even those which seem closest to the dominant assumptions of management as an occupation do not necessarily yield results which can be implemented. Yet the abandonment of even this form of social science by managers seems unwarranted and would be likely to leave us in the hands of the 'practical men' so roundly criticized by Fayol: except that today's practical men may well have set themselves up as 'gurus', cloaked in the garb of pseudo-science (Collins, 2000).

My own conclusion is twofold. First, it seems to me that generalization in the social sciences is possible, although, as contingency theorists have shown, the conditions under which generalizations about behaviour and organization can be shown to hold are difficult to determine with any precision. Nonetheless, even tentative generalizations derived from research in restricted contexts can provide crucial insights into managerial problems and these generalizations may often be as good or better than those derived from everyday experience or conventional folklore. It seems unlikely however that the integrated social science envisaged by Lupton is realistically possible. Quite apart from paradigmatic plurality, there is simply too much diversity even within the major paradigms. The chairman of the British Academy of Management, the club for management academics, has called for 'a coherent position on what BAM holds to be the nature of (and the future of) management research' (Wilson, 1998). A more orderly view of management might thus emanate from academia in the future. But few signs of this coherence have been forthcoming, perhaps because of the hyper-fragmented character of the field of management studies (Danieli and Thomas, 1999). Therefore managers will, as Watson (1986) suggests, continue to be faced with many different approaches to understanding organizational life and will have to cope with this by becoming adept at selecting from these according to the technical problems they encounter and their own personal values. To assume otherwise is simply wishful thinking.

Second, while many social scientists will continue to generate generalizations about behaviour and organizations, these will seldom if ever be so specific to the particular contexts of practice that they can be applied as if they were scientific laws. Hence the need for the reflective practice advocated by Schon. Management today need no longer be based purely on personal experience or conventional belief, but it will always be based on *improvisation*. By that I do not mean simply making it up as we go along, but, rather, the activity of fitting together all the various sources of knowledge that can inform practice in fruitful and productive ways. As Handal and Lauvas (1987) argue and as Burgoyne and Stuart's (1976) research showed, managers learn from many sources and bring many different kinds of knowledge to bear on their work. What distinguishes the thinking manager from the 'practical man' is not that the former applies the fruits of social science while the latter relies on more or less intelligent forms of guesswork. Both are engaged in improvisation. But the thinking manager incorporates the concepts, findings, methods and attitudes of the social sciences into the process of improvisation giving them their rightful place among other sources of insight and knowledge.

In my view, then, the social sciences can help managers but only if the nature of their contribution is properly understood. This is less in the form of the provision of technical, algorithmic knowledge which will enable managers to read off solutions to their problems than in the form of sensitizing frameworks – sets of theories, concepts, findings, and ways of seeing and thinking which alert the manager to alternative ways of understanding and hence of managing. This is probably as it should be in the messy and controversial worlds of social science and management.

Questions for discussion

1   What can the social sciences contribute to the management of organizations?
2   'There will never be a full and generally acceptable body of organizational or managerial theory' (Watson, 1986). If not, why not?

3   Can management ever be an 'evidence-based' profession like medicine?
4   An MBA should be a mandatory qualification for anyone who wishes to become a manager. Do you agree?
5   Does it make sense to think of managers as practical theorists?

Further reading

Eden, C. and Huxham, C. (1996) Action Research for Management Research, *British Journal of Management*, 7, pp. 75–86.

Klein, L. and Eason, K. (1991) *Putting Social Science to Work: The Ground Between Theory and Use Explored Through Case Studies in Organizations*, Cambridge: Cambridge University Press.

Shipman, M. (1997) *The Limitations of Social Research*, London: Longman.

Thomas, A.B. (1997) The Coming Crisis of Western Management Education, *Systems Practice*, 10 (6) pp. 681–701.

Tranfield, D. and Starkey, K. (1998) The Nature, Social Organization and Promotion of Management Research: Towards Policy, *British Journal of Management*, 9, pp. 341–53.

5 Principles of management
Valid or vacuous?

Without principles one is in darkness and chaos.

Fayol (1916)

The currently accepted 'principles of administration' are little more than ambiguous and mutually contradictory proverbs.

Simon (1947)

Some years ago, I was involved in a project that was concerned with the preparation of training materials for a group of professional employees. Amongst other things, we had to decide the content of the training; what sorts of information should we aim to communicate to our trainees? During discussions with the project director, whose knowledge and experience of the field was extensive, I made the suggestion that our problem would be readily solved if we simply taught the principles of the job. What could be simpler? Naively expecting this idea to be welcomed with open arms I was taken aback to hear his reply: 'We can't do that because there aren't any!'

At the time I found this mildly shocking. After all, there was nothing new about this profession. Indeed, it had been practised for hundreds, if not thousands, of years. Could it really be that in this field, one of the oldest of all, there were still no well-recognized principles that could be taught to newcomers?

Anyone approaching management for the first time might well be tempted to ask much the same question of it as I did – of teaching. Given at least a century of collective experience of industrial management, it seems reasonable to expect that there should be general principles upon which its practice can be based. Surely we must have learned something! Yet my colleague's scepticism about the existence of principles of teaching could as well have been applied to the occupation of management. If there aren't any principles of teaching can the same be said for management?

The controversy in brief

The idea of there being principles which might be used to guide human affairs has a long history, stretching back at least to the biblical story of Moses and the Ten Commandments. But the search for principles of management is a relatively recent development. Even though the problems of administering even quite large organizations, such as the military and government officialdom, were well known in, for example, Ancient Egypt (Breasted, 1909; James, 1985) and in early Imperial China (Loewe, 1968), systematic reflection on management is largely a product of the nineteenth and twentieth centuries. Nonetheless, the quest for management principles in modern times continues an age-old tradition and reflects an equally ancient human interest in reducing the uncertainties that are a perennial feature of human life. The identification of principles holds out the promise of control over events in a capricious and uncertain world.

The controversy over management principles is closely bound up with more general debates concerning the nature of science and in particular with the nature of social science. Science has come to be thought of as the best and perhaps the only way to obtain reliable knowledge of how the world 'works'. Managers clearly need to know how people and organizations work so a scientific approach to those problems has an obvious appeal. Thus the idea of developing a science of management gained considerable prominence with the expansion of the social sciences during the second half of the twentieth century and with the growing need to find more effective ways of managing in an increasingly hostile and competitive environment. Just as the natural sciences, like physics, have provided sound laws that enable us to act effectively on the natural world, so it has been hoped that social science might yield similar if less powerful laws which might constitute an effective and rational basis for the practice of management.

It was to this end or something like it that some of the best-known 'classical' writers on management aspired. People like Taylor and especially Fayol attempted to construct sets of scientific principles and techniques for the management of enterprises which, they hoped, would provide a better basis for managerial practice than mere custom and habit. But with the growing involvement of professional social scientists in the study of management, these early attempts to provide a science of management came under fierce attack with the result that they were virtually discredited.

The 1980s, however, saw a potent revival of interest in management principles among managers if not among management scientists. The publication of Peters and Waterman's *In Search of Excellence* (1982) offered a 'new' set of principles which seemingly offered the key to managing for excellence. Partly because of the enormous popularity of this book in management circles and the growth in 'guru' management theory which followed its appearance, the debate over the existence and validity of general rules for successful management sparked into life once more.

What we find, then, are two contending camps, one committed to the view that management principles are valid and the other that they are vacuous. Although this might seem like an arcane issue, mainly of interest to scholars and philosophers of science, it is an important problem for managers too. For if management principles do exist, knowing what they are and using them as a basis for the process of managing seems essential. After all, it would be a pretty bad engineer who chose to ignore the laws of physics, so can a manager who pays no heed to the principles of management hope to be effective? If, on the other hand, there are no real management principles to speak of, those who act as if there were seem to be in much the same position as the medieval alchemists, believing that they can turn water into wine by applying meaningless formulae. Were this so we are still left with the question of how management can proceed otherwise. In the absence of principles must the 'darkness and chaos' envisaged by Fayol inevitably follow?

The idea of principles

You may have noticed that so far I have talked about principles in a rather vague way, so some attention to the alternative meanings of the term seems appropriate. This is particularly necessary because controversies often involve disagreements on the meaning of terms, sometimes to the extent that disputes seem to be about little more than this. It is therefore important to be aware of some of the ways in which the key word 'principles' can be understood before we pursue the management principles debate.

There are at least four shades of meaning which are associated with the term 'principles'. One of these is the idea of fundamentals, foundations or basics. Someone claiming to know the principles of management might be taken to mean, at least in part, that they know its essentials and in making this claim they are also saying that they know important things about it. This idea is expressed in the titles of the introductory textbooks in many fields, such as 'Principles of Chemistry', 'Principles of Physical Geography', or whatever, which point to the intention of presenting the basic building-blocks of a discipline. An example in the management field is Fincham and Rhodes's *Principles of Organizational Behaviour* (1999).

A second meaning of 'principles' refers to ethics, morals or rules of right conduct. So to be 'unprincipled' or 'without principles' is to invite opprobrium whereas to 'act in accordance with one's principles' is a sign of moral probity. Management principles might therefore be understood as the moral rules which make up a code of ethics to which managers ought to adhere.

Third, 'principles' might be thought of as scientific laws or as generalizations based on scientific knowledge, as in 'the principles of thermodynamics' or 'biological principles'. In this case, to speak of management principles might be to imply that management can be understood scientifically.

Finally, we might think of principles as rules, as in the 'principles of chess'. In the case of management this might imply that there are certain rules which managers ought to follow if they are to be effective players in the game of management.

Contributors to the controversy over management principles have not always been clear about which of these meanings they are using. Indeed, the vague and inconsistent way in which some management thinkers have used the word has been a source of confusion and a valid point of criticism (Mouzelis, 1967). Nonetheless, the debate revolves largely around principles in the third and last meanings; are there scientific laws of management and can those laws be translated into rules for the conduct of managerial affairs?

To begin our exploration of these questions we must first examine the ideas of some of the early proponents of management principles who laid the basis for what has become known as 'classical management theory'.

The classical principles

The basic ideas of classical management theory were developed by writers in Europe and North America during the first half of the twentieth century. Among the best known of these contributors to management thought are Henri Fayol and Lyndall Urwick (both of whom we met in Chapter 2) and the Americans James Mooney and Alan Reiley.

A much less well known figure, at least for his contribution to management thinking, is Phineas T. Barnum (1810–1891), the famous showman and entrepreneur. So far as I know Barnum never wrote a management book, yet his 'Rules for Success in Business' (Box 5.1) published as an appendix to an early practical business book (Freedley, 1853), anticipated both in style and purpose the sets of principles that were to be produced much later by his more renowned successors. While the language and the content of Barnum's rules may seem quaint, at least one of them was reproduced in modern guise 130 years later in Peters and Waterman's bestseller! (I leave it to you to work out which one.) Furthermore, by the end of his career, Barnum had amassed a fortune of over five million dollars.

Like Barnum, the early management writers were closely involved in business and they wrote as managers rather than as social scientists. Their ideas on management were derived largely from their practical experience, just as Barnum's were, and they were chiefly interested in codifying these ideas into a body of precepts that would be of practical value to other managers. They wrote at a time when there was little general interest in the notion that management could be systematized as a body of knowledge and before the social sciences had shown much interest in it, so their

---

Box 5.1 P.T. Barnum's rules for success in business, 1853

'a few rules that I am convinced, from experience and observation, must be observed in order to ensure success in business':

1 Select the kind of business that suits your inclinations and temperament.
2 Let your pledged word ever be sacred.
3 Whatever you do, do it with all your might.
4 Sobriety. Use no description of intoxicating drinks.
5 Let hope predominate, but be not too visionary.
6 Do not scatter your powers.
7 Engage proper employees.
8 Advertise your business. Do not hide your light under a bushel.
9 Avoid extravagance; and always live considerably within your income, if you can do so without absolute starvation!
10 Do not depend on others.

Source: E.T. Freedley, *A Practical Treatise on Business; Or, How to Get Money*, London: Thomas Bosworth, 1853.

---

work needs to be seen in this light. They were in essence pioneers venturing into largely unexplored territory.

The classical management thinkers drew part of their inspiration from the example of the American engineer, F.W. Taylor (1856–1915). Taylor became famous, indeed infamous, for developing an approach to the organization and management of work which placed heavy stress on the need to specialize labour, to observe and measure work tasks 'scientifically' in order to identify the 'one best way' of executing them, to carefully select and train workmen, and to pay workers strictly according to output.

Although Taylor was an energetic advocate of his system of 'Scientific Management' and even though his ideas have been profoundly influential, their relevance to the concerns of the classicists was limited. Taylor's system was intended as a guide to the organization of all forms of work, but in practice it was most readily applied to job design at the shopfloor level where manual work tasks could be readily observed and measured. The classical management thinkers, however, were concerned more broadly with the tasks of general management and with the design of the total set of arrangements which make up an organization. So although Taylor used the language of principles in his writings and was explicitly acknowledged by some classical writers (Fayol called him 'the great American engineer'), the debate on management principles has tended to focus on these broader issues.

In 1887, Woodrow Wilson, the 28th President of the United States, made a bold call to the nation's scientists for the study of administration. This was urgently needed, he suggested, in order to 'rescue executive methods from the confusion and costliness of empirical experiment', by which he meant trial-and-error, 'and set them upon foundations laid deep in stable principle' (Wilson, 1887). Little could he have guessed that in far-away France Henri Fayol, the son of a construction foreman (Breeze, 1985), was about to embark on just such a study and one that was to lead to the formulation of an enduring though much criticized set of management principles.

Most of the classical writers built on Fayol's initial contribution presented in his book, *General and Industrial Management* (1916, 1949). There he wrote that 'the soundness and good working of the body corporate depend on a certain number of conditions termed indiscriminately principles, laws, rules'. It seemed, he suggested, 'especially useful to endow management with a dozen or so well-established principles, on which it is appropriate to concentrate general discussion'. These took the form of fourteen 'General Principles of Management' (Box 5.2).

Fayol was careful to point out the limitations of these principles. They were not to be interpreted rigidly and would have to be adapted to changing circumstances. They were not exhaustive; there was no limit to the number of principles that might be discovered. And they could not be applied in a mechanical way for it was 'a matter of knowing how to make use of them, which is a difficult art requiring intelligence, experience, decision and proportion'. He also acknowledged that the principles he had described had been derived largely from his personal experience and that they were not definitive but provisional. They were but one contribution to a theory of management which, he hoped, might be developed from general discussion and the pooling of the experiences of others. Even so, he was adamant on the need for principles. 'Be it a case of commerce, industry, politics, religion, war, or philosophy', he wrote, 'in every concern there is a management function to be performed, and for its performance there must be principles, that is to say acknowledged truths regarded as proven on which to rely.' For Fayol, then, principles were the key elements of a body of knowledge which could be taught to managers and which should be made the basis of management practice.

When Fayol's work is mentioned today, it is usually to acknowledge it as the first major analysis of the management function and the first modern statement of management principles. But it is seldom noticed that his main thesis was that management was a skill that could be taught. The first part of his book was titled 'Necessity and Possibility of Teaching Management', and although he introduced his famous definition of management there, this and the general principles were not discussed in detail until later.

In this opening section Fayol argued that even though management was a distinct and important function little or no provision was being made for

Box 5.2 **Fayol's general principles of management, 1916**

1 *Division of work*: tasks should be divided up and employees should specialize in a limited set of tasks so that expertise is developed and productivity increased.

2 *Authority and responsibility*: authority is the right to give orders and entails the responsibility for enforcing them with rewards and penalties; authority should be matched with corresponding responsibility.

3 *Discipline*: is essential for the smooth running of business and is dependent on good leadership, clear and fair agreements, and the judicious application of penalties.

4 *Unity of command*: for any action whatsoever, an employee should receive orders from one superior only; otherwise authority, discipline, order and stability are threatened.

5 *Unity of direction*: a group of activities concerned with a single objective should be co-ordinated by a single plan under one head.

6 *Subordination of individual interest to general interest*: individual or group goals must not be allowed to override those of the business.

7 *Remuneration of personnel*: may be achieved by various methods and the choice is important; it should be fair, encourage effort, and not lead to over-payment.

8 *Centralization*: the extent to which orders should be issued only from the top of the organization is a problem which should take into account its characteristics, such as size and the capabilities of the personnel.

9 *Scalar chain (line of authority)*: communications should normally flow up and down the line of authority running from the top to the bottom of the organization, but sideways communication between those of equivalent rank in different departments can be desirable so long as superiors are kept informed.

10 *Order*: both materials and personnel must always be in their proper place; people must be suited to their posts so there must be careful organization of work and selection of personnel.

11 *Equity*: personnel must be treated with kindliness and justice.

12 *Stability of tenure of personnel*: rapid turnover of personnel should be avoided because of the time required for the development of expertise.

13 *Initiative*: all employees should be encouraged to exercise initiative within the limits imposed by the requirements of authority and discipline.

14 *Esprit de corps*: efforts must be made to promote harmony within the organization and prevent dissension and divisiveness.

Source: Adapted from H. Fayol, *General and Industrial Management*, trans. C. Storrs, London: Pitman, 1949.

management education. Why was this? In practice, said Fayol, there was a recognition that management was a distinct activity requiring specifically managerial ability, for when it came to selecting people for management posts the choice was seldom made on technical grounds alone. Being a good engineer, for example, was not enough. But there was also a belief that managerial ability could only be acquired through practical experience; the idea that someone could be taught to manage was considered absurd. In Fayol's view this reason for denying the possibility of management education 'carries no weight' for 'managerial ability can and should be acquired in the same way as technical ability, first at school, later in the workshop'. 'The real reason for the absence of management teaching', he went on, 'is absence of theory; without theory no teaching is possible.'

His statement of management principles was therefore more than an attempt to provide managers with useful guidance on how to manage. It was part of a broader concern to establish a body of knowledge, to 'codify the data furnished by experience' which could form the basis for systematic education in management.

In the inter-war period several more works outlining management principles appeared. In the 1920s Oliver Sheldon, a colleague of the famous Quaker employer Seebohm Rowntree, published *The Philosophy of Management* (1923), and in the 1930s two General Motors executives, James Mooney and Alan Reiley produced *The Principles of Organization* (1939). But the next major event in the development and propagation of management principles was the publication of Lyndall Urwick's *The Elements of Administration* in 1943.

Before the publication of this book Urwick had written extensively on management matters and his thinking had been strongly influenced by both his wartime experiences and the ideas of both Fayol and Taylor. In a much cited paper (Urwick, 1933), he wrote:

> It is the general thesis of this paper that there are principles which can be arrived at inductively from the study of human experience of organization, which should govern arrangements for human association of any kind. These principles can be studied as a technical question, irrespective of the purpose of the enterprise, the personnel composing it, or any constitutional, political or social theory underlying its creation. They are concerned with the method of subdividing and allocating to individuals all the various activities, duties and responsibilities essential to the purpose contemplated, the correlation of these activities and the continuous control of the work of individuals so as to secure the most economical and the most effective realization of the purpose.

In the *Elements*, Urwick drew together the ideas of a number of classical writers including Fayol, Taylor, and Mooney and Reiley. Twenty-nine main 'principles of administration' were presented. These were discussed within

Fayol's framework of managerial functions and Urwick elaborated on both Fayol's ideas and those of later classical writers. One of the more contentious inclusions, as it turned out, was the span-of-control principle. This asserted that 'No superior can supervise directly the work of more than five, or at the most, six subordinates whose work interlocks.' The principle was based on the idea that the human 'span of attention' was limited; there were definite limits to the number of activities that any individual could keep under control. It was therefore necessary to take this into account when organizing.

Urwick felt that there was a 'remarkable consensus of agreement' on the part of those who had studied administration about the elements which made up its technique. But he warned against dogmatism in a field where there were 'so many unknown factors, so much territory unexplored'. In a section titled 'The Danger of the Easy Remedy', he warned of the dangers of relying on 'potted knowledge', and he added that 'there are no hints and tips and short cuts'. While books could help towards providing a first understanding of some principles, there was still a need for 'hard study and harder thinking, mastery of intellectual principles reinforced by genuine reflection on actual problems, for which the individual has real responsibility'. But like Fayol, Urwick was clear that administration needed to be improved and that this required theory, ideas and clearer thinking about the nature of administration, its methods and its principles. He was strongly committed to the belief that management skills could be taught, even though, like medical skills, they could only be refined and developed in practice. And he noted, as Fayol had done, that many 'practical men' would be impatient with such ideas. They would prefer to rely on habit and custom despite the fact that these were often 'highly irrational'.

The elaboration of management principles reached its high point with the publication of Ralph Davis's *The Fundamentals of Top Management* (1951); Davis presented more than a hundred principles! Although this growth in numbers could be seen as a sign of progress, the tendency for the principles to multiply, while extending their scope, also tended to weaken their impact and undermine their status as fundamentals. More concise lists therefore continued to appear.

In 1954, the American National Industrial Conference Board published a set of twelve Organization Principles (Box 5.3). These continued to be reproduced in various management texts in the 1960s and 1970s. In one (Richards and Nielander, 1969), the principles were introduced by saying:

> Like the engineer who builds his bridge to meet special needs, the organization planner, in designing a company structure, applies principles. For through years of experience it has been learned that if certain principles are followed, regardless of the size of the enterprise, the result will be good organization. Some of these basic laws follow.
> (Raube, 1954)

Box 5.3 Organization principles, 1954

1 There must be clear lines of authority running from the top to the bottom of the organization.

2 No one in the organization should report to more than one line supervisor. Everyone in the organization should know to whom he reports, and who reports to him.

3 The responsibility and authority of each supervisor should be clearly defined in writing.

4 Responsibility should always be coupled with corresponding authority.

5 The responsibility of higher authority for the acts of its subordinates is absolute.

6 Authority should be delegated as far down the line as possible.

7 The number of levels of authority should be kept to a minimum.

8 The work of every person in the organization should be confined as far as possible to the performance of a single leading function.

9 Whenever possible, line functions should be separated from staff functions, and adequate emphasis should be placed on important staff activities.

10 There is a limit to the number of positions that can be co-ordinated by a single executive.

11 The organization should be flexible, so that it can be adjusted to changing conditions.

12 The organization should be kept as simple as possible.

Source: National Industrial Conference Board, *Company Organization Charts*, New York: NICB, 1954.

The same list was included in books by Copeman (1962) and Hunt (1979) and is still drawn on by some of today's popular management writers. The classical writers did not form a close-knit, consensual 'school' but they did tend to share certain assumptions about the nature of management and management knowledge. First, they held a firm belief in the existence of general principles or rules which could and should be applied to the management of organizations. Their orientation was deliberately 'managerial' in that they wrote chiefly for, and usually as, practising managers and aimed to provide them with useful guidance.

Second, the various principles put forward by different writers pointed fairly consistently to a definite model of good organization. Nowadays this model is often referred to as the 'mechanistic' or 'military' model, invoking images of machines and armies. Terms such as 'discipline', 'command', 'orders', 'subordinates', 'personnel', 'esprit de corps' and even 'initiative' have unmistakable military associations. The principles can be seen as prescriptions for the tight control of behaviour by means of discipline, clearly defined tasks, carefully circumscribed spheres of authority, limited spans of control, and so on. They seek to reproduce the regularity, smooth functioning and orderliness of the machine in the human context much as Frederick the Great of Prussia had tried to do by organizing his armies on 'mechanical' lines (Morgan, 1997).

Third, there was a tendency to assume not just that there could be principles of management but that valid principles had already been arrived at through reflection on managerial experience. While some classicists were vague about the status of the principles they proposed others tended to treat them as established truths rather than as provisional generalizations. As Massie (1965) noted, the classical writers were not research-oriented and based their propositions largely on their personal knowledge instead of systematic research evidence. For example, despite his belief in the universal applicability of scientific method (Breeze, 1985), Fayol's conception of 'theory' seems to have been in terms of a set of principles which could be constructed by pooling the experiences of many managers and which would be evaluated by means of discussion.

Given the lack of formal research investigation into management and organization at the time, this somewhat unsophisticated approach to the development of sound principles was understandable. But could this be an adequate basis for an applied science of management?

The challenge of social science

From their first appearance, management principles proved controversial but this early criticism tended to come from the 'practical men' whose attitudes Fayol and Urwick were keen to challenge. These people tended to reject the possibility of the existence of principles of management because they believed that organizations were too dissimilar to allow useful generalizations to be made, and because they tended to see success in management as dependent upon personal leadership qualities which were difficult to define and impossible to teach. Management, on this view, was an art not a science. These 'empiricists', as Urwick called them, were therefore unimpressed by the notion of management principles.

After World War Two a second major line of criticism emerged from a different quarter, the social sciences. In 1947, an American professor of public administration, Herbert Simon, who was later to win a Nobel Prize for Economics, made what has come to be seen as the classic critique of management principles. In his book *Administrative Behaviour* (1947), Simon mounted a sustained attack on 'the so-called "principles" of classical organization theory'.

Taking the work of Urwick and his colleague, Luther Gulick, as his main reference point, Simon examined three of the classical principles: division of work (specialization), unity of command, and span of control.

He also looked at a further elaboration of the specialization principle which we can omit without doing violence to his main argument.

Specialization, said Simon, is simply a characteristic of any work based on group effort because it simply means different people doing different things. Work is always specialized but not necessarily in ways that are efficient. There are many different ways in which work can be divided up but the principle of specialization gives no guidance on which ways lead to efficiency and which do not.

Similarly, the principle of unity of command was always followed in practice, 'for it is physically impossible for a man to obey two contra-dictory commands'. But perhaps the principle was intended to mean that it was undesirable for a subordinate to be put in a position where he receives orders from more than one superior as Gulick had indeed stated. If so, this was at least a clear and unambiguous way of putting it. However, it then contradicted the principle of specialization without giving any indication of how the contradiction could be resolved. For example, unity of com-mand would mean that technical specialists working for a general manager could not be given orders on the technical aspects of their work by the technical manager. But employees may need to receive orders from a diverse set of specialists to work efficiently. Yet this violates the principle of unity of command.

As for the span of control principle, which 'is confidently asserted as a third incontrovertible principle of administration', it was possible to state an equally plausible 'proverb': that 'administrative efficiency is enhanced by keeping at a minimum the number of organizational levels through which a matter must pass before it is acted upon'. When the span of control (the average number of subordinates reporting to a superior) is narrow, the number of levels in the organization will tend to be greater than when it is wide. So any specified span of control will have implications for the number of levels in the organization. Narrow spans may promote efficiency by enabling closer control of subordinates; but this gain may be offset by the correspondingly large number of levels which will then exist in the organization. So to advocate a specific size of span as a principle leading to efficiency was misleading. In any case, the classicists disagreed among themselves on the ideal span – some said three, some five, some eleven – and gave no reasons for their choice.

Simon concluded that for each of the principles he had examined 'there was found, instead of a univocal principle, a set of two or more mutually incompatible principles apparently applicable to the administrative situa-tion'. They were vague, ambiguous and mutually contradictory, and little more than 'proverbs'. They could not provide a useful basis for practice and could therefore be dispensed with.

Although Simon rejected the classical principles, it is worth noting that he accepted that a science of administration might still generate principles. But this would take the form of statements relating different kinds of administrative arrangement to their effects on efficiency. They would not be based on a priori, 'armchair' reasoning but on experimental research using clearly defined measures. And although the results of administrative research might have implications for practice the first task was to describe and analyse administrative situations. Decisions about how to manage effectively presupposed a knowledge of the effects of management actions under different conditions. Efficient administration could only be based on this kind of knowledge, just as 'sound medical practice can only be founded on a thorough knowledge of the biology of the organism'.

Simon's rejection of the classical principles was largely based on a logical critique; the principles were contradictory and illogical rather than demonstrably false in the face of evidence of actual practice. But when the British organizational researcher, John Child, came to review the state of classical theory twenty years later (Child, 1969), he was able to draw on a growing body of research evidence. One study was particularly significant. Perhaps the most important challenge to the classical precepts came from the results of a research project carried out by Joan Woodward, Britain's first female professor of industrial sociology. This research set out explicitly to discover whether firms which adhered to the principles of organization proposed in classical management theory were, in fact, any more efficient than those which did not.

Woodward's study focused on a sample of 100 industrial plants with over 100 employees operating in south Essex in the mid-1950s. She found that although none of the plants displayed all the attributes advocated by the classicists about half of them had been organized along classical lines. But these firms seemed to perform no differently to those which ignored the classical prescriptions; 'conformity with the "rules" of management did not necessarily result in success or non-conformity in commercial failure' (Woodward, 1958). The classical principles, however reasonable and logical they might have seemed, were not indispensable to business success. So there could be 'no one best way of organising a business'.

If conformity with the classical principles did not have much impact on business performance, was there some other factor which did? Woodward found that when the firms were grouped according to the type of production technology they employed they tended to display common organizational patterns. For example, in mass-production firms, such as auto-assemblers, the span of control of foremen tended to be larger than in process production firms, such as chemical-makers. Differences in technology seemed to impose different requirements on organizations, and firms whose organization structures were closer to the average of the technological group to which they belonged performed better than those which deviated from it. Although there was no one best way of organizing, some ways were better than others provided that allowance was made for the technological conditions under which the firm operated.

Woodward's general conclusion, that a firm's organization has to fit the circumstances of its operations if it is to be effective, has been supported by a wide range of research studies. Later work showed, however, that technology was but one of many influences on organizational structure. Perhaps this finding is not too surprising. Indeed, it might appear to be rather obvious. But it certainly discomforted many of those who understood the classical principles as the basic laws of good organization. One college lecturer stated that 'Practical men will insist that there are principles of management, and I think that the social scientists who attack this idea are being academic and unconstructive' (quoted in Child, 1969). Nonetheless, as Rose (1988) noted, such studies appeared to have 'put paid to traditional administrative theory'.

Research evidence seemed, then, to give strong support to Simon's scepticism, for it indicated that 'the management principles and many elements in scientific management presented an appearance of established knowledge and unchallengeable (sic) expertise which subsequent analysis and investigation has shown to be largely spurious' (Child, 1969).

Child (1969) summarized the limitations of the classical approach as follows. It had proposed a standardized organizational model (the military or machine model) as the optimum but this was misleading. The classical prescriptions for tight control and narrow specialization of tasks had overlooked their negative implications for motivation. When work was organized in this way it could prevent employees from experiencing fulfilment and so lead to an unwillingness to contribute effort which would hinder rather than promote efficiency. The tendency to assert principles of universal application had had to give way to a situational approach. By concentrating on the formal structure of the organization, the 'blueprint' which could control behaviour, the classical theorists had ignored the processes of management such as decision-making, communication and conflict-management. And by its failure to acknowledge the complexity of organizational life, the classical approach had oversimplified the problems of management and had given it an aura of 'ease, rationality and uniformity which it rarely possessed in reality'. Thus, he concluded, 'Social science has today discredited some of the most important assumptions of management thought.'

In defence of principles

If Simon's comments can be regarded as the classic critique of management principles, the counter-arguments put forward by another American professor, Harold Koontz, might well be seen as the classic defence. It might also be called the 'neo-classical' defence because Koontz's position broadly reflects the modern stream of classical thinking.

In his paper 'The Management Theory Jungle' (1961), Koontz argued that the classicists, who had been 'branded as "universalists"' by their critics, could not reasonably be regarded as mere armchair theorists. Although their precepts had not been derived from rigorous empirical research they were nonetheless based on observations made over the course of lengthy practical experience. Their ideas had been called platitudes but 'a platitude is still a truism and a truth does not become worthless because it is familiar'. Often those who delighted 'in casting away anything which smacks of management principles' themselves offered generalizations which simply amounted to a restatement of the classical principles in a different guise.

One of the 'favourite tricks' of the critics, he said, was to use examples of the non-application of a single principle as grounds for rejecting the whole framework. Some critics seemed to have misunderstood and misapplied the principles which 'simply proved that wrong principles badly applied will lead to frustration'. In fact, Koontz proposed, management principles were far from being dispensable. They were, on the contrary, an essential part of management science and it would continue to be necessary to develop and test these fundamentals.

Koontz shared the classicists' belief that management science should be devoted to the improvement of practice, but unlike them he emphasized the need for rigorous empirical research. He elaborated his defence of principles in a series of textbooks written with his colleague, Cyril O'Donnell. In *Essentials of Management* (1974), they wrote that 'Principles are used here in the sense of fundamental truths applicable to a given set of circumstances which have value in predicting results.' These truths were provisional rather than final. Nonetheless, principles were 'believed to be a convenient and useful way of packaging some of the major truths that experience and research have found to have a high degree of credibility and predictability'. They were predictive and descriptive statements depicting relationships between variables which, when related in a systematic way, constituted a theory. Such a theory was not, as managers often seemed to assume, inherently impractical. On the contrary, it could be used to derive practical applications.

Management was an art but, like medicine or engineering, its practice could be improved by drawing on fundamental principles. But it was important to avoid applying them in a mechanical ways as if they were exact formulae. It was also important to recognize that no set of principles could deal with every eventuality because this would require complete knowledge. And when principles had contradictory implications this simply pointed to the need for compromise; the costs and benefits of applying or ignoring principles had to be assessed in any real-world situation.

Koontz regarded it as obvious that management principles could have 'a tremendous impact on the practice of management, simplifying and improving it'. Admittedly, no two management situations were ever identical but there might be common elements in different situations which could be abstracted from them and related to a general conceptual scheme. Causal relationships might then be identified. This knowledge could be used to manage future situations of the same type without the need to conduct costly original research or to engage in the risky business of trial-and-error. The identification and use of principles, then, promised more efficient and more effective management.

Like the early classical writers, Koontz argued for both the possibility and the necessity of management principles. Where he and later neo-classical writers have tended to differ from the early thinkers is in a greater recognition of the need for their empirical validation and in greater sensitivity to the idea that the conditions under which particular principles apply need to be identified. Koontz's definition of a principle reflects this. Similarly, a number of the principles discussed were presented in contingent form. For example, the 'correct principle' of span of control was given as that 'there is a limit in each managerial position to the number of persons an individual can effectively manage, but the exact number in each case will vary in accordance with the effect of underlying variables and their impact on the time requirements of effective management'.

The neo-classicists have also tended to distance themselves from the newer approaches to the analysis of management and organization which have developed within the social sciences. Koontz's original defence of management principles, reiterated in 1980 (Koontz, 1980) was also a complaint that the burgeoning social-science 'schools' of management were becoming unintelligible to managers and too far removed from their practical concerns. The emergence of new 'intellectual cults' had brought with it 'a kind of confused and destructive jungle warfare' that was threatening to obscure the existing achievements and potential for an applied science of management. As Lussato (1976) put it, the neo-classicists were in revolt against what they saw as a growing divorce between theory and practice 'or rather between the business manager and the organizational specialists'.

The continuing controversy

Before World War Two, the main protagonists in the management principles controversy were the classicists and the empiricists (the 'practical men'), but after the war it was the social scientists who increasingly challenged classical ideas. Their line of attack was similar to that of the 'practical men' in at least one respect because they too were sceptical of the possibility of formulating universal principles in the management field. Rather, they proposed a different approach which became known as 'contingency theory' (Lawrence and Lorsch, 1967).

Many people find the contingency approach or contingency theory puzzling at first sight but it is no more than an unfamiliar name for a very simple idea. It can be stated quite readily as an approach to the study of management problems which assumes that the effects of any managerial or organizational practice will differ according to the circumstances in which it is implemented. What 'works' in one context will not necessarily work in another so that the effects of a particular management practice are contingent upon the prevailing circumstances. Hence there are no universal principles.

Thompson (1956) put the matter clearly when he wrote:

> Much of our literature (on administration) is lore, spelling out how a procedure or technique is carried out in current practice or proclaiming that 'this is the way' to do it. This material contains rather bold and often implicit assumptions about the relationships between the procedure or technique under consideration and other things which take place within the organization. This type of literature frequently asserts that a certain device is proper, i.e. gets desired results, on the grounds that 'General Motors has it' or that the one hundred 'best-managed' companies use it. But a particular budgeting procedure, for example, may be appropriate for General Motors and not for Company X, and it may be appropriate for General Motors in 1956 but less appropriate in 1960. Any particular item, that is, may show a high correlation with 'success' when imbedded [sic] in one context but show a low correlation in a different context.

The contingency approach suggests that any organizational alternative, such as the classical mechanistic/military model, may work in some circumstances but not in others. The task of the organizational scientist is therefore to identify relationships between different types of managerial practice and organizational arrangements and business outcomes in different situations. Woodward's (1958) study provides an illustration, in that the mechanistic/military model worked for firms using mass-production technology but not for those using process technologies. The optimum form of organization therefore seemed to be contingent upon the type of technology in use.

Contingency theory came to be seen as a distinct alternative to the classical approach (Luthans, 1977; Child, 1977) and was the centrepiece of the emerging social science of organization. As the contingency approach crystallized, classical ideas tended to be relegated in the social science literature to a place in the pre-scientific history of the field. Thus the classicists, with their determination to remain faithful to their principles, seemed doomed to suffer much the same fate as King Canute, overwhelmed by the fast-rising tide of social science.

Developments in the 1980s suggest, however, that classical ideas have not only survived but have flourished to an unprecedented degree. In 1982, two business consultants, Tom Peters and Robert Waterman, published a 400-page book that has been described as 'a prime example of the success of the new management books' (Soeters, 1986). Within five years, *In Search of Excellence* sold over 10 million copies and seems to have sparked

Box 5.4 **Peters and Waterman's basic practices of excellently managed companies**

1   A bias for action
  - Project teams that tend to be small, fluid, ad hoc, and problem/action focused.
  - Communications are of the essence, and there is an important commitment to learning and experimentation.
  - Complex problems are tackled through a willingness to shift resources to where they are needed to encourage fluidity and action (chunking).

2   Close to the customer
  - The market-driven principle of commitment to service, reliability, and quality, based on an appreciation of 'nichemanship' and the ability to custom-tailor a product or service to a client's needs.

3   Autonomy and entrepreneurship
  - A principle which champions innovation, decentralization, the delegation of power and action to the level where they are needed, and a healthy tolerance of failure.

4   Productivity through people
  - The principle that employees are people and a major resource, and should be trusted, respected, inspired, and made 'winners'.
  - Organizational units should be small-scale to preserve and develop a people-oriented quality.

5   Hands-on, value-driven
  - Organization guided by a clear sense of shared values, mission, and identity, relying on inspirational leadership rather than bureaucratic control.

6.   Stick to the knitting
  - The principle of building on strengths and knowledge of one's niche.

7.   Simple form, lean staff
  - Avoid bureaucracy; build main commitments to projects or product division rather than to the dual lines of responsibility found in formal matrix organizations; use small organizational units.

8.   Simultaneous loose–tight properties
  - The principle that reconciles the need for overall control with a commitment to autonomy and entrepreneurship.

Source: G. Morgan, *Images of Organization*, Beverly Hills: Sage, 1986.

off an explosive growth in popular business publishing. Yet despite its modern style its approach closely resembled that of the classicists of old.

In this book Peters and Waterman described the characteristics that seemed common to 'excellent' US companies (Box 5.4). Their work was based on forty-three firms that had remained in the top half of their industries in terms of growth and profitability over a twenty-year period. Evidence on the characteristics of the firms which were claimed to account for their excellence seems to have been gathered mainly through interviews with some of the firms' managers and more generally from the authors' consulting experience.

Perhaps because of the extensive popularity of their book, Peters and Waterman's claims have been subjected to considerable scrutiny in the years since its publication. One prominent critic (Carroll, 1983) pointed to the methodological weaknesses of the study; confusion over which firms had actually been used to draw conclusions about excellence, vagueness about the ways in which data were obtained and analysed, and the absence of comparisons with non-excellent companies which might have helped to show whether the observed practices were causally related to excellent performance. A later commentator described the research underpinning the book as a methodological disaster (Lawler, 1985). In a report of a British study, Saunders and Wong (1985) were somewhat more charitable, seeing Peters and Waterman's volume as more important as a source of hypotheses concerning the possible determinants of corporate performance than as a statement of definitive findings. Even so their research gave only limited support to Peters and Waterman's conclusions.

In his commentary on *In Search of Excellence*, Child (1984) observed that its recommendations suffered from much the same limitations as had attended previous work in the classical tradition. By treating the attributes of the chosen firms as ones that would be displayed by any excellent company, no account had been taken of differences in firms' activities and situations. Since many of the firms in the study were high-technology and project management organizations, the excellent characteristics they showed might only be found in firms of that type and not, for example, in excellent firms in traditional industries such as coal and steel. Even then, high-technology and project management firms operating in different countries with different cultural assumptions and values might find it detrimental to implement some of Peters and Waterman's prescriptions. The delegation of authority, for example, is much less acceptable in some countries than it is in others (Hofstede, 1980b).

There was also a fundamental weakness in the design of the research as Carroll (1983) had noted. Studying only excellent companies made it impossible to tell whether their common attributes were uniquely associated with performance. If low-performing firms have the same characteristics as excellent ones what relevance could those characteristics have to excellence? Peters and Waterman's study, Child noted, did not provide an answer to this question so that they key issue of what it is that causes excellent performance remained unresolved. Furthermore, later analysis of the financial track-record of the supposedly 'excellent' firms showed that they did not stay excellent or even average for long. Makridakis (1996) commented that 'if the "excellent" companies could not even manage to stay average 10 years later, how can they teach lessons to other firms?'

In short, Peters and Waterman, like their classical predecessors, had generalized from the experience of particular types of firms in particular contexts to all firms in all contexts. Just as the classical mechanistic/military model of organization did not amount to the 'one best way' to manage neither could the 'excellence model'. It was not so much wrong as incomplete and therefore inadequate as a valid and reliable guide to management practice. As Thompson (1956) had pointed out nearly thirty years previously, prescriptions based solely on the grounds that 'the best-managed companies do it' were little more than folklore.

In search of suckers?

The publication of *In Search of Excellence* signalled a boom in the guru industry with its accompanying flow of popular business books. Farnham (1996) has estimated that by the mid-1990s more than 31,000 management 'gurus' were in business worldwide typically charging $10,000 a day or more for their consulting services. Although not necessarily couching their management recipes in terms of principles nor summarizing them in the form of Barnumesque sets of rules or checklists, the spirit of the approach of many of the most prominent business gurus has much in common with their most successful predecessors, Peters and Waterman. Among the most notable of these gurus are Stephen Covey, with his seven habits of highly effective people (1989), Peter Senge, with his five disciplines of the learning organization (1990), Michael Hammer, with his call for 'Reengineering Work: Don't Automate, Obliterate' (1990), and Rosabeth Kanter (1995), with her 3Cs of corporate global excellence (concepts, competence and connections).

The rise of the gurus has brought with it increasing critical comment on and scholarly scrutiny of their works (e.g. Abrahamson, 1991; Collins, 2000; Huczynski, 1993; Thomas, 1989). The limitations of much of the material produced by the guru industry have been summarized by Micklethwait and Wooldridge (1997):

> Management theory, according to the case against it, has four defects: it is constitutionally incapable of self-criticism; its terminology usually confuses rather than educates; it rarely rises above basic common sense; and it is faddish and bedevilled by contradictions that would not be allowed in more rigorous disciplines. The implication of all four charges is that management gurus are conmen, the witch doctors of our age, playing on business people's anxieties in order to sell snake oil.

These authors believe that all four charges are valid to a greater or lesser extent. But the main problem as they see it as the contradictory nature of much of what is on offer. This creates confusion in managers' minds. What Micklethwait and Wooldridge seem to be hankering for is a world of management theory devoid of awkward contradictions, a simpler and more straightforward world – a world with sound principles that managers can rely on.

In view of the inadequacies of guru management theory, how can its popularity be explained? Drawing on analytical work by Grint (1997), Jackson (2001) reviews four explanatory approaches to which he adds a fifth. These are the rational, structural, charismatic, institutional/distancing and rhetorical approaches. The rational approach argues that theories become popular because they 'work', for organizations, for managers or both. Huczynski (1993), for example, proposes that gurus and their writings fulfil certain key needs of managers who are working in the uncertain and capricious conditions of contemporary capitalism. These needs include understanding (of a rapidly changing and unpredictable world and of the behaviour of people), control (through the application of techniques to master uncertainty), and esteem (given their relatively lowly status in comparison with professionals like doctors and lawyers). The structural approach points to the importance of historical circumstances for conditioning the acceptability or otherwise of particular ideas and theories. The charismatic approach explains the influence and popularity of ideas as dependent on the persuasive qualities of individual gurus. The institutional/distancing approach depicts imitation and the 'bandwagon effect' as of key importance; if a leading organization adopts a guru's ideas, others tend to follow. Finally, Jackson explores the contribution of the rhetorical qualities of guru theories to explaining their widespread acceptability to managers.

All five explanatory strands, Jackson suggests, can help to illuminate the management guru phenomenon both for managers and social scientists. However, the era of the management guru may be over, at least for the time being, for the charismatic management evangelist is perhaps being superseded by the global consulting firm as a source of 'new' ideas, motivational inspiration and management principles. Yet though the channels of supply may change, the demand for 'instant' management theory seems undiminished (*Economist*, 1997).

Commentary

It was an accident of history that the earliest attempts to set out in a systematic fashion what was known about management took place at a time when the social sciences were little concerned with management and managers were little concerned with social science. But one consequence of this has been the creation of a sharp divide between the 'modern' management disciplines and the works of the 'classical' management theorists, with the latter often treated as if they were relics from the past and of purely historical interest. In their attempts to legitimate their own projects, managerial scientists have perhaps over-reacted against the 'unscientific' legacy of the past, much as the classical writers had attempted to establish their ideas by exaggerating the gap between the irrational, habitual outlook of 'practical men' and the new world of management principles. In any event the notion of management principles has continued to provoke considerable debate.

The classical principles have been subjected to extensive criticism over the years and, as with many controversies, the arguments have not necessarily been particularly clear nor altogether dispassionate. At this point we will try to isolate the underlying themes of the debate and offer some general comments. Our aim is not to adjudicate between the arguments of specific thinkers but to examine the major points of dispute within the controversy.

There are at least three major sources of contention in the management principles controversy. The first of these concerns definitions; how is the term 'principle' to be understood? Are we talking about universal scientific laws or perhaps general rules-of-thumb? The second is what might be called an existential issue; do or can principles of management exist irrespective of whether they actually exist now? The third is the validation issue; on what basis can a principle be claimed to be true? Clearly these issues are related and if we were to disagree about the first it is very likely that we will disagree about the second and third as well. Of course, in reality things are seldom quite as simple as this! Our discussion will therefore have to deal with several of these issues simultaneously.

As we saw at the start of this chapter the term 'principles' has a number of connotations but perhaps the most contentious one has been that of 'universality'. Critics of the classical approach claim that any assertion that principles are of universal application is unwarranted either because this leads to logical contradictions or because there is evidence of counter-instances or both.

A lot depends on how we interpret the term 'universal'. If we take this to mean literally something which applies at all times and in all places then there certainly cannot be any universal principles which can be demonstrated with evidence to be true because we can never obtain information on all past occurrences and certainly not on all future ones. Even if the notion of universality is given a more restricted meaning, for example as true for all known cases, anyone asserting such a universal principle is on inherently weak ground (Thouless, 1953). Anyone saying something like 'all x are y' or 'x always leads to y' is liable to be contradicted if it can be shown that there is even one counter-instance. If even one x is not y, then the universal claim is false. Not surprisingly, universal generalizations are difficult to sustain. If, however, the claim is softened to something like 'most x are y' or 'x usually leads to y' it becomes more robust but at the cost of losing some of the dramatic impact which tends to be associated with universal claims.

In criticizing the classical approach on the grounds that it claimed universal validity for its principles the critics therefore scored an easy point. Certainly some of the classical writers did make sweeping claims for their principles but it must be remembered that they were engaged in a polemical struggle with a management audience that was dedicated to a belief in 'empiricism' and which denied the possibility of forming any generalizations about management at all. The assertion of universality could therefore be seen as a potent weapon in their battle to be heard. As it turned out it was also one which could be turned against them by their later critics from social science. A charitable interpretation of the key idea of the classical view is that it claimed that it was possible to create generalized knowledge of management and organizations. Moreover, subsequent research studies indicated that the mechanistic/military model of classical theory probably *is* effective under certain circumstances. Woodward's study, for example, was widely understood to have destroyed the classical case. But among her conclusions was the finding that within the large batch and mass-production firms there *was* a relationship between conformity to the classical 'rules' of management and business success (Woodward, 1958). Thus valid generalizations about the relationship between management and business performance could be made provided that the conditions under which they held were specified. For large-batch and mass-production firms it was the mechanistic/military model which seemed to work best.

The contingency approach is often contrasted with the classical one but it shares with it much the same commitment to generalization. The contingency theorist aims to establish generalizations of the kind 'x usually leads to y under condition z'. If successful the result is not a universal principle but it is a principle, a statement about regularities between phenomena that can be observed, nonetheless. The difference between the two approaches lies not so much in their dedication to principles as in their definition of a principle, as a universally true statement or as a contingently true one, and in the basis upon which they are prepared to grant principles the status of knowledge. For the early classicists that basis emphasized generalization from experience whereas social scientists required validation by means of rigorously conducted empirical research. In that sense, the search for management principles has been continued by the modern contingency theorist.

Furthermore, the contingency approach does not eliminate the possibility that there may be some generalizations which apply irrespective of differences in context. Evidence to date suggests that this is a matter of degree. Some generalizations seem to apply only in highly specified contexts whereas others apply across such a broad range of situations that they can be considered universal at least in the weak sense of the word. That such a reconciliation of the classical and contingency approaches is possible is shown by evidence presented by Child (1974); five universal attributes of high performing organizations are stated together with five contingent ones. The contingency theorists' assertion that 'it all depends' is thus an assumption just as is the classical view that there are universal principles. Whether those assumptions are incompatible looks to be something that is best resolved by empirical evidence rather than purely by logical argument.

Another charge was that the classical principles were contradictory and that no guidance was given as to how these contradictions could be resolved. There does seem to be some truth in this but it is also apparent that contingency theory has not escaped this problem. It has been shown, for example, that large firms tend to work better when employees are more tightly controlled and that firms which are having to cope with change work better when employees are less tightly controlled. What then are the implications for a large firm which is having to cope with change, an increasingly familiar management dilemma? This sort of issue continues to be problematic for contingency theory and the problem of contradictions is therefore by no means restricted to the classical approach.

As Koontz noted, one way of claiming to have undermined the classical principles was by selecting one of them and showing that it could be contradicted. The span-of-control principle came in for particularly heavy criticism. Yet one review of a series of research studies on the span of control concluded that the revised version of the principle offered by neoclassicists like Koontz yielded a result remarkably close to that originally proposed by Fayol. Filley *et al.* (1976) found that the optimal span was somewhere between five and ten although larger spans were appropriate at higher levels of the organization. They commented that:

> Clearly, as suggested by early management theorists, there is a limit beyond which the size of a work group and the complexity of a manager's job cannot be extended without resulting in undesirable consequences for the organization, for the manager, and for the members of the work group. For managers whose subordinates' jobs interlock and require personal supervision, this limit has fairly consistently been found to be as originally stated by Henri Fayol – in the range of four to six.

Dismissals of the classical principles on empirical grounds seem unwarranted not only because of findings such as these but also because most of the principles have not, in fact, been subjected to systematic empirical test.

Despite, and perhaps because of, the 'challenge of social science', the notion of principles of management and organization has by no means been completely eradicated from management thought. Whereas the social sciences tend to offer more complexity, not less, more uncertainty rather than more security, more questions instead of more answers, management principles offer rules, procedures, solutions. Relinquishing entirely a belief in principles may prove just too much to bear.

Indeed the idea of principles appears to be remarkably resilient and will probably always be so as long as people continue 'searching for certainty' (Casti, 1992). As we have seen, the messages of the most influential popular management books tend to be cast in the mould of rules and principles and bear a strong resemblance to those of the classical texts (leaving aside the fact that the former were generally concise and short whereas the latter are frequently lengthy and verbose!). Notwithstanding the understandable scepticism of professional social scientists, the idea that there may be a limited set of fundamental rules of managerial conduct which promise 'results' seems likely to continue to exert a powerful fascination over the minds of ever more beleaguered managers. Frank (in Collingwood, 2001) argues that corporations have become so dominant in Americans' lives and so demanding of their time and dedication that they have to be depicted as 'special' and worthy of such commitment. 'That', he says, 'is why you have these hardheaded, no-nonsense managers reading this incredibly woolly minded stuff . . . they're looking to have their faith affirmed.'

Are there then any valid principles of management? If we take principles to mean literally universal generalizations then the answer must be no. If, however, we mean broad generalizations supported by substantial evidence then there seem to be quite strong grounds for saying that there are, depending on how much evidence of what kind you are willing to accept. Some of these generalizations apply across a broad range of contexts but others are specific to more narrowly defined situations. And always these generalizations remain provisional and open to revision in the light of new evidence.

The issue of management principles remains and controversial for the moment our verdict is an open one. At the very least we should continue to ask, as Rose (1988) has done, whether this question has yet been settled.

Questions for discussion

1   To what extent, if at all, are Henri Fayol's general principles of management applicable to modern organizations?
2   What are the advantages and disadvantages of imitating the behaviour of successful organizations in order to improve the performance of one's own?
3   Are there any principles of effective organization?
4   'Management gurus do more good than harm.' Do you agree?
5   Does the successful conduct of electronic commerce require new management principles?

Further reading

Farnham, A. (1996) In Search of Suckers, *Fortune*, 134 (7), pp. 78–84.

Jackson, B. (2001) *Management Gurus and Management Fashions: A Dramatistic Inquiry*, London: Routledge.

Micklethwait, J. and Wooldridge, A. (1997) *The Witch Doctors: What the Management Gurus Are Saying, Why It Matters and How to Make Sense of It*, London: Mandarin.

Miller, T.R. and Vaughan, B.J. (2001) Messages from the Management Past: Classic Writers and Contemporary Problems, *SAM Advanced Management Journal*, 66 (1), pp. 4–11, 20.

Numagami, T. (1998) The Infeasibility of Invariant Laws in Management Studies: A Reflective Dialogue in Defence of Case Studies, *Organization Science*, 9 (1), pp. 2–15.

6 Getting ahead in management
Meritocracy or myth?

Promotion should always be based on proven performance.

Drucker (1955)

One of the dominant myths surrounding the field of management is that 'successful managers' are equated with 'effective managers'.

Luthans, Hodgetts and Rosenkrantz (1988)

Many managers are fatigued by change, insecure, defensive in their career strategies, and highly political in their career behaviours.

Nicholson (1996)

One survey of management education and training in Britain reported that around 90,000 people enter management occupations each year (Constable and McCormick, 1987). Although we cannot know for sure how these new managers see their futures, it would be surprising if they were to look on their first post in management as the job they will hold for the rest of their working lives. It seems more likely that they will see themselves as having taken the first step towards a successful managerial career. Like their predecessors, today's new managers – with or without an MBA – therefore face an age-old problem: how to get ahead in management.

Getting ahead means different things to different people. To an actor it might mean playing increasingly prominent parts in better-known plays at more prestigious theatres. To a research scientist it might mean winning bigger research grants to finance ever-more sophisticated experiments. To a restless entrepreneur it may mean establishing a succession of ventures, moving on to the next fresh challenge as soon as the last has been successfully met. To a writer or poet it might mean writing one true sentence. But for managers it is more likely to mean gaining promotion in an organization. For most managers getting ahead involves climbing the organizational pyramid.

The controversy in brief

The trouble with pyramids is that they get progressively narrower the further one moves upwards from the base. Because there are fewer positions at each succeeding level in an organizational hierarchy, not all those who start at the bottom can subsequently be accommodated at the top. For example, Constable and McCormick (1987) estimated that out of a total of 2.5–3.0 million managers in Britain, 1.6 million were in junior management or supervisory posts, 800,000 were in middle management, and 350,000 were senior functional or general managers. So at the middle level there were half as many posts as at the base level, and at the top level there were roughly half as many posts as at the middle level. Organizations are therefore faced with a problem of selection; how are choices among candidates for promotion at each level to be made? And from the individual manager's point of view, the problem can be seen as one of how to become one of 'the chosen few' (Quinn *et al.,* 1968).

In principle, these concerns coincide. Organizations have an interest in making the most effective use of their personnel, allocating them to jobs in such a way that each post is filled by the person best fitted to carry it out. At the same time, if individual employees are to make the best use of their experience, qualifications and skills, they must be allocated to jobs which exploit their abilities most effectively. Both parties are likely to benefit if selection decisions are made in a way that yields both effective and fair outcomes. The organization achieves the most rational allocation of its 'human resources' and individuals receive a just return for the use of the skills they bring to the organization's tasks. On the face of it, selection on merit seems the best all round solution to the problem of deciding who should do what in organizations.

In practice, of course, things are seldom quite so straightforward. Even the most optimistic meritocrat would be hard put to make a convincing claim that there is a perfect match between people and their jobs. And in everyday life it is not uncommon to find a certain amount of scepticism being expressed as to the adequacy of many personnel selection decisions. Nonetheless, thousands of people are selected or rejected each year with profound implications both for organizations and their employees. It seems reasonable to ask how in fact these decisions are made.

When we ask how it is that some people get selected or promoted when others do not, we are asking for an explanation. What might be called the conventional explanation assumes, in effect, that something akin to the meritocratic ideal of fair selection on merit is generally realized, albeit imperfectly, in modern organizations. Elaborate selection procedures and techniques, designed to ensure that selection is both effective and fair, work in such a way as to distribute talent to its best uses. Unlike more feudal forms of organization, the modern corporation eschews the use of irrelevant, non-functional criteria when deciding who should be given the responsibility for the execution of particular tasks. It is not who you know but what you know that is held to determine the chances of selection. What counts is a track-record of achievement rather than family connections, membership of the old boy (or girl) network or pandering to the social prejudices of selectors. The conventional view, then, emphasizes the objective, rational character of selection decisions, achieved by the application of clearly defined, scientifically based selection procedures and techniques.

In contrast to this explanation, some observers have offered a second, more sceptical view. What happens in practice, it is argued, is that selection usually takes place on the 'me too' principle. Selection is determined less by merit than by the personal preferences of power-holders (usually for people like themselves) and by organizational politics. Thus Pfeffer (1981) writes:

> The common belief, or at least the commonly articulated value, stresses that career rewards, such as promotion and raises, go to those who perform the best and contribute the most to the organization . . . The data from both qualitative and quantitative studies consistently suggest the importance of contacts, linkages in social networks, social background, and being in the right department. In short, the importance of the factors associated with the power of various sub-units and the political skills of individuals to get themselves in the right place at the right time is stressed.

How then do managers get ahead in organizations? Is the ideal of meritocracy little more than a modern myth?

The normative approach: promotion as rational selection

By the 'normative approach' we mean a view of personnel selection which is less concerned with explaining how selection decisions are actually made than with advocating prescriptions as to how they ought to be made. This might be described as the 'textbook' approach to personnel selection (Wood, 1986). As such it represents not only the preferred view of personnel selection specialists but also the 'official' view of many organizations. A key tenet of this approach is that selection ought to be a rational process.

One of the features that has been widely assumed to distinguish modern organizations from their pre-industrial counterparts is their rational basis. In modern organizations work is systematically organized and controlled in order to attain the organization's goals in an effective and efficient manner. Whether it is a matter of choosing a new production technology, deciding on the best location for a new factory, or recruiting the latest batch of management trainees, modern organizations are expected to act rationally.

In essence, rational decision-making involves the application of explicit selection criteria to information on the alternatives from which a choice is to be made. In the case of personnel selection decisions the criteria are to

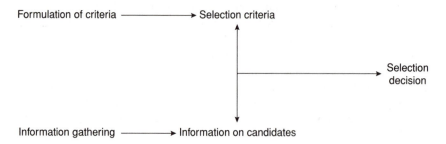

Figure 6.1 The essence of personnel selection

be derived from an analysis of the job requirements and specify the attributes which someone should possess to be able to carry out the job effectively. The alternatives facing the selector consist of the candidates. The selection process then involves obtaining information on each of the candidates which shows whether, or to what extent, they possess the attributes defined as necessary by the selection criteria, and using this to decide which of them is best fitted to the job in question. The overall process is depicted in Figure 6.1.

The normative approach emphasizes the importance of carrying out each step in the selection process in a careful and objective manner, the whole point being to avoid irrationality and bias. Typically the following procedures are recommended.

1 Selection criteria should be arrived at on the basis of a job analysis. To ensure that the criteria which will be used to select a suitable candidate are relevant to the job, it is necessary to develop a realistic job description. This should identify the tasks which are to be carried out, the conditions under which they are undertaken and any other relevant features, and so specify the job requirements. Job analysis may be carried out in a number of ways, but the main methods are: (a) analysis of current job descriptions, (b) obtaining information from current job-holders, (c) obtaining information from those whose work relates to the focal job and (d) direct observation of current job-holders' behaviour (Robertson and Cooper, 1983).

2 The job analysis should be used to prepare a personnel specification. This translates the job requirements into attributes which are required of someone if they are to be able to carry out the job effectively. So, for example, a job analysis of a sales position might show that this involves dealing with technical specifications written in certain foreign languages. The personnel specification would then define a knowledge of these foreign languages as an essential attribute of any candidate.

3 Once the required candidate attributes have been defined, appropriate

selection instruments must be chosen. These instruments are methods for obtaining from each candidate the information that has been defined as relevant. In the example of the sales job, candidates might be asked to submit evidence of their qualifications in foreign languages, or be given a language test, or perhaps be interviewed in French or German! A wide variety of selection instruments have been developed over the years. Mainstream methods include the interview, psychological testing, work sample tests and the use of assessment centres. Other 'fringe' methods, such as graphology (handwriting analysis) or even astrology are sometimes used but are seldom recommended by selection specialists (Anderson and Shackelton, 1986).

4 Once the requisite information on each candidate has been obtained, the selection decision is made by assessing the extent to which each of them measures up to the selection criteria. The candidate who best meets the criteria gets selected.

5 Ideally the whole process should be validated. The selection process should be checked to discover whether it does in fact select those who are best fitted to carry out the job.

The steps advocated by the normative approach are summarized in Figure 6.2.

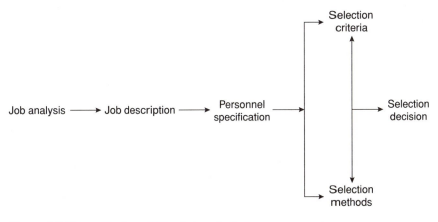

Figure 6.2 The normative approach to selection

The promotion process in practice

The normative approach to personnel selection is clearly an attractive one, combining as it does a concern with both the effectiveness and fairness of selection decisions. Collinson's (1988) statement of the rationale for the normative approach seems unexceptionable.

such as motivation and ability to get on with colleagues, were regarded as more important than experience, qualifications or intelligence as managerial selection criteria. Furthermore, while such 'nebulous and indefinable qualities' were seen as of secondary importance when selecting for specialist posts, they were of primary importance for middle and senior management positions.

In an illuminating American study, Quinn *et al.* (1968) found that 'non-ability' criteria were frequently used by managers during the management selection process. These criteria, such as social background, church attendance, and ethnicity, were officially proscribed by the companies' recruitment and promotion policies, yet they were widely applied by the selecting managers. For example, nearly half the managers surveyed said they would not rule out ethnicity when making a selection decision, and a fifth were prepared to consider a candidate's country of birth. Although criteria of a more clearly job-related kind were also used, this was not to the exclusion of 'non-ability' factors. Moreover, personnel managers were just as likely to refer to these extraneous factors as other types of manager; three-quarters of them, for example, said they took into account 'the right social background'.

Since managerial selection relies heavily on the interview, and because the interview is 'notoriously unreliable' (Seear and Pearn, 1983) as a means of assessing the kinds of nebulous attributes identified by Gill, willingness to adopt such vague criteria implies that practice departs somewhat from the normative ideal. The use of 'non-ability' criteria also suggests that prescription is not necessarily mirrored in practice.

The selection decision

While carefully designed procedures for defining and measuring relevant candidate attributes are indispensable to the realization of rational selection, the key stage in the whole process is the decision. At this point, information on candidates is compared with that defined as relevant to the job so that the person best fitting the defined criteria can be identified and selected.

Surprisingly little advice is available to selectors on how this decision-process should be managed, but we might expect that so long as it is carried out by personnel specialists the chances of reaching an objective decision will be increased. Because the power, prestige and professional identity of personnel managers is heavily bound up with a commitment to 'scientific' selection practices, they might well be taken to be best placed to take the selection decision itself, or at least to exert a decisive influence upon it.

In reality, management selection decisions are rarely taken by personnel specialists. Furthermore, their role in the decision process seems at best highly restrained. Gill's (1980a, 1980b) survey showed that final selection decisions were usually taken by the person to whom the new appointee was to be responsible, albeit with information and advice supplied by the personnel function. The way in which this advisory process actually works can be gauged from a research study on graduate selection.

Knights and Raffo (1990) observed the graduate selection processes of twenty major companies engaged in the university 'milkround' on the assumption that if discrepancies between theory and practice were found at this level they were likely to be even greater elsewhere. They found that at the point of decision the personnel specialists typically avoided making specific recommendations to line managers until they were confident that the line managers had decided on a preferred candidate. Line managers were thus left relatively unconstrained by the professional expertise of the personnel specialists. Partly as a consequence of this, Knights and Raffo conclude, it is 'acceptability rather than suitability that most often determine candidate selection outcomes'.

Evidence on managerial selection practices points, then, to a consistent set of conclusions.

1   Selection criteria are often included which refer to attributes which are difficult to assess objectively and/or which are of questionable relevance to job performance.
2   Interviewing is an unreliable method of making objective judgements of the suitability of candidates for managerial posts, and is particularly so when 'non-cognitive' factors are being assessed.
3   Nonetheless, interviews remain the most frequently used method of assessing candidates and are often used to assess non-cognitive attributes.
4   Psychological tests are much less likely to be used during selection, especially when selecting managers, and when they are used this is most often the point of initial recruitment and least often when making promotion decisions.
5   Even when formal selection procedures have been designed and implemented by personnel specialists, final decisions on whom to select are normally the prerogative of non-specialist line-managers, the more so the higher the level of the post being selected for.

Not surprisingly, this situation is a source of considerable angst among selection psychologists. As so often happens, organizational practitioners tend to get on with the job with little regard for the findings of social science. According to Anderson and Shackelton (1986), 'over the past fifteen years, there appears to have been minimal uptake of the advances in staff resourcing technology into organizational practices'. Or, as Robertson and Makin (1986) put it, 'the message does not appear to have reached practitioners in the UK that psychological research and theory have much to offer'. It is probable that the use of psychological tests for management selection has increased over the last ten years or so. More reliable interviewing methods are also being more widely used. However, these practices remain far from universal (Sisson and Storey, 2000).

The achievement principle

From the normative point of view, the current state of managerial selection practices is far from satisfactory. Although few selection specialists would claim that the methods they advocate can guarantee fair and objective decisions, such methods are nonetheless held to be superior to the alternatives. The need, it is argued, is to promote the greater use of the more objective techniques or at least to improve the unreliable but pervasive interview. By further developing selection technologies and by constantly pressing for their implementation, the ideal of selection by objectively assessed merit might be brought closer to reality. So even though the rational approach to selection is far from universally applied in practice, it could be applied if only organizational practitioners could be persuaded to do so.

This view of the problem has, however, been questioned by Offe (1976) who puts forward a radical critique of the rational selection model. He argues that the dominant rationale for the differential distribution of rewards from work in industrial societies is the 'achievement principle'. According to this principle, individuals ought to be rewarded according to their achievements and not on 'irrelevant' grounds such as their looks, family connections or religious beliefs. He suggests not only that rewards are often not distributed on the basis of achievement, but also that the conditions under which the achievement principle could be applied are ceasing to hold because of fundamental changes in the technical and organizational bases of work.

Offe distinguishes two forms of work organization. In the task-continuous form the tasks to be undertaken by job-holders at each level of the organizational hierarchy overlap so that the higher-level employees have an intimate understanding of the work of those below. Judgement of the performance of subordinates can therefore be based clearly on task-based criteria. For example, in the craft workshop the master knows how to perform all the tasks of the journeyman effectively and the journeyman has a similar understanding of the apprentice's work. But in the task-discontinuous form jobs at different levels in the organization differ greatly from each other. This makes it difficult to evaluate employees' suitability for higher-level posts on the basis of their current performance and it is not necessarily obvious that performance in the current job is a relevant basis for assessment of capacity to perform at the next highest level. As a result, Offe argues, promotion decisions in task-discontinuous organizations come to depend on 'extra-functional' criteria. And the increasing technical complexity of modern industrial organizations implies that the task-discontinuous form is becoming predominant.

Offe's analysis draws attention to two well-recognized problems concerning the evaluation of managerial employees. Because, as we saw in our discussion of the nature of management, managerial work is interwoven with that of many other organizational members it is frequently difficult to relate outcomes to individual actions. If a concert pianist plays a wrong note during a performance of a concerto there is no doubt as to who hit the wrong key. But when a sales department achieves record sales, or when a division returns a loss, there are likely to be problems in deciding who, if anyone, produced the outcome. Maybe it was a good, or bad, year. Maybe the unions or the government were to blame. Maybe it was sheer luck. There are always a lot of 'maybes', particularly when things go wrong.

Second, even when individual managers can be clearly distinguished in terms of their current performance, when the next job in the hierarchy is very different from that immediately below, current performance may not be reliable as a predictor of ability to carry out the new job. A typical case is that of sales managers. Good sales personnel have to be good at selling, but this is not sufficient to ensure that they will make good sales managers.

Under task-discontinuous conditions those who are faced with promotion decision have three choices. They can implement more sophisticated selection techniques which might distinguish more adequately between candidates' abilities and identify relevant attributes for the higher-level job. Current evidence indicates that this alternative is seldom taken up. Or they can select at random, for example by sticking a pin in a list of candidates. But this option goes so much against the notion of fair and rational selection that it can be considered a non-starter. The final choice is therefore to select on the basis of 'informal' criteria, these being ones which selectors find appealing but which cannot be firmly related to capacities to perform the job.

Informal factors in promotion

The use of 'informal' or 'non-ability' criteria in selection militates against the ideal of objective and fair selection. These factors are irrelevant to performance in the job although distinguishing among criteria in this way is not always a straightforward matter. Because of the sensitive nature of promotion decisions, relatively little evidence is available on the criteria which are actually applied during the selection process. Even so, the few studies that have been made suggest that the use of informal criteria is not unusual.

In a classic study of American industrial managers, Dalton (1951, 1959) observed a notable disparity between the 'official' view of the working of the promotion system in a large industrial concern and its actual operation.

In theory, promotions were awarded to managers on the basis of such attributes as their ability, effort and co-operativeness. But there were no clearly defined procedures for implementing these criteria. Instead, promotions appeared to be granted largely according to whether a manager conformed to the social preferences of higher management. In the case studies by Dalton these preferences included religious affiliation, ethnicity, political beliefs, participation in certain social activities, and membership of approved secret societies.

A second American study (Coates and Pellegrin, 1957–8) examined the organizational career patterns of 50 top executives and 50 foremen in 30 large organizations. One part of the study asked the participants what they thought about the prevalence and importance of informal factors in the promotion process. Four factors were regarded as of some importance although they were not thought to be consistently applied. These were: national origins, religious affiliation, membership of 'fraternal orders' such as the Masons, and political affiliation. A further eight factors were regarded as of universal significance by a majority of both executives and the foremen: family background and connections, membership of community and professional organizations, participation in recreational activities with other employees, inconspicuous consumption (a 'sober' lifestyle), acceptability of the employee's wife, conformity to the attitudes, values and behaviour patterns of superiors, cultivation of friendships with superiors, and having the loyal support of colleagues.

It is worth noting that many of these factors refer to an individual's membership of and participation in what have come to be called 'social networks'. As we shall see, more recent research has confirmed the significance of network participation to promotional success.

These and other studies, such as those of Powell (1963) and Bowman (1964), suggest that informal factors may well play a significant part in determining who gets promoted. The likelihood of this being so depends, however, on other conditions. In particular, as Coates and Pellegrin (1957–8) noted, informal factors are likely to play a strong part when formal criteria are indistinctly stated and difficult to measure objectively. Yet even when considerable efforts are taken to achieve formality and objectivity, less tangible influences may still prevail.

One of the few pieces of research to have examined the selection process at first hand dealt with the selection of army officers (Salaman and Thompson, 1978). This study was based on the observation of a three-day assessment using the Regular Commissions Board selection system. This system, the authors commented, was 'an impressive attempt to eliminate the personal and the subjective and to gather as much and as varied information about the candidate as is relevant and possible'. The selectors observed the candidates under varied conditions and interviewed them. They were also provided with a list of selection criteria and required to rate each candidate using a set of pre-established grades.

Despite the formality of the procedures and the intention of the selectors to be unbiased and fair, the selection process nonetheless gave preference to those public school qualities which were already firmly established in the culture of the officer corps. This came about not because the selectors were overtly biased in favour of those who were, in effect, from a similar background to themselves, but because the selection criteria, although formally designated, still had to be applied. When doing so, the selectors tended to interpret the evidence on each candidate in terms of their own, implicit class-based preferences. Thus, 'the results of the selection process are highly class determined; but all parties insist that they are operating solely on the basis of the formal, scientific selection scheme'.

Formalized procedures, then, are no guarantee of objective selections. As Collinson (1988) has pointed out, formalized selection procedures are necessary but are not in themselves sufficient because 'The need to judge and evaluate candidates will always afford selectors a substantial element of discretion regardless of the degree of bureaucracy and formality present in the selection process'. Given the inherent difficulties of specifying the precise nature of managerial skills and abilities and of clearly relating organizational outcomes to the action of specific individuals, it would not be surprising if managerial selection decisions were subject to consider- able ambiguity.

Who gets ahead?

Studies of selection and promotion procedures can tell us a good deal about how promotion decisions are made, but we can also learn something about the promotion process by examining selection outcomes. If we could compare, for example, the attributes of those who have been promoted within an organization with those who have not, this might enable us to infer something about the criteria which are applied during selection. Although there has been little research specifically aimed at making comparisons of this kind, a number of surveys have examined the back- ground characteristics, such as type of education and social origins, of both managers and company directors.

An early study (Acton Society Trust, 1956) examined the backgrounds and qualifications of managers in fifty-one large organizations. This showed that the background characteristics most advantageous for promotion were the possession of an arts degree from Oxford or Cambridge and having been a pupil at a major public school. These rated above the holding of technical or scientific qualifications. The most disadvantageous attribute was to have been a foreman.

Although the social origins of the managers were not closely analysed in this study, the combination of public schooling and an Oxbridge arts degree implies that those who got on did so at least in part because they possessed social attributes that were attractive to selectors. Social acceptability seems to have been an important influence on the chances of promotion, though not necessarily to the exclusion of 'competence'.

The advantage conferred by public schooling is particularly significant. These schools, which are attended by a tiny minority of the population, have long been renowned for inculcating and developing the type of 'leadership skills' favoured by the upper classes, and have been heavily patronized by families of high social status. The Acton research showed that public schooling was increasingly important at the higher levels of management. Whereas 14 per cent of junior managers and 19 per cent of middle managers had attended a public school, 33 per cent of top managers had done so. As McGivering *et al.* (1960) noted, this suggests 'that top managers tend to be of a different "social type" from middle managers and that class background is a factor influencing movement from middle to top management ranks'.

Subsequent studies by Clements (1958), Clark (1966) and Leggatt (1978) tended to confirm the importance of social attributes for getting ahead. The findings of studies focused exclusively on company directors (Copeman, 1955; Heller, 1967, 1970, 1973, Thomas, 1978), usually in large firms, have also generally been consistent with those of research on managers. Former public schoolboys have been heavily over-represented among directors and Oxbridge graduates have tended to outnumber graduates from other universities. These studies suggest that social credentials have traditionally been of considerable relevance to the prospect for getting ahead in British management.

There has been considerable speculation on the extent to which this picture is changing in the wake of post-war reforms in education and broader changes in management and society, but up-to-date evidence is lacking. One newspaper study indicated that among the chief executives of the largest firms, the dominance of those with private secondary education may be lessening. There may also have been some reduction in the proportion of Oxbridge graduates (Hughes and Steiner, 2001).

An American study (Useem and Karabel, 1986) has emphasized the importance of social attributes to advancement within the ranks of top management. Drawing on data on 2,729 senior managers from 208 major corporations, these authors showed that upper-class origins conferred advantages even among those with identical educational backgrounds. Although prestigious educational credentials were also relevant, they concluded that 'coming from an upper-class background remains an important resource in gaining access to the highest rungs of the corporate world'. This, they argue, might be because high social origins give access to 'strategic elite networks'. In addition, one of the most valued requirements of potential top managers, who are to be given access to the levers of corporate power, is that they be 'trustworthy'. One way in which strategic elites might reassure themselves that their selection decisions realize this is by selecting those who are from a similar social and educational background as themselves.

The use of such criteria seems to be at odds with the meritocratic ideal. Social origins are conferred by birth and strongly influence the likelihood of access to elite educational institutions. This may account for the reluctance of firms to subject top management appointments to the same formalized selection processes as are used at lower levels of the organizations. As Bonis (1972) has suggested, modern psychological methods are rarely applied to the selection of top managers because they do not take into account an individual's commitment to the values of the organization's dominant cadre. Hence, 'when it comes to choosing managers at the highest level, selection is made by co-opting small subgroups that have a very strong sense of loyalty to the organization'.

Managerial effectiveness and managerial success

The achievement principle proposes that rewards and promotions should be awarded on the basis of merit, whilst the normative approach to selection advocates formal, scientifically rational procedures as the appropriate means to the realization of this end. Were these ideas to be implemented in practice, it would be expected that those who receive greater rewards are at the same time those who have been clearly identified as the most able. In the case of managers this would lead one to expect that there would be a close relationship between managerial success and effectiveness.

Somewhat surprisingly there have been relatively few attempts to examine this important assumption. Instead there has been a widespread tendency to take for granted the rationality and efficacy of managerial promotion practices. But a study by Luthans *et al.* (1988) has tackled this issue head on. These authors conducted an elaborate investigation of the work of 457 'mainstream' managers in a variety of public and private organizations in the United States. Using interviews, questionnaires and observations of the managers at their places of work, they compared the managers according to both their 'success' and their 'effectiveness'.

As a measure of 'success', Luthans *et al.* created a success index. This was defined as the ratio of a manager's current job level in the organization to the length of time spent working in it. In effect, this is a measure of 'speed' of promotion where speed equals distance travelled (the number of organizational levels traversed) divided by the time taken (the number of years spent in the organization). More rapidly promoted managers were therefore regarded as more successful than those who had been promoted slowly or not at all.

To measure 'effectiveness', an assessment of the performance of the manager's organizational unit was combined with data on the degree of satisfaction and commitment displayed by the manager's subordinates. Effective managers were thus defined as those who both 'delivered the goods' and maintained high employee morale. Using these measures, Luthans *et al.* found that very few managers were both highly successful

Table 6.1 The activities of successful and effective managers (% of time devoted to four clusters of activity)

	Successful	Effective	Successful and effective	All managers
Traditional management	13	19	34	32
Routine communication	28	44	31	29
Human resource management	11	26	15	20
Networking	48	11	20	19

Source: Adapted from F. Luthans, R.M. Hodgetts and S.A. Rosenkrantz, *Real Managers*, Cambridge, MA: Ballinger, 1988.

and highly effective. Of a sample of the 60 most successful managers, only fifteen were highly effective. Moreover, successful managers behaved differently to effective ones.

The success and effectiveness indices were related to data on the distribution of attention given to four major clusters of work activity. These clusters were: 'traditional management' tasks, such as planning, decision-making and controlling; 'routine communication', such as exchanging information and handling paperwork; 'human resource management', such as staffing, training and managing conflict; and 'networking' which included interacting with outsiders, socializing and politicking. As Table 6.1 shows, successful managers differed markedly from effective ones in the way they allocated time to these activities. Whereas effective managers paid most attention to communications and human resource management, successful managers invested heavily in networking. Indeed the more successful a manager was, the greater the involvement in networking.

Although the authors of this study are cautious in assuming causal links between the patterns of activity, effectiveness and promotional success, the message for the ambitious manager comes over clearly. If you want to get ahead, get into networking, because 'networking and communication skills seem to be the most important keys to success'. But from the point of view of social and economic well-being a more disturbing implication is that 'the wrong people are being promoted'.

The politics of promotion

The frequently noted disparity between 'official' accounts of managerial promotion processes and observed practices and outcomes suggests that the normative approach to promotion is inadequate as an explanation of promotion processes. As Lee and Piper (1988; see also Lee, 1985a, 1985b) have pointed out, concentration on the formal aspects of promotion systems tends to encourage an overly-simple and mechanistic view of what are, in fact, complex, subtle and highly charged human activities. In particular, the normative model of promotion underplays the active role which those seeking promotion may play in securing advancement and the micro-political interests of selectors. Hence much of the technical literature on personnel selection implicitly depicts candidates as inert raw materials processed by a formalized system run by dispassionate automatons.

An alternative to this decontextualized, mechanistic view is to see promotional opportunities as scarce organizational rewards which are highly valued by many, though not all, managers. As such, they become a focus of acquisitional struggles in which individuals deploy various personal resources in order to improve their chances of success. These resources include not only those which are recognized by the formal system, such as good 'track record', but also informal resources of the kind noted earlier. Acquaintance with higher-level managers, family connections, participation in organizational networks, even gender skills, may be used to influence the outcomes of promotional processes.

Of these, network participation appears to be of particular importance. Kakabadse (1983) defines networks as 'interest groups which are formed for non-organizational reasons' and identifies four types of network – practitioner, privileged power, ideological and people-oriented – although these are best seen as examples rather than as an exhaustive list.

Practitioner networks link those who share a common training or professional concern. They may be formalized in professional associations or consist of loose groupings of employees who share a common professional identity. Access to such networks therefore depends heavily on possession of the appropriate qualifications and familiarity with the cultural assumptions, language and values of the practitioner group. Privileged power networks, on the other hand, draw together those who possess substantial positional power, and operate as exclusive 'clubs' in which the mighty celebrate and enhance their elite status. Access is strictly by invitation. Ideological networks draw people together on the basis of their shared concern to advance certain broad policies or objectives. Access is afforded on the basis of commitment to shared ideals and programmes. Finally, people-oriented networks form around shared feelings of personal warmth and familiarity, and persist largely so long as their members find their continuing association personally worthwhile. Hence they can be seen as friendship groups to which new members are admitted on the basis of their personal identification with existing participants.

Although the boundaries of these groups may coincide with recognized organizational groupings, such as departments, they are frequently informal structures sustained by the fluid participation of their members. Nonetheless, these networks can operate powerfully to promote the interests of their participants. The key significance of network participation for promotion is that it may provide access to information otherwise unobtainable through the official system and to influential superiors who are in a position to influence or to make promotional decisions.

Unlike the normative approach, which places the formal selection system at the centre of the promotion process, the political model emphasizes the importance of informal processes and criteria. This leaves a question-mark over the official selection system: what role does it play? The political approach suggests that a key function of the official system and its meritocratic ethos is legitimation. As Pfeffer (1981) puts it, 'A belief in the merit-based and non-political aspect of careers is important in order to maintain the legitimacy of the organization's internal labour market and to help assuage the feelings of those who earn less than others in the organization ... This value is articulated repeatedly, and comes to be believed by those involved in the process.'

Barlow's (1989) discussion of the latent functions of management appraisal systems is of relevance here. Based on the results of a field study of seventy managers in a petrochemical company, Barlow noted a divergence between the officially stated aims of the company-wide appraisal system and managers' perceptions of what actually happened in practice. Although the system was officially geared to the identification and assessment of potential, and while managers overwhelmingly perceived reward in terms of promotion, few of them saw much relation between the two. Thus, 'despite formal declarations concerning the objectives of the appraisal system, managerial potential for career development in fact was evaluated by a process of social selection, rather than by independent assessment of aptitudes, characteristics, skills and learning abilities'. Managers believed that the appraisal system served neither as a motivational nor as a control device. Rather, these functions were executed by the 'network of colleague relations' linking operating managers to each other and to their superiors. In particular, the capacity to influence higher-level gate-keepers who were believed to control access to the promotional ladder was seen as a more effective means of improving the likelihood of promotion than the formal appraisal system.

Barlow concludes that the appraisal system functioned essentially as a legitimating ritual; legitimating, because the existence of the system symbolized the organization's commitment to rational, fair and effective treatment of its personnel, and a ritual because its operations were disconnected from the real processes which largely determined the fates and fortunes of employees. These rested heavily in the hands of higher management. The appraisal system operated less as a constraint on the exercise of higher managers' discretionary powers than as a facilitator of it. For example, disgruntled managers who had been passed over for promotion tended to discharge their hostility not onto higher management but onto the official owners of the system, the personnel department.

The politically charged nature of performance appraisal systems also becomes clear from Gioia and Longenecker's (1994) interviews with eighty-two American executives. The executives' beliefs about the operation of management appraisal included that it is subject to political manipulation and that it is 'a "political tool" used to control people and resources'. The researchers note that 'politics plays an especially sinister role in executive performance appraisals'.

Commentary

The last few decades have seen substantial changes in the organizational landscape as firms have come and gone and those which remain have restructured (Wheatley, 1992). Some of the career ladders which managers have been accustomed to climb have been broken or even cast away (Osterman, 1996), perhaps throwing the managerial career system into crisis (Newell and Dopson, 1996; Nicholson, 1996; Thomas, 1983). Nonetheless, as Guest and Mackenzie's (1996) research shows, many traditional career ladders remain in place albeit at steeper angles. The struggle for advancement in organizations will continue.

The clearest conclusion to be drawn from this discussion is that the conventional assumption that organizational promotions are governed by a rational principle, which ensures that access to posts is afforded to those who are best fitted to fill them, is at best too simple and at worst a contemporary myth.

The political perspective usefully draws our attention to the fact that organizations are structures of control (Clegg and Dunkerley, 1980). Promotion, particularly at the higher organizational levels, is not simply a matter of fitting technicians to roles. The movement of individuals between positions of power and influence in organizations has broader political implications. In this process, supporters and confidants may be lost or gained, alliances and coalitions may be reinforced or weakened, group and individual interests may be advanced or retarded. Since promotion processes cannot be divorced from this organizational context, it seems unreasonable to expect that advancement will often occur on the grounds of 'merit' alone, especially at the higher levels.

It might be wrong to conclude, however, that promotional processes amount to no more than a political game. Insofar as managers do make a difference to organizations' performance, promotion without reference to ability is likely to be self-defeating in the long run. Whilst managerial expertise is notoriously difficult to define and measure by standardized methods, this does not necessarily mean that it does not exist nor that it cannot be identified by informal means. As Wood (1986) has pointed out, informal selection methods are not necessarily capricious or irrational.

It seems plausible to propose that in management what you know and what you have achieved will seldom be sufficient for getting ahead. Having an MBA, for example, may only get you an entry ticket to the promotion race. Knowing and being known in the networks of influence both for what you have achieved and for who you are may be essential if you are to progress. Perhaps, then, it is not a matter of suitability or acceptability but suitability *and* acceptability. Of course, even this conclusion might well be considered controversial.

Questions for discussion

1 Can fair selection decisions in organizations ever be guaranteed?
2 Are psychological tests the only way of obtaining objective information on managers' abilities?
3 Should selection interviewing for management posts be banned?
4 How can managerial effectiveness and managers' career success be more closely aligned?
5 Why is it difficult to assess a manager's performance?

Further reading

Collinson, D.L. (1990) *Managing to Discriminate*, London: Routledge.

Gioia, D.A. and Longenecker, C.O. (1994) Delving into the Dark Side: The Politics of Executive Appraisal, *Organizational Dynamics*, 22 (3), Winter, pp. 47–58.

Luthans, F. (1988) Successful vs. Effective Real Managers, *Academy of Management Executive*, 2 (2), pp. 127–32.

Robertson, I.T. and Makin, P.J. (1986) Management Selection in Britain: A Survey and Critique, *Journal of Occupational Psychology*, 59, pp. 45–57.

7 Gender in management

Must men manage?

The world of employment, particularly at senior organizational levels, is dominated by male values, needs and perspectives on the world.

Marshall (1984)

Evolutionary theory predicts that men will tend to exhibit greater status-seeking, competitiveness, and risk-taking than women, and that women will exhibit more nurturance and affiliative behaviour. These predictions are borne out in every known human society.

Browne (1995)

There is a conspiracy called evolutionary psychology going on against women.

Moore (2001)

In the early 1970s an interesting book about middle-class careers appeared called *Managers and Their Wives* (Pahl and Pahl, 1971). Is there anything about that title that strikes you as problematic? If there is, you may be someone who sees the gendered character of management as an issue. If not, you may believe that everything has changed since the days when men managed businesses and women managed homes and families. A study of managers today, you might suggest, would show that there are just as many female managers in business as male. Gender is therefore no longer a problem for managerial careers. Alternatively you may think that it is natural and obvious that management is a masculine occupation and that managers ought to be men.

Whatever your response, it would be hard to deny that over the last thirty years or so, sex and gender have been consistently hot topics in management. The problems of sexual harassment at work, equality of opportunity and equal pay have been a focus of continuing attention. Such issues are, of course, one part of a broader concern with women's rights and roles in contemporary society. Since the 1960s in particular, that concern has produced a voluminous literature, both theoretical, empirical, policy-related, and polemical. It has spawned a political movement to advance women's interests and has stimulated the formulation of organizational policies and national laws to promote equal opportunities and combat gender discrimination. But despite these developments the position of women in management continues to provoke considerable discussion and research.

The question of what is to count as controversial in this field looms large. It is not too difficult to understand why Connell (1995) observed that when writing about gender 'the issues are explosive and the chances of getting wrong answers are excellent'. There are disagreements, for example, about the extent to which men and women are different, about the reasons for such differences, and about their consequences. With the possible exception of leadership (see Chapter 8), the 'gender and management question' has probably generated more debate and has certainly raised more passions than any other controversy in management. No one chapter nor even several books could do justice to the material available on these wide-ranging issues. It must be said immediately, then, that here we deal with just one important gender question in the context of managing organizations; why are there so many men in management, especially at the higher levels? How is this situation to be explained? Is it inevitable? Must men manage?

The controversy in brief

Once it was more or less taken for granted in managerial circles that management was a male occupation, and mostly it still is. The fact that women and men are differentially distributed across occupations and within organizational hierarchies in most if not all industrial societies is a well-established observation and is not seriously in dispute. Men tend to be over-represented in management occupations and to predominate at the most senior levels. What *is* in dispute is the explanation for this state of affairs and, in turn, what might be done about it.

One long-standing school of thought argues that women and men have different 'human natures' which stem from their biological constitutions and their biological roles in the reproduction of the human species. Under the rubrics of sociobiology and evolutionary psychology, this school depicts humans as 'hard-wired', with fixed constitutions established through the evolutionary process of natural selection. Women and men are biologically programmed with separate traits which give rise to distinct temperaments, preferences and styles of action. Under the competitive conditions of free-market capitalism, these distinct traits are held to differentially advantage males in the competition for access to positions of power in organizations. Men are 'naturally' aggressive, competitive and risk-taking whereas women are 'naturally' placid, collaborative and risk-avoiding. It is no surprise, on this view, that the captains of industry as well as the occupants of the other command posts in society are predominantly men, for it is men who are naturally best fitted to occupy them. Any proposals for changing this situation are therefore seen as problematic.

Against this view, social constructionists, as well as many feminists, have tended to argue that although women and men play biologically separate roles in human reproduction, other significant differences, in behaviour attitude and orientation, are not a direct consequence of biology but are social artifacts. Men and women *learn* how to think, feel and act as males and females according to the rules and expectations which prevail in their society. Much that we take for granted as essential differences between the sexes, built into each person's biology, are, on the contrary, socially constructed, created during a person's upbringing in a particular social context. People are born into their sex but are socialized into their gender. They are more a product of culture than of nature. However, work organizations, it is sometimes claimed, are arranged and governed largely by men and for men within a patriarchal society, with the result that women have encountered significant barriers to their progress to positions of organizational power. Once these constraints are removed, men and women will compete on a level playing field so that one day members of both sexes will be found at the top in more or less equal numbers. This will promote both justice and efficiency by making best use of the talents available in society.

From a constructionist point of view, the biologically based ideas of the evolutionists are likely to be regarded as both inadequate and as outdated. They may be seen as a flawed ideology which flourished in the pre-feminist era but which was soon overturned during the feminist resurgence of the 1960s and 1970s. But it would be a mistake to see the evolutionary perspective today as simply an obscure and outmoded branch of the sciences that is concerned with the behavioural implications of biological sex differences in animal species. On the contrary, it may have a significant impact on management. For example, it has recently been used to account for the differential success of men and women as managers and, its critics would argue, to justify unacceptable inequalities (Welch, 1998). Moreover, in the guise of evolutionary psychology it is now being used to underpin prescriptions for the management and design of organizations (Nicholson, 2000).

Men and women in management

Before we explore explanations for the disparity in the numbers of men and women in management, it is important to examine its existence and extent. To do so we can draw on evidence from international labour-force surveys as well as studies which have looked in some detail at the gender structure of the managerial workforce in individual countries and corporate sectors.

Although women and men are represented in almost equal proportions in the world's population, participation in employment, or at least paid employment, is less evenly balanced. World Bank estimates show that about 59 per cent of the world's labour-force are male and 41 per cent female (World Bank, 2001). If a person's career chances were unrelated to their gender, then we would expect to find men and women represented in similar proportions to these across industries and occupations. This is far from being the case.

Across the world, men are over-represented in industries such as manufacturing and construction, and in many industrialized countries women are over-represented in the services sector. So, for example, in the second half of the 1990s in the UK, 86 per cent of the female labour-force worked in services compared with 60 per cent of the male labour-force, whereas only 13 per cent of working women were employed in the industrial sector compared with 38 per cent of men. This situation is very similar to that found in the USA (World Bank, 2001).

Table 7.1 shows the proportion of men and women in both the labour-force and in managerial and administrative occupations for a selection of industrial nations in 1999. Because the occupational definitions used by different countries vary somewhat, and because management is notoriously difficult to define precisely, these figures should be treated with caution since they permit only fairly crude comparisons to be made. Even so, it is clear that in most cases men are significantly over-represented in management ranks compared with their representation in the labour-force as a whole. Only in the case of the USA do the proportions approximate equivalence. In sharp contrast, management in Japan is an overwhelmingly male preserve, with fewer than one in ten management posts being held by women. What these statistics show, then, is that even when we allow for the fact that there are more men in employment than women in these countries, men are typically over-represented among managers and women under-represented.

When we turn to top management, global figures are harder to come by but single-country surveys show that the tendency for men to predominate in managerial occupations is much accentuated at the higher organizational levels. A directory listing more than 10,000 'decision-makers' in British industry found that fewer than 2 per cent were female (Margetts, 1991). Holton's (1995) survey of the boards of directors of the 200 largest private sector industrial companies in the UK showed that 75 per cent of the boards were all-male and 96 per cent of the directors were men. In another survey Olins and Steiner (1997) obtained data on 15,000 British company directors of whom 95.4 per cent were men. Ninety-nine per cent of the CEOs of the top 100 firms were male. Similarly, an Institute of Management study (1998) reported that over 96 per cent of the directors covered were male. Thomas (2001) studied the composition of the boards of directors of Britain's largest retail companies. In a sector which might have been expected to be 'female-friendly' in the light of its predominantly female labour-force, it was found that in 1997 men held 89 per cent of

Table 7.1 Men and women in the labour force and in management, selected countries, 1999 (%)

	Total employment		Managers/Administration	
	Men	*Women*	*Men*	*Women*
Australia	56.53	43.47	75.21	24.79
Canada	54.13	45.87	64.87	35.13
Denmark[a]	54.23	45.76	76.60	23.40
Finland	52.95	47.04	71.31	28.69
Germany	56.75	43.25	73.69	26.31
Greece[a]	63.12	36.88	75.06	24.94
Ireland	59.52	40.48	66.09	33.91
Italy	63.89	36.11	81.18	18.82
Japan	59.28	40.72	90.70	9.30
Netherlands[a]	57.98	42.02	77.23	22.77
New Zealand	54.65	45.34	62.67	37.33
Russian Federation	52.18	47.81	62.78	37.22
Sweden	52.15	47.85	71.20	28.80
United Kingdom	55.16	44.83	66.70	33.30
USA	53.52	46.48	54.90	45.10

Source: International Labour Organization, *Yearbook of Labour Statistics,* Geneva: ILO, 2000.

Notes: [a]Data for 1998. Figures calculated from data given in Table 2C. Definitions of 'managers/administrators' vary according to the classification system adopted – see source for details. This table can be usefully compared with Table 3.1 in Antal and Izraeli (1993).

the directorships, 96 per cent of the executive directorships and all the CEO posts. Even today only one of the top 100 quoted companies in Britain is headed by a female chief executive. In short, wherever you look in British business the story is much the same.

Studies such as these have tended to show that the numbers of women holding top management appointments has grown but that the rate of change is slow. Holton *et al.* (1995) commented that if change were to continue at the rate they had observed in their researches, it would be 2017 before all of the top 200 firms in Britain had at least one woman board member. In the USA, Daily *et al.*'s (1999) survey of the boards of the *Fortune 500* companies found that board membership by women had increased substantially between 1987 and 1996. But 98 per cent of the CEOs were still male, and women comprised 0.006 per cent of insider/exec-utive directors. They commented that 'not only have women made no progress in their ascension to the executive suite; there is no evidence that such progress is likely to be forthcoming for many years' (Daily *et al.,* 1999).

Cross-national research by Antal and Izraeli (1993) indicates that the situation in Britain and the United States is not greatly different in many other developed industrial countries. They reported that the proportion of top or senior managers who were women was less than 10 per cent, and often much less, in countries such as France, Germany, Holland, Norway, Denmark, and Israel. In Japan it was fewer than 1 per cent. In general, then, the position is clear. As Wajcman (1998) has put it, 'men continue to monopolize the elite level of corporate power in almost all regions of the world'.

Why men manage: the evolutionary perspective

The idea that women and men's differing biological constitutions entail different psychological and social attributes has a commonsense appeal as can be seen from the success of best-selling popular books highlighting sex differences (Gray, 1993; Pease and Pease, 2001). Recently this idea has been given the backing of scholars working in the fields of evolutionary psychology and its progenitor sociobiology, for they too emphasize the influence of our biology on the way we think and act. I shall refer to these fields jointly as the 'evolutionary perspective' and to their adherents as 'evolutionists'. In part this is a matter of convenience but it is also because, despite differences in detail, these fields constitute a relatively uniform and distinct school of thought.

The evolutionary perspective adopts a number of basic assumptions about people and their behaviour which are derived from the framework developed by Charles Darwin (1809–1882) and his neo-Darwinist successors in the field of evolutionary biology. Of key importance is the assumption that humans should be considered as animals, and *homo sapiens* (wise, or reasoning, man) as but one among many animal species. This enables human behaviour to be brought under the same explanatory scheme as that of other 'organisms', a move seen as highly controversial in Darwin's day as it is indeed today.

The evolutionary perspective was given its modern form by a Harvard biologist, E.O. Wilson, in his influential text *Sociobiology: The New Synthesis* (1975). Wilson applied Darwin's insights into the development of animal species through evolutionary processes of natural selection to the explanation of social structures and patterns of behaviour. Wilson's sociobiology was concerned to develop a general theory of animal behaviour, but later writers focused more specifically on the biological determinants of the behaviour of humans. Meanwhile cognitive psychology was attempting to understand the human brain as a complex computer and was faced with the problem of explaining how such complex entities could have come into being. Evolutionary biology provided an explanation for the development of complex biological structures – natural selection. The structure of the human psyche could thus be seen as an outcome of evolutionary processes. In this way the evolutionary perspective combines elements of evolutionary biology with those of cognitive psychology.

Natural selection and sex differences

Evolutionary theory proposes that biological organisms possess features that can be passed on from one generation to the next through their encoding in the genes. The process of natural selection entails selective retention whereby those features which promote the survival and repro- duction of the organism are retained and transmitted to subsequent generations whilst those which do not are discarded. It is crucial to under- stand that in the case of humans both physical and psychological charac- teristics are assumed to be subject to natural selection. As humans adapt to the challenges presented to them by the environment in which they develop, both their bodies and their minds are shaped by their experiences. Evolutionary psychology therefore aims to identify evolved psychological mechanisms, 'behavioural predispositions that evolved to solve particular problems in the environment of our Pleistocene hunter-gatherer ancestors' (Browne, 1995). Since evolutionary processes occur over lengthy time scales, it is inferred that the basic psychological structure of modern humans was formed some hundreds of thousands of years ago and has not changed significantly since. As Nicholson (1998) has put it, 'you can take the person out of the Stone Age, evolutionary psychologists contend, but you can't take the Stone Age out of the person'.

Crucial to the process of natural selection is differential reproductive success. This means that some members of a species will produce more offspring than others, and that the genes of these more successful members will be more predominant in the succeeding generation. On this view, males and females adopt different 'reproductive strategies' in order to improve their chances of reproductive success: whereas males can increase their chances of successfully passing on their genes by mating with as many females as possible, females can do so by investing their efforts in nurturing the offspring they bear. The males of a species are thus depicted as 'mating specialists' and the females as 'parenting specialists'.

Because of these different reproductive strategies, males and females develop temperamental and behavioural differences. To be successful in mating, males display greater tendencies to risk-taking, aggressiveness and promiscuity than do females. So according to Browne (1995) 'in society after society, men increase their reproductive success by engaging in risky activities and increasing their wealth and status ... women increase their reproductive success by devoting the bulk of their energies to investment in children rather than the acquisition of resources'. These tendencies, it is claimed, were established in the distant past but continue to function in contemporary society. Men and women exhibit 'grossly different tempera- mental styles' and these, says Browne, are very likely to be biologically based rather than to arise from differential socialization. If anything, the way individuals are brought up reflects differences produced by natural selection rather than being constitutive of them. Since these differences are built into the human character, there seems very little likelihood of changing them.

Sex differences and patriarchy

The American sociologist, Steven Goldberg, has produced a theory of patriarchy which seeks to explain 'why men rule' (Goldberg 1974, 1993). He argues that biologically based differences between men and women, rooted in their differential hormonal endowments, lead inevitably to the dominance of men over women in all organized spheres of life – political, economic, religious or social – as well as in family relationships. Leadership and authority have, he claims, been the preserve of men in all societies and this is to be accounted for primarily by men's greater propensity to 'aggression'. By aggression, he explains, he refers to a tendency to competitiveness, single-mindedness of purpose and endurance, a willingness to make sacrifices to attain control and power, self-assertion, the need to impose the will on the environment, resistance to the influence of others, and domination in relationships with women.

Men and women's differential propensity to aggression arises from 'the hormonal-central nervous system differentiation between males and females', that is to say their different biological constitutions. 'The male hormonal system,' he argues, 'engenders a greater male "aggression" that results in a male superiority at attaining roles and positions given high status . . . so that it is inevitable that positions and roles of leadership and status will be attained by men.' Rule by men, or patriarchy, is thus unavoidable given humans' evolutionary history as biological entities.

Sex differences in management

Kingsley Browne is neither a biologist nor a social scientist but a professor of law, yet he has brought the evolutionary perspective to bear specifically on the issue of women in management (Browne, 1995; 1998a; 1998b). He addresses what are widely regarded as two key issues: the 'glass ceiling', which denotes the under-representation of women in management, especially at the higher levels, and the 'gender gap', which refers to the observation that women's earnings are, on average, substantially lower than those of men.

Against the background of the evolutionary perspective, he says:

> I should at this point say exactly what I am arguing. It is my central thesis that much of what we call the glass ceiling and gender gap is the product of basic biological sex differences in personality and temperament. These differences have resulted from differential reproductive strategies that have been adopted by the two sexes during human history

and are every bit as much a product of natural selection as our bipedal locomotion and opposable thumbs. Although these temperamental traits evolved in our hunting-and-gathering ancestral environment, they remain with us today whether or not they remain adaptive.

(Browne, 1995)

Browne points out that in the USA at least, women are represented in management in accordance with their numbers in the labour-force as a whole (see Table 7.1 above). In senior management, however, they are significantly under-represented. Studies of executive careers have shown, he argues, that to be successful managers must be willing to take risks, to work long hours and to put their work at the centre of their lives, and that women who have reached the top have usually displayed these male qualities. But in general 'men are more inclined to take risks, are more oriented toward attainment of status and resources, and are more single-minded in achieving these goals', whereas women 'are more nurturant and empathic, and more centred on relationships than on power and dominance'. These temperamental differences, he suggests, may explain to a significant degree the different career outcomes for men and women in organizations.

Citing evidence from the Federal Glass Ceiling Commission report (1995), Browne notes that women managers and professionals tend to be employed not in the high-risk private sector but in the low-risk public and not-for-profit sectors and in less risky staff positions rather than in line management. 'Staff positions and positions in the public and non-profit sector,' he says, 'tend to carry with them lower career risk, less pressure to relocate, and probably fewer irregular hours.' If women are found more frequently in such positions this may reflect their preferences as much as the existence of barriers to access to riskier and more demanding posts.

Turning to proposals for change advocated by some feminists, Browne is pessimistic about the likelihood of their producing the desired effects. It would seem that organizations must change or women must change or both. But Browne thinks neither is probable.

All else being equal – and in the absence of some prohibition – an employer will generally prefer a worker who puts in more hours to one who puts in fewer; it will prefer a worker who will travel or relocate to one who will not; and it will prefer a worker whose career is not interrupted by lengthy absences from the labour market to one who is. Those employees are simply more valuable ... In sum, as long as women are, on average, less single-minded about their careers than men, employers will continue, on average, to reward them less, unless, of course, the government prevents them from doing so.

As for changing women's temperaments so that they more nearly match men's, Browne is again sceptical. Since their outlooks are derived more from their biological inheritance than from their education and upbringing, the likelihood of change seems slim.

The gender gap in earnings, Browne proposes, can also be explained in part by evolutionary theory. Women's earnings are, on average, less than men's. But, on average, women are employed for fewer hours than men, have a lower level of job-related education and experience, and commit more effort to household responsibilities than do men. Moreover, women have chosen to avoid the jobs that entail high risks, whether physical or career risks, and which attract premium rates of pay. Browne concludes:

> The underlying answer to the [gender gap] question is in large part a biological one. For evolutionary reasons, men and women are not the same; they have different temperaments and values. These differences in turn cause them to behave differently in the labour market, and these behavioural differentials have economic consequences.

Finally, Browne takes issue with what he terms the feminist critique of the status of women in the workplace. Feminists argue that the demands of existing workplace structures disadvantage women by forcing them to choose between work and family. But disadvantage is relative and reflects the different choices men and women make. Women are less concerned with the rewards of money, status, and power than men are and so choose to invest more in the domestic sphere than men do. These different criteria of personal success are 'biologically ingrained'. Moreover, men also have to choose between work and family and pay a price, as women do, for the choice they make: longer hours at work, less contact with their children and shorter lifespans. Under-representation in a particular job category, such as senior management, does not necessarily imply discrimination as feminists claim, but reflects the decisions men and women make about how to lead their lives.

Why men manage: from biological determinism to social construction

The claims of the evolutionary perspective have been confronted both directly and indirectly and by both feminist writers, politically committed to the advancement of women's interests in society, and by 'neutrals' who do not identify themselves with any such interest. In general, these writers start off from a position directly opposite to that of the evolutionists, since they tend to consider biological influences on human behaviour as of relatively little significance compared to social factors. Cooper (1989), for example, says that: 'There is now a wealth of empirical evidence, both anthropological and historical, confirming that the social position of the two sexes is not biologically determined but is shaped by social and historical processes.' Similarly, Hearn and Parkin (1988) comment that

' "Women" and "men" and femininity and masculinity are socially and culturally produced and vary with the society and the social context.'

Shortly we will review the social constructionists' alternative explanations for male dominance in management, but first we examine the arguments against the evolutionary perspective which deal specifically with its claim that biology determines or is at least a principal influence upon human behaviour.

Beyond biological determinism

Social scientists may find themselves at a disadvantage when trying to respond to biological arguments because few of them possess a deep knowledge of the biological sciences. But some biologists and geneticists have themselves directly attacked the biological reasoning that underlies the evolutionists' claims. For example, Anne Fausto-Stirling, who is a professor of biology and medicine and also a feminist, and Steven Rose, director of the Brain and Behaviour Research Group at the Open University, have argued that the evolutionists' biological theories of human development and of human society are fundamentally flawed.

Goldberg's theory of patriarchy places heavy emphasis on the role of the hormone testosterone in generating the aggression in men which leads to their dominance in all spheres of life. Fausto-Sterling (1992), however, points out that individual hormones do not act alone but as parts of interrelated hormonal systems in which testosterone is simply one among many hormones such as cortisone, thyroid, estrone, insulin and so on. It makes little sense, she indicates, to single out one hormone and treat it as the cause of behaviour. She finds little research evidence to support the claim that differences in hormone levels are actually related to aggression and achievement whether in humans or other primates. Such evidence ranges, she says, 'from weak to non-existent'.

Similarly, the idea that 'genes cause behaviour' is also problematic. Just what 'genes' are has been a matter of dispute in biology, but they are not simple switches which are turned on at the moment of an organism's conception and which then determine its structure and behaviour. Rather, they are complex entities which do not operate in isolation but in interaction with the environmental conditions to which an organism is exposed. As with hormones, a person's genetic makeup does not directly predict their physical characteristics nor their behaviour. In short, the biological bases of human differences, including sex differences, are much more complex than the evolutionists claim. So, Fausto-Sterling concludes, 'referring to a genetic ability to perform math or music, or to a biological tendency toward aggressive behaviour obscures rather than informs.'

The evolutionists' use of evolutionary theory is also held by Fausto-Sterling to be seriously inadequate. There are significant disputes among biologists concerning evolution but these, she argues, are played down as if there were a single agreed evolutionary view. The evolutionists also claim that the different reproductive strategies of men and women arise from their different biological 'investment' in producing on the one hand sperm and on the other ova. Men produce millions of sperm but women produce relatively few eggs, so it is claimed that women have 'put more' into their reproductive capabilities than men. However, this sex-based difference is treated as if it were an obvious fact, but no actual evidence in support of it is given. Furthermore, among the supposedly universal behaviours which are held to accompany such differences, it is impossible to distinguish those which have arisen from natural selection from those which have arisen through social conditioning or by chance. Claims that such differences are biologically determined are spurious.

Rose *et al.* (1990) make a similar point. Although it can be accepted that biology plays some role in explaining human behaviour and that not everything is a result of cultural development, it is impossible to disentangle these influences since humans, although biological organisms, never exist outside culture. Evidence from non-human species cannot be assumed to apply to humans. These authors conclude that 'we do not know the limits that biology sets to the forms of human nature, and we have no way of knowing'.

Finally it is argued that claims about how people behaved in prehistory, some hundreds of thousands of years ago, must necessarily be fragmentary and speculative. The social organization of our 'hunter-gatherer' ancestors can only be inferred from the limited physical evidence that remains, for there are, of course, no written records and there is no possibility of obtaining observational data. Humanity's distant past can at best be only fleetingly glimpsed.

Needless to say, these basic controversies about biology have not been resolved. Indeed, the issues have recently been taken up once more by some of the leading protagonists (Goldberg, 1993; Rose and Rose, 2000). For the moment then, we will leave aside these biological disputes to consider an alternative explanation of men's dominance in organizations that has been prominent in recent feminist work, the 'gendered' character of management and organizations.

The social construction of management

> The code is this: you milk the plants, rape the businesses; use other people and discard them; fuck any woman that is available, in sight, and under your control; and exercise authoritative prerogatives at will with subordinates and other lesser mortals who are completely out of your league in money and status.
>
> (An upper-middle level male manager, Covenant
> Corporation, quoted in Jackall, 1989)

Most recent feminist approaches to management and gender pay little direct attention to the evolutionary perspective. Although the question of whether men and women are 'different' has sometimes been an important issue for feminist writers, rather more attention has been given to organizational factors that facilitate men's progress in managerial careers but obstruct women's.

In their international survey of women in management, Adler and Izraeli (1988) identify several 'barriers' which help to explain gender inequalities. Primary among these is the existence of management as a masculine domain; 'managerial roles are filled by men, popular beliefs about the requisites of management are socially constructed from stereotypically masculine traits, and the social codes that govern interaction in the managerial arena are forged from the collective experience and interests of men'. In addition, they argue, societies differ in the cultural constraints they place on women's access to management. In Japan, for example, women have traditionally been required to relinquish paid work on marriage – arguably a very convenient tradition from a male point of view. Expectations of women's involvement in the domestic sphere, the pattern of growth in opportunities across industries and occupations, and policies concerning women's rights, the provision of childcare services and access to education, especially higher education, are also important influences on women's career chances. Finally, organizational policies and practices concerning the selection, development and deployment of employees within management significantly affects women's opportunities and progress.

Feminists have increasingly argued that the factors sustaining male dominance are deep-rooted and located not simply in organizations' formal selection and promotion policies but in the established structure and culture of management, organizations and managerial careers. These are, it is claimed, inherently masculine. This conclusion has been reached in part because, despite the widespread introduction of equal opportunities policies and the decline of overt sex discrimination, male dominance in management and especially senior management persists.

In an influential contribution, Kanter (1977) combined a descriptive study of the behaviour of men and women in a large, American manufacturing company with a theoretical explanation of that behaviour. At the company, Industrial Supply Corporation, she found that, as elsewhere in American industry, management ranks were overwhelmingly filled by males although a few women had started to trickle through. In the early years of American industrialization, she argues, a 'masculine ethic' came to be established in management whereby certain attributes – tough-mindedness, analytical ability, unemotionality and brainpower – were associated specifically with the occupation. Since nearly all managers were men, it was assumed that these were male attributes. Women, it could therefore be argued, could justifiably be excluded from management on the grounds that they 'obviously' lacked the necessary qualities.

Kanter explained the perpetuation of this male dominance in functional terms. The uncertainty surrounding commercial operations generates a need for high trust among those in controlling positions and this leads their occupants to recruit those who are like themselves socially. This 'homosocial reproduction' in an occupation dominated by men, leads to a situation in which 'the men who manage reproduce themselves in kind'. In such a situation, the few women who do enter management become 'tokens' subject to special pressures. Because there are so few women managers they tend to stand out and to be scrutinized more closely than their male colleagues.

The relative positions of men and women in management can be explained by reference to the structures and situations in which an organization's members are placed. Sex differences, Kanter argues, play little part, for anyone would be likely to behave in similar ways in similar situations irrespective of their sex. Women's 'typical' ways of behaving in organizations are not due to their female characteristics but are 'very reasonable – and very universal – responses to current organizational situations'. Kanter thus concluded that her 'examination of how forms of work organization, and the conceptions of roles and distributions of people within them, shape behavioural outcomes leaves very few verifiable "sex differences" in behaviour that are not better explained by roles and situations'. Since 'to a very large degree, organizations make their workers into who they are', the way to change behaviour is by changing organizations, their structures, policies and procedures. These conclusions are, of course, very different to those reached by the evolutionists to account for differences in men's and women's work behaviour.

Kanter's study focused on women's and men's experiences in the corporation, but more recent work has incorporated a broader and more historical account of the gendered division of labour. This shows that the emergence of formal organizations, with their hierarchies of jobs, took place in a social context dominated by men. As these organizations developed women were allocated the supporting roles while the central, leading tasks were appropriated by men. This allocation process took place both inside the corporation and outside it in the wider society. Outside the corporation women provided the domestic services – shopping, housework, child-rearing – which enabled men to devote themselves to developing their careers. Inside the corporation women undertook servicing tasks as secretaries, clerks and 'tea-makers' which freed male managers from routine work and helped them to concentrate on the 'real' tasks of management. In this way, it is argued, organizations function on the basis of an implicit 'sexual contract' (Pateman, 1988) which gives males a privileged position and which excludes females from access to positions of influence and power. Such is the basis of patriarchy in society.

In a patriarchal society organizations are infused with what Connell (1995) terms 'hegemonic masculinity', that is, with practices which legitimate and express the power of men over women. The quotation at the start of this section illustrates one way in which this dominance may be expressed through an organizational rhetoric that is hard, harsh and exploitative of both things and people, especially women. On this view, both organization structures, cultures, the idea of a managerial career and managerial work itself are seen to embody and sustain male outlooks and preferences. Under these conditions, women are always in the position of being outsiders, of being 'travellers in a male world' (Marshall, 1984). The provision of equal opportunities leaves the basic situation largely untouched since at best it amounts to an equal opportunity to play a game that is organized according to someone else's rules.

Some feminists, however, taking the position that 'women are different', have argued that current trends are driving organizations towards a more female-friendly orientation (Rosener, 1990). The emergence of the flexible firm, with a looser, flatter structure, a greater emphasis on collaboration, teamwork, the value of 'human resources', and on the need for initiative and leadership at all levels, opens the way for women's advancement. Since strong interpersonal skills, communicative ability, and a cooperative style are of key importance in the new, non-hierarchical world, and since these are held to be skills at which women are particularly adept, hegemonic masculinity is claimed to be under threat.

These possibilities have been examined in detail by Wajcman (1998) in her study of senior managers in five multinational companies located in Britain. These firms operated in technologically advanced industries and all were seen to be operating best-practice equal opportunities policies, yet the ranks of senior management continued to be filled mainly by men.

Wajcman argues that a key aspect of the explanation for this state of affairs lies in the gendered nature of managerial work. Thus the ethos of hegemonic masculinity, strongly associated with aggressiveness and violence, dominates the management culture even though 'managerial work clearly does not require physical prowess'. Male symbolism is dominant in conceptions of the manager as 'action man' and in definitions of the attributes required for managerial success – lean, mean, tough and forceful. This male image of the manager is used as a standard or norm against which women are compared. To succeed women therefore have to 'manage like a man' at considerable cost to themselves. The successful female senior managers Wajcman studied were 'compelled to deny aspects of themselves' and became 'not so much representatives of, as exiles from, their sex'. Moreover Wajcman found little evidence to support the view that organizations are shifting away from 'hard' structures and cultures to 'softer' forms. In the firms in her research traditional hierarchical models of authority and aggressive management styles prevailed. Women found it difficult to participate in the informal networks which, as we saw in Chapter 6, are so important to promotional success. Successful women managers, it would seem, have to manage their work, their careers and their selves very much on male terms.

Commentary

The gender-and-management problem exemplifies the messy nature of management issues that we highlighted in Chapter 1. So, for example, even the terms in which to discuss the differences and similarities between men and women have been disputed. Should we be thinking of sex and gender as significantly different concepts, as most contributors accept? Or is Browne (1995) correct when he suggests that gender is a redundant term? In addition, connections between causes and effects are frequently unclear and have proved difficult to establish with conviction: the extent to which temperamental differences between men and women are due to biology and/or upbringing is a case in point. Also values are not obviously agreed: if organizations run by women were less financially efficient than those run by men, would that be 'a price worth paying' for gender equality or not? Even to raise such questions is to risk obloquy. At this point it seems worth repeating the comment by Connell (1995) that I mentioned earlier: when writing about gender 'the issues are explosive and the chances of getting wrong answers are excellent'.

Attempts to explain the relative success of men and women in management have used a variety of approaches, but they can broadly be divided into those which stress the 'external' factors of organization and society, and those which stress the 'internal' ones of biology and psychology. Each approach emphasizes a particular factor while usually acknowledging the influence of others. So, for example, evolutionists do not claim that biological differences are the only differences that count, just as social constructionists rarely argue that biological differences are totally un-important.

These differences of emphasis nonetheless have significant implications for the politics of work and organization. Evolutionists tend towards a conservative position, seeing efforts to produce change as 'going against the grain of human nature'. Some of their critics, such as Rose *et al.* (1990) accuse them of advancing reactionary, right-wing political agendas behind a cloak of scientific neutrality. Social constructionists and feminists, on the other hand, generally seek to promote change. 'Liberal' feminists have argued for significant but relatively modest changes to organizations' HRM policies and practices in order to promote equal opportunities and equal pay. 'Radical' feminists, on the other hand, have advocated radical restructuring of the wider society and culture as the only solution to women's oppression.

These different approaches are also reflected in views of how gender equality in management might be achieved. The 'equity model' assumes that managerial competence is gender neutral. Since women are as capable of managing as men, the problem is to secure fair, meritocratic access to managerial positions by such means as equal opportunities policies. The 'complementary contribution' model, on the other hand, assumes that men and women bring different but complementary ways of managing to organizations. From this perspective the need is to gain recognition for the unique contribution women can make and find ways of combining it with that of men so as 'to form new and more powerful managerial processes and solutions to the organization's problems' (Adler and Izraeli, 1988). Without this unique female contribution, management operates sub-optimally.

The extent to which men and women are, for whatever reason, 'different' has continued to be a troublesome issue within the gender-and-management debate. Kanter (1977) proposed that they are not very different and that observed differences in the behaviour of men and women in organizations is largely a product of their differing situations. In that case, were women to have access to managerial posts in large numbers they could be expected to manage like men; put them in the same situations as men and they will respond in similar ways. Others, such as Ferguson (1984) and Marshall (1984), have argued that women and men are indeed different, so that what is needed is organizational structures which facilitate women's way of managing rather than suppressing it. There have been a number of research studies in addition to those already mentioned which have examined men's and women's ways of managing and leading, but so far they remain inconclusive. Even so, most academic empirical research appears to support the no or only small difference view (Alvesson and Billing, 1997).

In what has been a complex debate engaging strongly held views, it is clear that neither of the perspectives we have discussed here can be said to have proven its case. As Crompton (1997) has argued in the broader context of explaining women's and men's overall employment patterns, a multi-theoretical approach is most likely to illuminate the gender-and-management controversy. Indeed, Crompton's discussion of gender and employment in the medical profession indicates how, in practice, elements of the evolutionist and constructionist arguments interrelate in organizations. In medicine, male exclusionary practices are used to keep women out of the ranks of surgeons, but women also seem to choose medical specialities which enable them to combine paid employment with domesticity or which are culturally associated with women. Radiology and psychiatry, for example, do not demand the irregular hours that surgery requires, and paediatrics is concerned with the medical care of children. In all three specialities, women are relatively strongly represented. To what extent their choices can be considered 'free' is, of course, a point of controversy. Constructionists might argue that this is a choice made in the face of limited childcare provision and that this acts as a barrier to women's progress. If childcare facilities were more readily available, would women confronted with such career choices take a different path? Evolutionists might well respond by saying that 'the call of the genes' would predispose women to choose as they do now.

As is often the case when studying the social world, getting definitive answers to the questions associated with the gender-and-management controversy has proved difficult or impossible. A recent review of the research on women in management has concluded that 'the accumulation of studies has not so much meant convergence and agreement as increased variation and uncertainty' (Alvesson and Billing, 1997). Moreover, there does not seem to be much prospect of resolving these disputes in the fore-seeable future. Fausto-Sterling (1992) has called for experimental research, but that is highly problematic in the case of managerial work and organizational careers.

Personally I think there is good reason to be suspicious of the 'genes with everything' view which seems to be gaining increasing popularity as a means of explaining human behaviour. We should not accept too readily the claims of those who assert that their views are based on 'science', for what counts as 'science' is now strongly questioned and scientists can no longer expect automatic deference to scientific authority. Quite apart from their scientific adequacy, the biological arguments taken by themselves are too simple. The same can be said for the more strident versions of constructionism. What is needed, of course, are approaches that transcend simplistic dichotomies (Shakespeare and Erickson, 2000) but it seems entirely possible that controversies such as this may never achieve public resolution.

The central source of this complexity is ourselves as persons. The androgynous or 'cocktail' view of gender (Billing and Alvesson, 1994) depicts men and women as being equipped with much the same capacities, but subsets of these are socially designated as more appropriate to one sex or the other. The subsets may differ from society to society and historically so that there are various kinds of femininities and masculinities, different ways of being men and women. Individuals come to largely accept these social definitions as central to their identities, and enact them in daily life. These enactments serve in turn to reproduce these social identities but they are, nonetheless, potentially open to change. But it is not only a matter of gender because we never encounter 'men' or 'women' in reality. These are abstract categories. Any real person is a complex of sex, gender, social status, age, ethnicity, nationality, experience and a host of other characteristics, any of which may be significant for behaviour and all of which may affect how that person acts in particular situations. This controversy reminds us of the sheer variety of ways of being human.

Evolutionists assume that humans are just one among many species of 'animal' and charge their opponents with having 'exalted' humans to a unique position in the animal kingdom (Browne, 1998a). I do not agree. On the contrary, I would contend that there is, as Schumacher (1995) has argued, a distinct 'ontological break' between animals and humans, so that humans and animals are distinct types of being. This is not to deny that humans have something in common with animals in the sense of being biological entities, but, rather, is to make the positive claim that we are much more than animals. Some animals may possess the rudiments of language or even of culture, but there does not seem to be much sign of science, music, philosophy or even of good cooking! The members of the animal kingdom still have a long way to go.

Having reviewed the evidence on gender and employment in Britain, Crompton (1997) has concluded that we can expect a continuing 'blurring of the stereotypical boundaries' that currently divide men and women at work. That process has been under way in management for some time, but whether it will reach as far as the executive suites and corporate board-rooms of the world's leading firms remains to be seen. Would it be controversial to suggest that the sooner management is reconstructed in the image of women, the better it will be for all of us?

Questions for discussion

1 Why has management traditionally been regarded as 'men's work'?
2 What evidence is there to show that human biology is a major influence on human psychology?
3 Why are there international differences in the gender composition of management?
4 If women controlled major companies, would it change the way firms are organized and managed?
5 Why are there so many men and so few women in top management?

Further reading

Alvesson, M. and Billing, Y.D. (1997) *Understanding Gender and Organizations*, London: Sage.
Browne, K. (1998) *Divided Labours: An Evolutionary View of Women at Work*, London: Weidenfeld and Nicolson.
Connell, R.W. (1995) *Masculinities*, Cambridge: Polity Press.
Nicholson, N. (1998) How Hardwired is Human Behaviour? *Harvard Business Review*, July–August, pp. 135–47.
Wajcman, J. (1998) *Managing Like a Man: Women and Men in Corporate Management*, University Park, PA: Pennsylvania State University Press.

8 Organizational leadership
Does it make a difference?

When little men embark on great enterprises they almost always reduce them to the level of their own mediocrity.

Napoleon I (1804–15)

The successful organization has one major attribute that sets it apart from unsuccessful organizations: dynamic and effective leadership.

Hersey and Blanchard (1977)

Leaders tend to operate on the premiss – which is usually false – that what they do can determine the future of their organization, but we know this is seldom if ever the case.

Grint (2000)

Anyone who is interested in understanding the problems of managing organizations has to contend, sooner or later, with the vexed question of leadership. Although it is a subject that has attracted a great deal of attention and which has spawned a voluminous literature, it remains one of the most confused and confusing areas in the whole field of management.

One thing that is generally agreed is that leadership is a topic of substantial significance. Most managers, for example, would probably support the view that leadership in organizations is important. In their survey of successful British companies, Goldsmith and Clutterbuck (1984) commented that few of them 'make a song and dance about leadership, yet in all of them managers down the line pinpoint effective leadership at chairman or chief executive level as a key to their own motivation and to the company's success'. One American survey (Rahim, 1981) showed that managers generally agreed that leadership was not only an important topic but the most important topic of all in the field of organizational behaviour. Similarly, many social scientists, and especially psychologists, have shown a consistent interest in leadership over many decades. Bass's (1990) revised edition of Stogdill's authoritative *Handbook of Leadership* lists several thousand references to leadership studies and hundreds of new articles appear each year. In general, then, both managers and social scientists attach considerable importance to leadership. But could they perhaps be mistaken?

The controversy in brief

On the face of it, concern with leadership seems to be well justified. Every organization has its leaders whether they are called chief executives, head-teachers, archbishops, generals, prime ministers or whatever, and as the occupants of the top-most positions of organizational authority they appear to be the key actors upon whose decisions and behaviour an organization's performance and well-being may depend. If leaders have the capacity to make or break organizations there is every reason to be interested in leadership and especially in the determinants of leader effectiveness. Most leadership research has, indeed, been directed at this issue (Bryman, 1986).

Leader effectiveness studies have sought to identify the characteristics of effective leaders. The emphasis has often been on leadership in small groups, with effectiveness defined in terms of group outputs such as productivity and members' satisfaction. The earliest approach to this problem concentrated on 'traits' which might distinguish leaders from non-leaders. These include physical characteristics (such as height or appearance), personality characteristics (such as dominance or self-confidence), and ability characteristics (such as intelligence or knowledge). Although this tradition of research continues today, it has been largely superseded by approaches which concentrate on leader behaviour. These have been directed either at the identification of a distinctive and universally effective leadership style, or at a range of styles which may be more or less effective depending on the situation facing the leader. On the latter view, what makes for effective leadership is heavily dependent on circumstances.

Despite the substantial efforts that have been devoted to the study of leader effectiveness the results have been widely regarded as disappointing. Handy (1993), who provides a concise review of the main findings, describes the leadership research scene as one of confusion in which 'the search for the definitive solution to the leadership problem has proved to be another quest for the Holy Grail in organization theory'. For whatever reason, the secrets of effective leadership have proved elusive.

In the face of this disillusionment some have suggested abandoning the traditional approach to the study of leadership altogether (Miner, 1975). But another response, stemming partly from theoretical developments in the wider field of organizational studies, has been to shift the focus of leadership research away from its emphasis on small groups and leaders' attributes and towards an examination of the role of leadership in its organizational and societal context. In doing this the problem of leader effectiveness becomes recast at the macro level. Traditional approaches have tended to assume that leaders do have a substantial impact on the performance of an organization via their influence on subordinate groups within it. The problem of leadership is then defined in terms of the need to find better ways of exercising this influence by means of improved leader selection and training. Recently, however, some organization theorists have seriously questioned the extent to which leaders can influence organizational performance, and have raised the possibility that leaders may not matter much after all. On this view, leadership is not so much unimportant as much less important than is commonly believed.

What is leadership?

One of the problems that has bedevilled the study of leadership is that of definition. Stogdill (1974) may have been overstating the case when he suggested that there were as many definitions of leadership as there were writers on the subject, but the concept is nonetheless notorious for its ambiguity and vagueness. This is partly because it is usually necessary to make reference in any definition to a number of concepts which are themselves difficult to define such as 'influence', 'control', 'authority' and 'power'. Mintzberg (1983), for example, has concluded that attempts to define power are fruitless while Dahl (1957) referred to the study of power as 'a bottomless swamp'. But without clear and agreed definitions, meaningful discussion is difficult and the accumulation of research findings becomes problematic.

Even in everyday usage the term 'leadership' is ambiguous. It is used to refer to the holders of certain formally defined positions in an organization, as when speaking of 'the party leadership' or 'the union leadership'. But it is also used to denote a particular type of behaviour; when someone is commended for displaying 'outstanding leadership' it is their actions that are being praised. Such a person may or may not occupy a position of leadership. On the other hand, a formally designated leader need not necessarily behave as a leader and in extreme cases may hardly be said to behave at all. So, for example, it has been claimed that Leonid Brezhnev (1906–1982), a former head of state of the now defunct Soviet Union, was barely alive in the later years of his premiership, let alone an active force capable of exerting decisive influence over events.

If leadership is an inherently ambiguous term, clear communication might be easier if it were simply dropped altogether. We do not, for example, talk about 'teachership' or 'managership' but about teachers and teaching and managers and managing. Similarly we could use 'leading' to refer to certain forms of behaviour, and 'leaders' to refer both to those who occupy positions requiring this behaviour and to those who exhibit this behaviour even though it is not a formal requirement of their position. In other words, leaders include those who are formally designated as such and 'informal' leaders who engage in leading even though they are under no formal obligation to do so. This usage points to the fact that while informal leaders are, by definition, engaged in leading, this cannot be safely assumed in the case of formally designated leaders. However, in practice it is difficult to avoid using the word 'leadership' despite its ambiguities, but these distinctions need to be kept in mind throughout our discussion.

When taken as a way of behaving, leadership has often been associated with the process of influence. According to Bryman (1986), a widely used working definition of leadership is that it 'involves a social influence process in which a person steers members of the group towards a goal'. As he notes, this definition has several drawbacks. In particular, the notion of a social influence process is extremely broad and includes certain kinds of actions which are not normally regarded as acts of leadership. The threat of physical force, for example, is one way of exerting influence, but it has often been thought that a distinguishing characteristic of leading is its orientation towards securing voluntary compliance on the part of followers rather than forced obedience. For the purposes of this discussion, however, this rather fragile distinction between voluntary and involuntary compliance is less important than the general idea that leading is centrally concerned with influence. Thus the question of the significance or otherwise of leaders in organizations can be posed in terms of the extent to which they are capable of influencing organizational outcomes.

The image of leadership as an influence process exercised by a group leader over its members suggests that leaders exist at many levels within an organization. Because organizations may contain many groups, such as shopfloor work-groups, project groups, departments, committees and boards, the linking of the idea of leadership with groups means that organizations have many leaders. Indeed, if the group element of the definition is dropped it seems that any and possibly every member of an organization can be engaged in leading. Thus Katz and Kahn's (1978) definition of leadership as 'the exertion of influence on organizationally relevant matters by any member of the organization' indicates just that. Similarly, Mintzberg (1973) includes leadership as one of his managerial roles and, as we have seen, these roles are held to characterize all forms of managerial work. But this approach to leadership has the disadvantage of being so broad as to define the concept of a leader almost out of existence. I therefore prefer to retain the association between leadership and the exercise of influence over groups.

Clearly there are some positions of influence in organizations that are potentially of greater significance than others. As Hall (1987) says, 'most important for the organization is the leadership (or lack of leadership, in some cases) that occurs at the top of the organization'. We could say that there are leaders and Leaders. Middle and junior managers, supervisors and perhaps some employees at lower levels may act as formal or informal leaders, but they clearly do not have the scope of responsibilities nor the degree of formal authority possessed by top executives and directors. Even though the chairman of a company board and the foreman of a work group are both in positions of influence over groups, the chairman's attempts to secure agreement on, say, an acquisitions policy is potentially more likely to have significant consequences for the organization than is the foreman's attempt to gain commitment to a quality circle. Of course, this is a matter of degree. But because high-level leaders are most likely to be able to influence an organization in significant ways, it seems sensible to focus our attention on this level if our aim is to assess the importance of organizational leadership. Our interest, then, is in top leaders or with members of what Giddens (1974) has called 'elite groups' which consist of 'those individuals who occupy formally defined positions of authority at the head of a social organization or institution'.

Historical views of leadership

Before we go on to examine some of the more modern contributions to the debate on the significance of leadership it is worth pausing to consider two early, fundamentally opposed views. These views are not simply of historical interest because they express, in a general way, basic differences in outlook on leadership which are still current today.

In May 1840 the social thinker, Thomas Carlyle (1795–1881), delivered a lecture entitled 'Heroes, Hero-Worship and the Heroic in History'. In a famous passage he declared:

> the history of what man has accomplished in this world, is at bottom the history of the great men who have worked here. They were the leaders of men, these great ones; the modelers [sic], patterns and in a wide sense creators, of whatsoever the general mass of men contrived to do or to attain; all things that we see standing accomplished in the world are properly the outer material result, the practical realization and embodiment, of thoughts that dwelt in the great men sent into the world.
>
> (Carlyle, 1841)

This great man theory of leadership places leaders firmly at the centre of the stage. These 'great ones' are depicted as the prime movers in society, founders of empires, winners of wars, and instigators of revolutions, who by virtue of their heroic qualities are able to create and transform organizations or even whole societies. In particular, leaders are seen as the primary source of innovation and change.

Although seldom advanced in such a grandiose form, echoes of great man theory can still be heard today. For example, the popular belief that leaders possess natural, inborn leadership qualities reflects the idea that leaders are 'sent into the world' rather than made in it. One army recruiting slogan ran 'If you've got it in you, we'll bring it out of you', which assumes, of course, that you must have 'it' in you to begin with. Ongoing interest in the biographies of business leaders can also be seen as an indication of popular enthusiasm for great man theory.

Even some of the more 'technical' books on leadership adopt a heroic conception of the leader. The following passage by Chorafas (1988) presents this idea in almost Wagnerian tones:

The indispensable man, the man who commands the enterprise, is not a mere technician. He is the animator, the promoter, the organiser, the person who values above all the qualities of hard work, of objective imagination, of internal drive, and of unbiased judgement. Perfection in the preparation, daring in the execution, submission to the facts and impartiality in regard to his own interests will be found in varying degrees in all great industrial leaders. There exist people who do things well and accomplish their distant objectives; there exist people who bring, wherever they go, order, clarity, and success. There exist others who bring confusion and unhappiness . . . The *gifted* executive prepares himself over long, tedious periods of time to become the man at the centre of industrial destinies.

While great man theory implies that leaders run the affairs of the world, Tolstoy offers an account of leadership which is diametrically opposed to this view. Although better known as a novelist than as a writer on leadership, Leo Tolstoy (1828–1910) has much to say that is relevant to the student of organization. Indeed, Kassem (1978) has made a convincing case for saying that Tolstoy's works, and *War and Peace* in particular, contain many of the fundamental ideas which are now an accepted part of modern organization theory.

In the Second Epilogue to *War and Peace*, Tolstoy (1957) takes issue directly with the great man theory of leadership. He argues that although leaders are commonly believed to command events and appear to be the causes of them they are in fact merely 'labels' used to explain outcomes that otherwise seem inexplicable. In war, for example, commanders cannot control the progress of battles because what happens on the battlefield depends on the actions of thousands of individual soldiers who can only obey the commander's orders if their immediate circumstances allow it. These local circumstances are beyond the commander's control; indeed, he cannot even know about them in any detail. So the relationship between the commander's orders and the behaviour of those who determine the outcome of the battle, the soldiers, is tenuous. The real role of leaders, according to Tolstoy, is less one of determining the course of events than one of justifying the collective activity that leads to such outcomes as revolutions and wars. By relieving those who actually produce these outcomes, the soldiers, from moral responsibility for their behaviour, the commander enables them to commit heinous acts.

In a striking passage Tolstoy likens the role of leaders to that of a bow-wave surging ahead of a ship. The wave always moves ahead of the ship whichever way it turns so that 'the surge which neither directs nor accelerates her movement will always foam ahead of her and at a distance seem to us not merely to be moving on its own account but to be governing the ship's movements also'. For Tolstoy, the concept of the leader as a figurehead would have seemed particularly apt.

In conclusion, Tolstoy writes:

> historians have assumed that events depend on commands. But examining the events themselves and the connection in which the historical characters stand to the masses, we have found that historical characters and their commands are dependent on events.

Carlyle's great man theory and Tolstoy's 'figurehead' theory remain controversial to this day even though they are seldom systematically discussed by modern thinkers. Carlyle has been criticized for greatly exaggerating the significance of 'great men' (Marwick, 1981) whereas Tolstoy has been faulted for greatly understating it (Mills, 1956). But despite the obvious limitations of each view, both of them, and especially Tolstoy's because of his explicit interest in the relationship between leaders' commands and subordinates' behaviour, draw attention to an important issue: to what extent can leaders control the internal functioning of organizations?

Leadership and internal control

Organizational outcomes can be seen as the product of the interaction between an organization and its environment. Organizations are open systems dependent on interchanges with their environments for their continued functioning and survival, and both their structures and behaviour are strongly influenced by conditions external to them. At the same time they must find ways of regulating the behaviour of their members so that they contribute effectively and efficiently to the production of the organization's primary outputs. There is thus a requirement for internal control. For this reason, organizational structures normally include elements which are intended to facilitate the control of employees' work behaviour and it is through these elements that leaders exert influence over the internal functioning of the organization.

At their most basic, control systems in human organizations are comprised of three elements: goals, information systems, and sanctioning systems. First, the entity being controlled must be goal oriented. If the system is not directed at some reasonably well-defined end then it cannot be the subject of purposive control because control of a process implies selection and reinforcement of activities and this requires some criteria for choice. In principle, these criteria are derived from the system's goals. Second, the system must contain an information system. This is to enable instructions to be communicated to members which, if followed, will direct their behaviour towards the attainment of the system's goals. It also enables feedback to be obtained on the extent to which the instructions have been followed and their results. Finally, because we are dealing with human organizations, there must be a sanctioning system which is intended to secure compliance with instructions. This system distributes rewards and penalties in accordance with compliance or deviation from the required behaviour. Looked at from the point of view of leadership we can say that, given the existence of a goal, the capacity of leaders to control organizations depends on the effective workings of both the information and sanctioning systems.

Although these are the basic requirements for the purposive control of an organization, there is no guarantee that any of them will be realized in practice. Leaving aside the question of whether organizations do have workable goals, there may be many imperfections in both the information and sanctioning systems. Information may be poorly communicated, misunderstood, distorted or lost. Furthermore, human beings are not mechanical cogs in a great organizational machine whose compliant response to control can be assumed. The internal control of organizations is always problematic, partly because of imperfect communication, but also because employees are capable of exercising resistance to control.

Organizational constraints on leader influence

Great man theory, in its more extreme form, tends to portray the leader as a person largely free of constraints. Leaders are depicted as men (seldom women) of heroic stature partly because they seem to be able to overcome obstacles which ordinary mortals cannot. But because organizational leaders are found at the top of organizations, they head a structure that simultaneously enables and constrains their capacity to exert influence. For example, leaders may be faced with well-established reward systems which prove difficult or impossible to change except at very high cost. Or there may be formal limits to the scope of their authority, elaborate policies and operating rules, and a firmly rooted culture which includes definite expectations about appropriate and inappropriate methods of control. Although leaders can exert influence through the established structure and culture of organizations, they are at the same time constrained by them.

The extent of these organizational constraints varies, however, according to a number of conditions. Here we consider five of these: the organization's age, size, task complexity, structural form and operating situation.

Hall (1987) has pointed out that leaders are likely to be particularly influential when an organization is being formed. At this stage strategic options are open so that decisions about what to produce, where to produce it and how to produce it are relatively unconstrained. Information and sanctioning systems can be tailor-made according to the demands of the situation and the leader's preferences, and the organization's culture is unformed. At the moment of its birth leaders can put their stamp on an organization with lasting consequences. Older organizations, on the other hand, are likely to become set in their ways and resistant to leader initiated change.

It is perhaps a commonplace observation that small organizations are more open to the influence of top leaders than large ones, but the reasons for this are less obvious. They stem from the effects of size on the operation of the control system. In a small organization, with perhaps a few dozen employees working in the same location, the leader (very probably the owner) can issue instructions, obtain feedback, and administer rewards and penalties directly. Small size also enables the leader to maintain face-to-face relationships with the employees which obviates the need for impersonal control methods. The leader can bring personal influence to bear on subordinates, invoking loyalty and respect rather than mere obedience or submission to orders. In addition, a small organization is likely to be dedicated to only one activity, or a small and related range of activities. The task complexity facing the leader is therefore low. For these reasons the potential for leader influence in a small organization is relatively high.

As organizations grow, internal control becomes more problematic, the more so if its operations become geographically dispersed and technically diversified. Technical diversification in either products or production processes is likely to carry the organization's activities into areas that are beyond the experience of its leader. As this task complexity increases, the leader's competence to handle it is reduced. Furthermore, with a growth in the number of employees direct control ceases to be viable. The leader cannot be in many places at once! A typical response is to formalize the information and sanctioning systems and delegate their operation to a set of intermediaries, the managers. Rules, regulations and written communications replace personal observation and 'management by walking about'. And managerial relationships with employees come to displace personal acquaintance with the leader. Since the leader must now exert influence indirectly, through intermediaries and by impersonal methods, rather than directly, the likelihood of a weakening of leader control increases. This is partly because the introduction of intermediaries between the leader and the led creates a further potential source of resistance to leader control.

The significance of the growth of an organization for the exercise of leader control is therefore substantial. As the size and complexity of an organization increases, the number of intermediaries and the specialized expertise which they derive from their positions also grows until a point may be reached where control is executed 'from below'. In the case of large public bureaucracies, Weber (1946) argued that control from the top was problematic because 'the "political master" finds himself in the position of the "dilettante" who stands opposite the "expert", facing the trained official who stands within the management of administration'. The intermediaries come to know more about their specialities than any leader can and at the same time develop a sense of their own identity and interests. Galbraith (1967) presents a similar diagnosis of the modern corporation in which power shifts away from entrepreneurial leaders and towards a diverse 'technostructure' of managers and technical specialists. By virtue of their capacity to filter the information which reaches the leaders from within the organization, members of the technostructure come to *make* the decisions while leaders merely *take* them.

Different structural forms of organization also condition the potential impact of leadership. For example, an organization with a centralized policy-making structure concentrates formal authority in a few hands, or even a single pair of hands, at the top of the organization as is often the case with an army at war. In other organizations there may be widespread opportunities for participation. Cohen *et al.* (1972) have portrayed some types of organization, such as universities, as 'organized anarchies' in which organizational goals are complex and ill-defined, the technologies for achieving them are unclear, and participation in decision-making processes is fluid, with different interests tending to coalesce around different policy issues. Under these conditions influence over decisions does not clearly stem from a central source selecting from available means to realize specific goals. Rather, 'the flow of individual actions produces a flow of decisions that is intended by no one and is not related in a direct way to anyone's desired outcomes'. Formal leaders are in a weak position because where goals and means are ambiguous the legitimacy of any particular preference is difficult to sustain; there is no 'obvious solution' to which leaders can expect widespread assent.

Finally, the impact of leaders is likely to be influenced by the type of situation facing the organization. Under normal operating conditions, the organization can be seen to be rather like an aircraft flying on autopilot. So long as it encounters only minor changes in its environment, established routines carry it along on a level course. But when the organization faces novel conditions, particularly in the form of a 'crisis', innovative responses are called for. At such times, leaders may have a crucial impact (Hall, 2002). In crises leaders may be expected to take a more directive role in organizational affairs and the existence of a crisis gives powerful grounds for the introduction of change. But given that crises are exceptional events the implication for leadership of varying situational conditions is that they are typically highly constraining.

Employee resistance to leader influence

If leaders are subject to constraints arising from the organization's structure and situation a further limitation is the capacity of employees, or subordinates, to resist leaders' influence. Even under conditions of close control backed by the most extreme sanctions people are still capable of resisting effectively as the behaviour of inmates of civilian prisons and wartime prison camps shows. In military organizations, where obedience to authority is a central value inculcated in recruits by means of elaborate training schemes and reinforced by rigorous military codes, obedience to orders cannot be guaranteed. Instances of personal disobedience and collective mutiny are many as are more passive forms of 'combat withdrawal' such as simply refusing to fire weapons (Holmes, 1985; Keegan, 1976). One authority on World War Two has estimated that few American infantrymen actually fired their rifles during combat (Marshall, 1947). In the Vietnam War resistance sometimes took the more extreme form of killing those of one's own side who showed themselves too ready to engage the enemy; perhaps as many as 20 per cent of all the American officers killed during the war had been 'fragged' by their own troops.

Resistance to control can take many different forms, some of them more visible than others. At the extreme, employees may simply absent them-selves from the workplace either temporarily (absenteeism) or permanently (quitting) or withdraw their labour by striking, but less overt forms of psychological withdrawal may also take place. Employees may quietly 'turn off' and 'go through the motions' in a more or less ritualistic fashion. Although resistance by shopfloor employees tends to attract the greatest attention, a number of studies have shown that it can occur at any level within the organization including the higher ranks of management.

One of the first and most influential studies to draw attention to shopfloor resistance to control was the Hawthorne studies. This research, carried out at the Hawthorne works of the Western Electric Company in Chicago between 1927 and 1932, has itself proved controversial (see Rose, 1988), but the main point of interest here is the 'discovery' that shopfloor workers tended to develop a spontaneous group organization which had no place in the formal structure but which regulated the behaviour of its members. In particular, work groups practised output restriction, deliberately circum-venting managerially imposed output targets in favour of their own. This observation sparked off a considerable amount of research on output restric-tion, and drew attention to the capacity of shopfloor employees to resist managerial control without recourse to the more obvious forms of resist-ance through trades union organization. It also promoted interest in supervisory leadership which was seen to have a greater contribution to make to the harnessing of workers' commitment than had previously been recognized.

While resistance by lower-level employees is a frequent source of concern to managers, managers themselves may be no less active in asserting their autonomy. As in the case of shopfloor employees, managers may develop informal group relationships in order to augment their influ-ence as individuals. In a long-term observational study of American managers, Dalton (1959) found that they tended to form themselves into cliques that were used to advance personal and sectional interests irre-spective of the official goals of the organization. Similarly, Burns (1955) distinguished defensive cliques and aggressive cabals, the former tending to develop among older managers and the latter among the younger. Harvey *et al.* (1984) also found important divisions within management based on age groups. In one firm they studied, the older managers formed an 'old school' which clashed with the younger and shorter-serving managers of the 'new school'.

Studies of managerial behaviour at the highest levels are rare, particularly those involving observation of top decision-making processes. At this level we are dealing less with resistance to leader control than with conflicts and dissension among the leaders themselves, so it is not particularly surprising to find that researchers have had great difficulty in gaining access at the top. However, Pettigrew's (1985) monumental study of ICI showed clearly and in considerable detail how top leaders' intentions can be frustrated over long periods not least because of the resistance of senior colleagues, and Pahl and Winkler's (1974) observations of boardroom behaviour have provided some rare insights into the power games that most of us normally glimpse somewhat more distantly from the pages of the business press.

These sorts of studies have highlighted the political aspects of management. Managers cannot be assumed to accept the goals of the organization as set out by their leaders. And even if they do accept them, they do not necessarily give them priority when they conflict with more personal ambitions and interests. Furthermore, even the formal leadership may be divided in its aims and unable to exert concerted influence over the organization it heads.

A final element of constraint on the ability of leaders to exercise control within the organization is inertia (Hannan and Freeman, 1984). Because organizational structures exist in order to regularize and stabilize behaviour they carry an in-built tendency to resist change. If a given type of structure persists for any length of time those who work within its confines tend to become adjusted to its requirements so that 'the way we do things around here' becomes 'the way we *ought* to do things around here'. As Quinn (1988) puts it, ways of organizing become 'competing moralities, ways of seeing the world that people hold implicitly and about which they feel intensely'. To attempt to change an organization's structure may therefore mean challenging cherished values and deeply held beliefs.

In their study of a Yorkshire mining community, Dennis *et al.* (1969) reported the experience of one ex-miner who had started a bookmaker's business on the strength of his gambling winnings. Having been subjected to the harsh treatment of the coal-owners during his years as a miner he was determined to 'rule by kindness' in his own business. Alas he found that his employees had the same expectations of him as he had had of the coal-masters; kindness resulted in his being swindled and he had to resort to ruling with an iron hand if he was to stay in business. Even though he was the owner now, he had little real choice about how to manage his employees.

In such ways methods of organizational control also constitute constraints on control for if they are found wanting it may be very difficult to change them. Not only may leaders experience resistance to existing control methods, but also resistance to modifying those methods in ways which might yield greater control.

What all this points to is that even if leaders possess clear goals and have both information systems and sanctioning systems at their disposal, employees may still resist control. And very often it seems they may well succeed. Leaders can undoubtedly exert influence over those within the organization but seldom control. Indeed they may appear to be more *under* control than *in* control. Thus Carlson (1951) commented of his research on chief executives:

> Before we made the study, I always thought of a chief executive as the conductor of an orchestra, standing aloof on his platform. Now I am in some respects inclined to see him as the puppet in a puppet-show with hundreds of people pulling the strings and forcing him to act in one way or another.

External constraints on leaders

A reminder of the internal constraints which muffle the capacity of leaders to influence organizations usefully counterbalances the tendency to exaggerate the significance of leaders inherent in the great man view. However, there has been a growing emphasis on a further source of constraints on organizational leaders, which stem not from within the organization but from outside it. The significance of these constraints for organizational leadership have been especially emphasized by the resource dependence approach.

The resource dependence model (Pfeffer and Salancik, 1978) depicts organizations as open systems which must engage in transactions with their environment if they are to survive. Organizations are continually faced with the problem of maintaining a flow of the resources they need and the problems of achieving this depend on factors often outside the organization's control. Whether, for example, resources are abundant or scarce will depend partly on the size of the resource pool and how many other organizations are competing for them. What happens in an organization is therefore 'not only a function of the organization, its structure, its leadership, its procedures or its goals', but also 'a consequence of the environment and the particular contingencies and constraints deriving from that environment'. On this view organizational outcomes are very heavily constrained by external factors.

Leaders may be thought to be able to wield decisive influence over the fate of organizations but there are a number of limitations on their freedom of action. They may not, for example, be able to influence matters which do impact on performance and which are in theory within their control. More importantly many things which determine performance may simply be out of the leader's reach.

The resource dependence model places heavy emphasis on the dependent position of organizational leaders but they are not entirely at the mercy of external forces. Three roles can be identified for them: responsive, discretionary and symbolic. Whereas traditional theories of leadership have assumed the first two of these to be the key components of leader behaviour the resource dependence model attaches particular importance to the third, symbolic role.

The responsive role of leadership is concerned with adapting the organization to the demands and constraints imposed by its environment. The leader's task is threefold. First the leader must obtain information on the state of the environment and estimate its implications for the organization's functioning. Then the leader must identify the appropriate organizational responses such as modifications to the organization's strategy or structure. Finally the leader has to implement the required changes so as to bring the organization into line with its environment. The leader's responsive role is essentially one of accommodating the organization to external forces and pressures and is therefore 'at variance with the image of great managerial leaders directing the organization, making decisions, and through the sheer force of will transforming organizations to achieve success' (Pfeffer and Salancik, 1978).

While the responsive role of leadership is concerned with changing the organization, the discretionary role deals with changing the organization's environment. So, for example, leaders may lobby government to secure legislation more favourable to their organization's interests or may negotiate mergers with competing organizations. Although some organizations may be in a position to make significant changes to their environments, resource-dependence theorists argue that this is only possible for a few very large ones. For the vast majority of organizations the option of changing the environment to suit the organization rather than changing the organization to suit the environment is not a realistic one.

The third leadership role is symbolic. As a symbol the leader personifies personal and individual control over the organization and its behaviour and acts as a focus of accountability. Even though a leader's actual capacity to influence events may be slight, the leader is treated as if he or she were responsible both for producing the organization's successes as well as its failures. People tend to attribute organizational outcomes of whatever kind to leaders although leaders themselves tend to attribute successes to themselves and failures to external circumstances. Leaders thus serve to fulfil a general social expectation that individuals can control the world they live in. If they succeed they become management heroes and if they fail they become scapegoats. As symbols they help to sustain the belief that organizations are controlled by people rather than by the impersonal forces of the environment (Meindl and Ehrlich, 1987; Pfeffer, 1977; Schwenk, 1990).

In general the implication of the resource dependence view is that although leaders are important to organizations they are much less important than is generally believed. Because options for organizational change are heavily constrained by the environment, leaders generally mediate between the environment and the organization and symbolize the capacity for personal control. They are, however, neither the primary initiators of change nor the guarantors of organizational outcomes.

The impact of leaders

The practical implications of these contending theories are potentially significant. If it is the case that leaders generally have little impact on performance outcomes, not only have most leadership researchers been engaged in a trivial pursuit in their attempts to find better ways of selecting and training leaders but the efforts of organizations to ensure 'sound' leader recruitment decisions seems equally misplaced. So much for the arguments. What can the research evidence tell us about this problem?

Before we look at some research findings three general points need to be made. First, there have been very few studies that have tested these competing claims directly. Despite the importance of the issue it has seldom been made the subject of systematic research (Beatty and Zajac, 1987). Second, of the studies which have been conducted a substantial proportion have not dealt with commercial organizations. A good deal of work has in fact been directed at sports teams, specifically baseball and basketball teams, not because they are of great significance in themselves but because they are particularly convenient vehicles for research. Third, research in this area is marked by considerable differences in method and problem definition so that it is by no means always a straightforward matter to decide whether a particular study's findings are actually relevant to the general issue. As Hall (1987) has said, 'Studies of leadership in organizations are confusing (if not downright chaotic) even to those who are well-versed in the literature', a comment that may be found comforting or disconcerting according to taste.

To bring some order to our review the research can be examined under two broad headings. One type of study approaches the problem from the point of view of leader change or 'succession'. Broadly speaking leader succession studies try to assess the impact of changes in an organization's leadership on performance outcomes. It is assumed that if leaders make a difference then we should be able to detect different levels of performance for different leaders. If, on the other hand, we were to find that performance levels remained much the same irrespective of changes in leader we might conclude that it doesn't matter much who leads an organization. Succession studies are, then, most directly relevant to our problem when they deal with whether leaders can be distinguished from each other, although they have also dealt with other issues (see Gordon and Rosen,

1981). If some leaders really are great men then this should be reflected in close association between periods of high performance and the bounds of leaders' periods of office.

A second type of study asks, in effect, an additional question. This is: what effects do leaders have on performance relative to other factors? In this case the issue is defined not in terms of whether leaders differ in their impact on performance but in terms of how much of an impact they typically make in comparison with, for example, the effects of changes in general economic conditions. Such studies can be conveniently labelled 'leader contribution' studies because they aim to establish the extent of leaders' contribution to performance outcomes.

Leader succession studies

Leader succession studies originate in the work of Grusky (1960, 1963). Drawing on the meagre evidence available at the time, Grusky suggested that leader succession is always disruptive. At a minimum the appointment of a new leader brings a different person to the head of the organization who is not well integrated with other top personnel and who will have some new ways of applying policies and interpreting established procedures. In the short run this can lead to conflict and lowered morale. The extent of this disruptive effect is likely, however, to vary according to a variety of circumstances. Most of these are not within the leader's control. The implication, then, is that it is the succession event itself which has disruptive consequences irrespective of the abilities of the new leader.

From this point it is but a short step to propose that organizations which experience frequent leader changes will perform less adequately than those where leader change is infrequent. This hypothesis was confirmed when Grusky examined the frequency of succession of managers of major baseball teams in relation to the teams' end of season position in the league tables. Teams which changed managers more frequently tended to occupy lower positions. But a second study of baseball teams by Gamson and Scotch (1964) showed that managerial change had little impact on team performance. These authors suggested that the replacement of managers represented a form of 'scapegoating', a ritual sacrifice which served to assuage disgruntled individuals. Changing the manager did not, however, lead to any consistent change in team performance.

Eitzen and Yetman's (1972) research on basketball teams yielded similar conclusions. This study showed that the impact of a new team coach was related to how well the team was performing prior to the appointment. Where teams were doing well before succession their performance tended to decline after the appointment of a new coach and vice versa. But when these effects were compared with chance expectations they could not be attributed to succession. Similarly, in a study of major baseball teams over the period 1920–73, Allen *et al.* (1979) concluded that changing managers had only a slight impact on team performance. Brown (1982) reached much the same conclusion from his study of coach succession among teams in the National Football League.

In general these studies support a sceptical view of the significance of organizational leaders. Variations in sports teams' performance seems to be governed largely by factors other than leadership skill. But we may well wonder whether findings based on studies of basketball and baseball teams can be applied to major industrial companies. Fortunately two further studies of leader succession throw some light on the generalizability of the sports team findings.

Samuelson *et al.* (1985) conducted an ingeniously designed study using 122 large US corporations as their sample. These firms were grouped into pairs so that the firms in each pair were similar in terms of size and product market. Measures of performance, such as sales value and return on assets, were obtained for a seven year period for each firm. In one of the firms in each pair the same chief executive was in office throughout the seven year period but in the second a new chief executive had been appointed in the mid-year of the period. Because the firms were studied over the same period and were arranged in matched pairs, the research design heightens the chances that any differences in performance can be attributed to leader succession rather than to the characteristics of the firms and their environments.

The findings of this study are generally consistent with those of the sports team studies. Although there were some variations in impact on the various performance measures, in general performance did not change substantially after the appointment of new leaders. On the contrary, these authors concluded that 'there is very little evidence that changes in top management affect, in important ways, the magnitude of such traditional performance measures as sales, income and rates-of-return'.

Finally, Beatty and Zajac (1987) examined the impact of changes in chief executives in 209 large firms on stock-price movements and strategic change. Their study showed that stock market reactions to announcements of changes in leadership were usually negative. A change in chief executive was generally perceived as a negative indicator of the firm's future earnings, a finding which supports Grusky's view that succession events are disruptive and have negative consequences for organizations. To that extent this study refutes the implications of much previous research; leader change does seem to make a difference.

It is difficult to draw any firms conclusions about the impact of leadership from these succession studies. Although research on sports teams has generally implied that leaders do not have much impact on performance it is not clear that the findings can be generalized to other types of organization, and the results of company-based studies are contradictory. Moreover, succession studies generally deal only with the short-run impact of new leaders rather than the performance records of leaders for the whole of their leadership careers. Whether some leaders can consistently turn in a superior performance across contexts remains an open question.

Leader contribution studies

Leader contribution studies address the problem of whether leaders make a difference in a different way to the succession research. Here the issue is not so much whether changes in leader are associated with changes in performance but with how much of an impact leaders make in comparison with other factors. Since an organization's performance will be subject to many influences, such as the state of competition in the industry in which it operates, general economic conditions, legislative restrictions, the firm's size and so on, the impact of leaders on performance needs to be seen against this background. If it were possible to assess the contribution of each of these factors to performance outcomes then the relative significance of leadership could be identified. At least that is the theory; in practice things are rather less straightforward than they might seem.

This approach to the leadership problem was first applied by Lieberson and O'Connor (1972) in a paper which has had a long-lasting impact on the debate. These authors obtained data on performance values for sales, profits and profit margins for 167 major American firms drawn from thirteen industries over a twenty year period. Details of the periods of office of the chief executives were also obtained for each firm. They then subjected their data to an analytical procedure which enables the relative contribution to organizational performance of general economic conditions, industry factors, organization-specific factors and leadership to be assessed.

The results of this study are complex and open to various interpretations but nonetheless have seemed 'startling' to those who really believe in leadership (Hall, 1977). For what they showed was that each of the performance measures was very heavily influenced by environmental conditions and influenced very little by leadership. Organizational performance seemed to be heavily constrained by general economic conditions, the state of an organization's industry and the nature of the organization itself so that leaders had relatively little impact on performance outcomes. Like corks bobbing on a choppy sea, organizations could be seen as largely driven by powerful economic currents rather than being directed masterfully against the elements by potent leaders.

Lieberson and O'Connor's study has been widely understood to have shown that organizational leaders have a relatively insignificant impact on performance. This view has been reinforced by a study of the impact of mayors on city budgets (Salancik and Pfeffer, 1977) which suggested that they too were heavily constrained in their capacity to influence budgetary expenditures. Yet further work on this issue has qualified the conclusion that organizational leaders don't make a difference.

Weiner (1978) undertook a replication of Lieberson and O'Connor's work by conducting a study of 193 American manufacturing firms over the period 1956–74. Using the same analytical techniques, Weiner showed that the results could be reversed if a different approach to the analysis was used and concluded that the findings of Lieberson and O'Connor's original study could be regarded as spurious. In a second paper, Weiner and Mahoney (1981) reanalysed Weiner's data and concluded that in contrast to previous studies it could be shown that leaders did have a substantial impact on some performance outcomes. As with the succession studies, attempts at assessing leaders' contribution to performance have tended to produce contradictory findings.

Elsewhere (Thomas, 1988) I have argued that these seemingly contradictory results can be reconciled. A full understanding of the explanation for this requires an appreciation of some rather technical aspects of the analytical methods used in previous studies, but since this is beyond the scope of our present discussion I will concentrate on the main conclusions of this work.

On the basis of a re-examination of the methods and interpretations of the studies of Lieberson and O'Connor (1972), Salancik and Pfeffer (1977), Weiner (1978) and Weiner and Mahoney (1981) and an analysis of some original data on leadership and performance in large British retail firms, I offered the following conclusions. First, that leaders do differ significantly in the impact they make on the financial performance of the firms they head and that leaders therefore do make a difference. However, performance differences between companies are largely to be accounted for by differences in the firms' sizes which serve as constraints on individual leaders' capacity to make a difference. For example, larger firms typically make larger absolute profits than smaller ones irrespective of differences between leaders. In that sense leaders are heavily constrained by the characteristics of the firms they lead: each firm has a performance capacity which limits the levels of performance that can be achieved by any given leader just as the performance of a Grand Prix driver is constrained by the characteristics of the car he or she drives. But within these constraints the characteristics of leaders do matter; in the driving analogy some drivers will be able to take their car nearer to its limits than others even though no driver will be able to go as fast as someone in a car with an engine twice as powerful.

Some support for the notion that leaders do matter is given by the studies of Smith et al. (1984) and Beatty and Zajac (1987). One conclusion of the latter study was that the chief executives of large firms did make a difference by influencing the longer-run strategies of their firms. The belief in the importance of the chief executive expressed by, among others, writers on strategic management was supported by Beatty and Zajac's analysis.

Smith et al.'s research drew, like the sports studies examined in the previous section, on a somewhat unusual sample, Methodist Church ministers. Fifty ministers who had presided over a number of different congregations over a twenty year period were designated as effective or ineffective according to their salary levels. It was then assumed that effective ministers would have a greater effect on performance outcomes, such as numbers attending services, number of members registered with the congregation, and total charitable income received, than ineffective ministers. The results showed that this was indeed the case; some ministers produced superior results not only with a single congregation but repeatedly as they moved from congregation to congregation during the course of their careers. This suggests that leaders do differ in their abilities and that they can have a substantial impact on performance although, as these authors are careful to note, this is not to say that the ministers were great men in the heroic mould. Some of them were effective leaders of their congregation but this does not necessarily mean that they would have been effective as leaders of other types of organization.

Leader contribution studies offer a confused picture with much the same tendency to produce contradictory findings as we have noted for the succession studies. What is clear from both types of research, however, is that the whole problem is conceptually ambiguous, complex and difficult to translate into decisive research designs that will provide clear and indisputable answers. With that thought in mind we turn from the empirical research to reflect again on the vexed problem of leadership.

Commentary

This controversy is undoubtedly one of the most difficult and intractable in the whole field of organizational behaviour. The problem is both resistant to unambiguous definition and elusive in the sense that it is not at all clear what kinds of evidence would be needed to illuminate it. Located within an area of inquiry, leadership studies, that has been 'in a state of ferment and confusion' (Yukl, 1989), the problem of whether leaders matter seems, to borrow Winston Churchill's phrase, like a riddle wrapped in a mystery inside an enigma!

It seems inherently implausible that leaders are either so powerful that they can control everything or so powerless that they cannot control anything, yet we can probably point to instances of leaders who have approached these extremes. The case of Leonid Brezhnev has already been mentioned as an example of the impotent leader and while omnipotence is usually an attribute we associate with gods rather than human beings it is not too difficult to suggest individuals who do seem to have been peculiarly influential figures in their time. It seems unhelpful, though, to address the problem in these terms. What we need to ask is not so much whether leaders make a difference as under what conditions leaders make a difference?

That question can be answered in the abstract quite readily and in an earlier section we suggested some factors that impinge on leaders' capacity to exercise control. Provided that leaders have both the will and the skill to lead, the more constraints they face the less difference they can make and the fewer the constraints the greater their potential impact. Where leaders are subject to few constraints they have many options open to them which means they have maximum freedom to make an impact whether positive or negative. But where leaders are hemmed in by constraints they can only go along with the tide of events and wherever that tide sweeps the organization it will not be because of its leaders. What distinguishes leaders who make a difference from those who don't might, then, be their capacity to transform constraints into options. Great men were conceived as those who could transform all constraints into options, so giving them maximum possible scope for changing the world. Figureheads, on the other hand, might be seen as those who are unable to loosen any constraints and so find themselves prisoners of circumstance. In reality it seems that no leader, whether man or woman, can ever be fully in the position of the great man nor of the figurehead but that most will find themselves wrestling with the varying constraints imposed on their actions by the circumstances in which they find themselves.

These rather trite observations are in fact accepted by most investigators in the field for there is hardly anyone who now adopts one or other extreme position. Modern-day equivalents of Carlyle and Tolstoy are few and far between. Demonstrating the validity of these propositions by means of systematic research is, however, another matter.

As yet there has been little work on the impact of organizational leadership under different conditions. In part this is because of the difficulties of gaining access to the boardroom and executive suite where top leadership can be observed at first hand, but also because the difficulties of carrying out controlled investigations of organizations are formidable. In the sports team research, Jacobs and Singell's (1993) study of basketball teams used some sophisticated methodological control techniques and showed that managers do have an important effect on team performance. In the commercial context, a Canadian study has found that the impact of leadership on the financial performance of credit union branches varies considerably according to the size of the branch (Savoie *et al.*, 1996). No doubt further innovative research designs will be forthcoming that will shed further light on these issues. Meanwhile Hall's (2002) conclusion is apposite:

> From the perspective of the total analysis, it is clear that top leadership is important for the organization as a whole as it seeks to be effective. We cannot specify how much more or less important it is, however, or under what conditions it is important, when compared with some of the other factors considered. These factors include the existing organizational structure, informally derived power relationships, pressures from the environment, and relations with other organizations. We can state,

however, that it is important and we can hope that future research will begin to assess the relative strengths of these factors under various conditions.

If you detect a note of desperation in that final sentence that would not be surprising. For in the absence of compelling evidence on the significance of leadership we are forced back to a considerable extent on our convictions and beliefs, and a belief in the potency of leaders is perhaps one of the most deeply rooted and magical of human assumptions. Even if it were to turn out that 'effective' leadership does not exist it might just be necessary to invent it!

Questions for discussion

1 What, if any, is the difference between 'managing' and 'leading'?
2 What distinguishes effective from ineffective leaders?
3 Under what conditions is a leader likely to have a greater or lesser impact upon the organization he or she leads?
4 'When leaders look down from the top of the tree in the jungle, all they see is their organization staffed by monkeys. When followers look up at their leaders from their position at the bottom, all they see is bums' (Grint, 2000). What view of leadership does this imply and what is the alternative?

Further reading

Bass, B.M. (1990) *Bass and Stogdill's Handbook of Leadership: Theory, Research and Managerial Applications*, New York: Free Press.

Goffee, R. and Jones, G. (2000) Why Should Anyone Be Led by You? *Harvard Business Review*, September–October, pp. 63–70.

Grint, K. (2000) *The Arts of Leadership,* Oxford: Oxford University Press.

Kets de Vries, M. (1996) Leaders Who Make a Difference, *European Management Journal*, 14 (5), pp. 486–93.

Thomas, A.B. (1988) Does Leadership Make a Difference to Organizational Performance? *Administrative Science Quarterly*, 33, pp. 388–400.

9 Managing all over the world
One way or many?

Despite the ups and downs of the business cycle in Japan, there remains a core of world-class companies in Japan that have evolved manufacturing management systems that companies throughout the world have been striving to emulate.

Liker, Fruin and Adler (1999)

It is predicted that distinctive Japanese HRM practices will be phased out by approximately 2010 and will assume forms that are similar to those prevailing in the West.

Mroczkowski and Hanaoka (1998)

Shortly before the collapse of the Soviet Union in 1991, I took a brief mid-winter vacation in Russia. One evening I was invited to meet with some students who were keen to practise their language skills on a native English-speaker. During our conversation I was asked if I was an American. 'No,' I replied, 'I am from England.' 'I see,' came the response, 'and where is that?'

It was a real surprise to me to find that these young Russians had very little idea of where England was. As I began to explain, I realized that if you were to look at a map of Europe centred on Moscow, Britain would appear as a rather insignificant little island on its extreme western edge! This was a useful reminder to me of how easy it is to become ethnocentric, taking it for granted that one's own country and culture are at the centre of everyone's world.

The controversy in brief

The world of management and especially management theory has by no means been immune from ethnocentrism. Since modern industrialism first developed in the West, management theory has been dominated by western thinking and thinkers. Until very recently it has been implicitly assumed that western management, especially American management, is to be equated with successful management.

But with the growth of international and now global business and the emergence of powerful non-western economies such as Japan, there has been growing interest in the relationship between national cultures and management practices and in the possibility of transferring successful practices between countries. If businesses are to be run efficiently, must they be organized and managed in the same way in all countries, or do organizations need to adapt to local circumstances? And can management practices that work well in one part of the world be readily implemented or transferred to others?

These questions have become associated with the issue of convergence: to what extent are management and organization in different countries becoming more alike? If there is only one way of effectively organizing and managing modern production technologies, then as more countries industrialize they should be seen to adopt a common set of managerial practices. According to this 'convergence thesis', the management system utilized in well-established and successful countries will be 'transferred' to newly industrializing countries as they adopt the latest industrial technologies.

When the first industrial nations began to emerge in the nineteenth century, the idea that they would progressively come to develop similar structures and cultures was widely shared by social theorists (Kumar, 1978). The industrial society was seen as a distinct type with a set of related characteristics; urbanism, a complex division of labour, secular values and so on. Any country embarking on industrializing its economy was thus seen to set off a chain reaction which would eventually affect all its institutions in a similar way.

In the 1960s this view was restated by Kerr *et al.* (1960) who argued that modern societies are driven by a 'logic of industrialisation' which leads them to converge in the long run. On this view, investment in industrial technologies necessitates complementary changes in organization such as the adoption of systematic planning and management systems. One implication of this view is that the social environment into which industrial technologies are introduced adapts to support the operation of those technologies and does so in very similar ways. Variations in organizational and societal forms should thus diminish over time as societies converge. In the long run, the world's management systems will end up more or less the same, irrespective of current cultural differences among countries; management systems around the world should display increasing homogeneity.

If, on the other hand, like Tolstoy's unhappy families, every industrializing country manages production in its own way, industrial countries will exhibit and maintain distinct management systems; countries will not converge and may even become increasingly divergent. From this 'non-convergence' point of view, while countries may well learn new approaches and techniques from foreigners, these will seldom be directly transferable but will have to be modified to fit with the cultural assumptions that underpin management in their country. Organizations and management practices are, on this view, not culture-free but soaked in cultural values, beliefs and assumptions.

It is worth emphasizing that this management-and-culture controversy is no idle academic dispute. Attempts to implement 'foreign' management approaches involve altering the way organizations are run and influencing the behaviour and work experiences of those employed by them. If those approaches are truly context free, there should be, relatively speaking, no problem. If, however, their efficacy depends on a close fit between the approach and the context into which it is introduced, a poor fit spells trouble. The stakes are therefore high: both employees' quality of working life, firms' industrial competitiveness and even nations' economic survival are likely to be affected. Getting it right may be crucial, especially for newly industrializing countries and the former soviet economies. Understanding the problems and prospects for managing in different cultural contexts is therefore of considerable practical importance.

National cultures and management systems

If you're having trouble carrying out a difficult task, then turning to a successful performer to see if you can learn how it's done looks like a sensible move. Once upon a time the world's top business performer was Britain, but that position has, of course, long since been relinquished to the United States.

As the world's most successful industrial capitalist nation, the United States of America has had a profound influence on industrial management and organization outside its own borders. In part this has been through the direct investment by American firms in other countries' economies, as well as through foreign 'aid' and military 'assistance'. A further important channel of influence has been management education and management consulting together with the books and other means of broadcasting management ideas that go with these activities. America has succeeded not only in exporting the products of its industry but also its ideas on how to run business (Lawrence, 1996), and many less successful nations have been keen to learn from America's experience.

The influence of the American approach to management was particularly potent after 1945 during the long process of post-war reconstruction that took place in Europe and the Far East. The only way to compete with America, it seemed, was by learning from the American way of managing. But by the early 1980s, the boot was on the other foot. Following the two oil shocks and in the face of faltering economic growth, it was America itself that sought to learn from its increasingly successful competitor, Japan. Whereas in the past managerial knowledge had passed chiefly from West to East, now the process was to be reversed. Perhaps for the first time,

American business had to confront the possibility that a country with a very different management system could outperform it. It also posed the pressing question of whether a system that worked in a different cultural context could and should be adopted in the USA.

Until the early 1980s very few management thinkers displayed much interest in culture, despite a considerable history of cross-national research on organizations (Child, 1981). But growing awareness in America that its position as the world's leading industrial nation was being challenged by Japan created a sudden and substantial concern with culture and management. There could hardly have been a more propitious time for the appearance of a major research study on just this issue, and this was supplied by a Dutch academic, Geert Hofstede.

In 1980, Hofstede published the results of a major cross-national survey of 'culture's consequences', the impact of national cultural differences on organizational structures and management practices (Hofstede, 1980a, 1980b). This classic study was based on a large-scale questionnaire survey of IBM employees in forty countries, including most of Western Europe, North America, Central and South America, Australia, the Far East and some other major Asian countries.

Hofstede defined 'culture' as 'the collective mental programming' of a people whereby a society's members are equipped with a common set of values and beliefs. Data from 116,000 respondents showed that countries could be distinguished in terms of the prevalence of certain key values. A country's position in respect of these values represented the 'norm' for that country, though individuals would differ in the extent to which they held them.

Initially Hofstede identified four key 'cultural dimensions' to which he later added a fifth (Box 9.1). Countries' positions on these dimensions were associated with different preferences for types of organizational structure and management style. So, for example, both the UK and the USA exhibit low power distance, favouring egalitarian relationships, and low uncertainty avoidance, being relatively tolerant and comfortable with uncertainty. An organization that is decentralized, sharing power, and informally managed, without rigid rules and regulations, seems to fit best within this type of culture. By comparison, France and Japan exhibit high power distance and high uncertainty avoidance. The type of organization which best fits those values is centralized and highly structured by rules. However, this does not mean that all organizations in a country will fit that country's cultural preferences, for management has to take account of other factors in addition to culture when designing the organization's structure and style.

Hofstede's research indicated that there was no globally applicable management system. American management theories and hence practices did not necessarily apply abroad, for each country's organizations seemed to be shaped by its cultural environment. National culture should

---

Box 9.1 **Cultural variables**

Power distance: the degree to which equality in the distribution of power is valued.

Uncertainty avoidance: the degree to which certainty, conformity and lack of ambiguity is valued.

Individualism: the degree to which independence is valued in relationships rather than collective interdependence and co-operation.

Masculinity: the degree to which assertiveness, heroism and material success are valued over modesty, relationships and caring for others.

Time orientation: the degree to which long-term goals are given preference over short-term ones.

Source: G. Hofstede, *Culture's Consequences: International Differences in Work-Related Values*, Beverly Hills, CA: Sage, 1980; and G. Hofstede and M. Bond, The Confucius Connection: from Cultural Roots to Economic Growth, *Organizational Dynamics*, 16 (4), 1988, pp. 4–21.

---

be considered as another consequential contingency to be added to those already identified by previous researchers. Moreover, since cultures change only very slowly and with great difficulty, national cultural differences are likely to persist and so, therefore, will differences between organizations in different countries.

Others pointed out that there is no necessary connection between technologies and organizational forms (Jamieson, 1980). Technologies are 'neutral' or at least permit a wide variety of ways of using them so that the global spread of industrialism does not in itself give grounds for expecting convergence in management systems. Furthermore, the recent success of a number of eastern industrial economies, structured along very different lines to those in the West, seems to demonstrate that there is not one 'logic' but a whole series of 'logics of industrialisation'. Indeed there are differences among western countries as well as between East and West. Different countries and different cultures adopt industrialism in different ways (Hickson and Pugh, 2001). This might suggest that convergence is a myth and that a variety of national management systems, firmly rooted in their own cultural contexts, will continue to deliver the goods in their own manner.

To explore these rather complex problems we will examine one of the most researched examples of a national management system, that of Japan.

Learning from Japan

The culture-and-management controversy arose against a backdrop of growing penetration of western and especially American markets by the Japanese in the late 1970s and early 1980s. An early warning note was sounded by Kahn (1970), a prominent 'futurologist', who pointed to the impending emergence of Japan as a new 'superstate'. Some years later, Vogel (1980) developed the theme of Japan's rapid growth and its discomforting implications for American business. Japan was not only challenging the world's leading industrial nation, but seemed likely to overtake it in the near future.

The story of Japan's post-war recovery is certainly remarkable. Defeat at the hands of the Allies in 1945 left the Japanese economy in ruins. In 1947 the nation's output stood at about one-third of its pre-war level, and most observers agreed that Japan's prospects were bleak (Reischauer and Craig, 1979). But by the late 1950s the pre-war position had been regained, and during the 1980s Japan was challenging the United States as the leading economy in the 'free world'. Japan had achieved the impossible: staggering rates of economic growth, low inflation, minimal unemployment and a perfunctory level of industrial unrest. In an era of 'economic miracles', Japan's rise from the ashes of war could well be seen as 'the greatest miracle of all' (Pollard, 1982).

Although Japan's economic success has been attributed to many different factors, one explanation has been particularly popular in management circles. Japan's 'secret', it has been widely claimed, lies in its approach to management. Could it be, then, that the key to successful competition with Japanese industry lay in the adoption of the Japanese way of managing by western business? Or is Japanese management effective only within the confines of Japanese society?

In 1981, two books appeared that may well have done more to draw the attention of western managers to Japanese management than any before or since. Ouchi's *Theory Z* (1981) and Pascale and Athos's *The Art of Japanese Management* (1981) rapidly became bestsellers. Although differing in detail, both books asserted that America's problems were rooted in its management and that much could and should be learnt from the Japanese. Within a short space of time, the 'learn from Japan' boom was well under way (Dore, 1984).

But critical responses soon followed. Sullivan (1983), for example, produced an 'Anti-Theory Z' in which he questioned Ouchi's interpretation of the Japanese management system. The following year Sethi *et al.* (1984) published a detailed review of both the theory and evidence for the transferability of Japanese management, concluding that American business had little to gain by attempting to emulate the Japanese. With the battle lines drawn, albeit far from clearly, the debate has rumbled on ever since.

On the face of it, the controversy revolved around the matter of 'transferability'. Could the Japanese system be applied outside Japan with equally dramatic effects on industrial performance? Yet hardly anyone seriously suggested that the entire Japanese approach could be transferred. The real question was whether certain elements of it could be transferred. If the full-blown Japanese system could not be expected to be transplanted to foreign soil, perhaps Japanese-style management could.

Although the debate tended to be conducted in terms of 'transferability', the underlying issue was this: why was it that large Japanese manufacturing companies were more productive and more competitive than their western counterparts? The question of 'transferability' was to some degree secondary to this issue. For without a sound explanation of the superior performance of Japanese corporations, it was difficult to specify what, if anything, of the Japanese way was worthy of emulation.

Advocates of learning from Japan tended to argue that a major part of the explanation could be found in the way the Japanese managed. In particular they focused on Japanese employment and personnel practices. They also proposed that key elements of these practices could be transferred in modified form to the West, citing similarities between successful western and Japanese corporations as evidence that this was so. To them it was clear that the Japanese way could and should be adopted in the West, so promoting the convergence of the American and Japanese systems.

Critics of this view took up a variety of positions, but two main strands of argument can be identified. One was that the significance of Japanese employment practices had been overstated, and that what really counted were such things as their approach to manufacturing management, marketing and strategy. From this point of view, the most prominent advocates of learning from Japan were teaching the wrong lesson. Another drew attention to the domestic environment in which Japanese business operated, emphasizing the dependence of the management system on supportive cultural and institutional factors. Since these factors did not hold in the West, attempts to transfer Japanese practices were doomed to failure even if those practices were at the root of Japan's success. Both viewpoints seriously questioned the validity of the advocates' explanation of the success of Japanese corporations. They also cast doubt on the likelihood and desirability of a growing convergence between American and Japanese practices.

Ironically, as interest in Japanese management grew, the Japanese economy's reputation for spectacular performance weakened. At the start of the 1990s the economy was in significant difficulties following the collapse of the bubble boom. Japan's problems were soon compounded by the onset of the wider economic crisis in South East Asia which erupted in 1997. By early 2002 the economy was in its fourth recession in ten years with unemployment at record levels, the stock market standing at a quarter of its 1990 level, and the country struggling with a severe domestic debt problem. For some this economic deterioration implied that the Japanese management system was obsolete and would have to be replaced by western methods. Japanese 'exceptionalism' was at an end and convergence with western capitalism was under way.

What is the Japanese management system?

Before we can examine these issues, we need to establish a provisional understanding of the Japanese management approach. This section therefore outlines the main management practices that are broadly agreed to have applied in Japan until recently, at least in large firms in the manufacturing sector. As we shall see later, the system as described here is currently undergoing significant change.

Employment and personnel practices

One of the most striking features of the Japanese management system is lifetime employment. The term is, however, something of a misnomer and is better described as long-term employment with a single firm. In contrast with much western practice, large firms in Japan aim to recruit all their employees, both blue and white collar, directly from the education system. 'Regular' employees enter the firm at its lower levels and are then expected to remain with it for the rest of their working lives. Although some movement between firms is tolerated, this is usually restricted to young employees at the start of their careers. Beyond this, there is an understanding between employer and employee that to leave the firm amounts to a severe breach of mutual obligation. This system is self-maintaining because large firms seldom recruit personnel from other firms. Once the initial 'exploration' period is over, employees cannot leave without severely damaging their career prospects.

To westerners, lifetime employment seems puzzling, not least because it seems to constrain a firm's ability to adjust its labour costs in response to changing business conditions. But the system is underpinned by the use of temporary workers who can be laid off as the need arises. Lifetime employment is therefore far from universal in Japan, even in large firms. Furthermore, women are excluded from the system. Some estimates have indicated that only 40 to 60 per cent of those working in large manufacturing companies and trading houses are covered by lifetime employment (Sethi *et al.,* 1984).

Given the long-term commitment of Japanese firms to their 'core' employees, it is not surprising that considerable care is taken over their selection. Selection methods combine both interviews and stiff examinations which each firm sets for itself. The main considerations are general ability and the likelihood of fitting in, something which is made more likely by the practice of recruiting from the same schools and colleges each year.

The most prestigious firms prefer to recruit only from the most prestigious of these, so that there is a close link between the type and level of education a person has received and their chances of joining the best firms. Competition within the education system is correspondingly intense.

The emphasis given to general ability rather than specific vocational skills during selection reflects a preference on the part of Japanese employers for 'blank pages' on which the firm can press its own imprint. New employees are given intensive technical training as well as a more general induction into the firm's culture covering such matters as its history and philosophy. Further training is provided during each stage of the employee's career, and is expected to be taken very seriously. For example, promotion to higher levels may depend on successful completion of the firm's promotion examinations.

The reward and promotional practices of Japanese corporations are one of the least understood aspects of Japanese management, but both pay and advancement are heavily dependent upon an employee's length of service with the firm. This *nenko* system tends to allocate rewards chiefly on the basis of seniority, although individual merit and ability do play a part.

According to Clark (1979), large firms operate a system of standard ranks akin to the hierarchy of grades that are found in the British civil service. Each rank is divided into a dozen or so grades forming a ladder which stretches from the bottom to the top of the organization. On entry to the firm, each employee is given a grade, higher or lower according to age. This grade determines the employee's basic salary, to which substantial bonuses may be added. For regular employees, advancement within the hierarchy is automatic at the lower levels but becomes more competitive once the ranks of management are reached. Temporary workers, however, are not eligible for promotion.

Curiously, an employee's position in the ranking system need not reflect his position in the job structure. An employee with the rank of department head, for example, may not be in charge of a department! To encourage flexibility, employees are discouraged from identifying with 'jobs'. Their status in the firm is given by their rank rather than their job, something that is likely to change frequently because of the extensive use of job-rotation both within and across departments. Job-rotation is not restricted to shopfloor levels and continues throughout an employee's career.

In addition to the rewards of job-security, pay and status, Japanese firms provide a wide range of welfare benefits. These may include financial assistance with housing and education, medical services, free transport, and social facilities. Retirement benefits are, however, meagre by western standards. As with lifetime employment, welfare provisions express the paternalistic relationship between employer and employee, although temporary workers are not entitled to receive these benefits. They are also excluded from membership of the enterprise union.

The enterprise union is the main unit of labour organization in Japan. Each firm has its own union to which all lifetime employees, other than those who have reached management grades, are required to belong. One consequence of this is that a firm's managers will have spent many years as union members. Although enterprise unions do operate as bargaining units and sometimes organize brief strikes, disputes tend to be ritualistic, family affairs. Co-operation is encouraged by the lifetime employment system which ties the fate of the workforce indissolubly to that of the company.

Finally, the Japanese approach to decision-making involves extensive communication and consultation. Proposals for change are circulated within the organization and elaborate attempts are made to secure agreement from the parties that are likely to be affected. Suggestions for improvement to operating procedures are encouraged from below and are considered at each level until a consensus is achieved. This *ringiseido* approach to decision-making is time-consuming, but enables swift implementation of decisions once agreement has been reached. The process operates as a 'top-down' means of communicating decisions that have been authorized at high levels and as a 'bottom-up' means of communication from below.

Taken together, practices such as lifetime employment, continual training and job-rotation, seniority-based pay and promotion, extensive welfare provisions, and consensus decision-making provide core employees with employment security, continuous improvements in pay and status over a long period, extensive all-embracing welfare benefits, skills development through training, and a degree of participation in decision-making. In return, employees are expected to display a total dedication to their work and to their firm.

Production methods

Although these employment and personnel practices have been seen as the most distinctive elements of the Japanese management system, there has been a growing recognition that Japanese production methods are also of vital importance. Early in the debate Hayes (1981), for example, argued that the success of Japanese firms rests on their efforts to perfect the basics of the manufacturing process.

Japanese manufacturers have sought to eliminate waste, inefficiency and errors from manufacturing operations by emphasizing 'total quality control' (Oliver and Wilkinson, 1988). To achieve this, a combination of techniques are used such as 'just-in-time' methods, tight in-process controls and quality circles. The just-in-time system aims to eliminate stock-holding by producing each item of production only at the precise moment it is needed. Outside suppliers, for example, may be required to deliver parts daily, or even hourly, so that only very limited stocks are on hand to support each stage of the manufacturing process. During manufacture, machines are subjected to statistical process controls which predict variations in output quality and eliminate them before defective items are produced, so reducing scrap and reworking costs. Finally, the goals of reliability and quality are further stressed by the use of quality circles, which consist of small groups of workers who are encouraged to identify problems in the production process and to devise improvements.

These methods are associated with a significant reduction in manufacturing costs and consistently high-quality production. The system is, however, very vulnerable to disruption given the absence of buffer stocks. Successful operation depends heavily on highly disciplined behaviour on the part of the production workers, both those of the firm and its suppliers. In part this is promoted by the employment and personnel practices outlined above.

Making sense of Japanese management

Apart from a few scholars, not many westerners showed much interest in Japanese management until the early 1980s. The American management guru, Peter Drucker, writing in 1971, had asked what could be learned from Japanese management (Drucker, 1971) but this does not seem to have aroused unusual interest. The same could not be said of Ouchi's *Theory Z* (1981) when it appeared a decade later.

Theory Z and the Seven Ss

In *Theory Z* (1981), Ouchi stated that the root cause of America's industrial decline was to be found in the social organization of the business corporation. In America, he suggested, large firms tended to be organized in accordance with classical bureaucratic principles which gave them seven major organizational characteristics.

1 *Short-term employment*: employees spend relatively short periods in employment with any one firm, and this promotes impersonality in relationships at work.
2 *Rapid evaluation and promotion*: rapid labour turnover means that the firms must assess new hires quickly and promote promising individuals fast before they become impatient and leave.
3 *Specialized career paths*: specialization is encouraged by the need to transfer between firms; firm-specific skills are less marketable.
4 *Explicit and formal control mechanisms*: impersonal relationships and specialization encourage the use of distant, formal methods of control; there is little room for unspoken mutual understanding.
5 *Individual decision-making*: individuals are responsible for decisions.
6 *Individual responsibility*: responsibility for success or failure rests with designated individuals.

7   *Segmented concern for employees*: the relationship between the firm and the employee is confined to work-related matters.

These characteristics, said Ouchi, foster excessive individualism. They inhibit intimacy, trust, co-operation, involvement and loyalty, and limit the economic effectiveness of the firm.

The Japanese approach represents a sharp contrast. There the firm is organized on the model of the 'industrial clan' rather than the impersonal bureaucracy. Employment is on a lifetime basis which means that evaluation and promotion need take place only after an extended period with the firm. Career specialization is discouraged by means of lifelong rotation between jobs and across functions. Long acquaintance with fellow employees promotes close understanding of the firm's goals and philosophy, and this fosters implicit co-ordination and control. Decisions are made slowly but participatively, with a sense of shared responsibility for outcomes. Collective values are stressed and the firm seeks to bind its employees together in a 'holistic relationship' by blurring the divisions between work and social life. 'People who live in a company dormitory, play on a company baseball team, work together in five different committees, and know the situation will continue for the rest of their lives will develop a unique relationship', one based on intimacy, trust and understanding.

The industrial clan promotes loyalty, commitment and co-operation, and discourages interpersonal rivalry and conflict. It therefore seems better suited to the demands of modern, large-scale industrial production which requires large numbers of people to work together harmoniously. 'In a sense,' said Ouchi, 'the Japanese can better cope with modern industrialism.'

Ouchi was well aware of the fact that some features of the Japanese model probably would not work in the West. But he went on to argue that many of America's most successful firms already had characteristics that were very similar to those of the Japanese industrial clan. These 'Type Z' organizations emphasized continuity of employment rather than lifetime employment, slow evaluation and promotion as in Japan, fairly generalist careers, implicit control combined with explicit measures, consensual decision-making but with individual accountability, and a holistic concern for employees. He also claimed that they were superior performers in comparison with the more conventional bureaucratic firms. The Type Z form of organization was one that could and should be widely adopted.

Like Ouchi, Pascale and Athos (1981) asserted that the key lesson to be learned from the Japanese was how to manage. 'A major reason for the superiority of the Japanese,' they wrote, 'is their managerial skill.' And, like Ouchi, they claimed that many of the best American firms were managed in a very Japanese manner.

The similarities and differences between the Japanese and American ways of managing were discussed in terms of the 'Seven-S' framework.

This depicts the management process as one that involves the manipulation of seven 'levers': strategy, structure and systems (the 'hard' Ss) and staff, skills, style and superordinate goals (the 'soft' Ss). Drawing heavily on a comparison of Matsushita Electric Company and International Telephone and Telegraph (ITT), Pascale and Athos argued that while Japanese and American firms were equally adroit at the 'hard' Ss, the Japanese were particularly skilled in the 'soft' ones. This was because Japanese culture was more attuned to coping with the inherent ambiguity, uncertainty and interdependence of organizational behaviour. Whereas the Japanese accepted these as inevitable, Americans tended to see them as things to be eliminated. Uncertainty and ambiguity were to be overcome and independence, rather than interdependence, was to be encouraged. By working across, rather than with, the grain of these 'existential conditions' of organizational life, American managers placed themselves and their firms at a disadvantage when competing with the Japanese.

Pascale and Athos saw America's managerial decline as an effect of its culture. This hampered the systematic integration of the Seven Ss. Outstanding American companies were, however, very similar to their Japanese counterparts. They paid attention to each of the managerial levers and ensured that they were consistently related to each other. In particular, they were strong on the 'soft' Ss of staff, skills, style and superordinate goals. As a result, these firms had 'staff members who have a high degree of shared understandings and beliefs about their company, about what takes priority, about what is expected of them, and about their high value to the enterprise'.

Both Ouchi and Pascale and Athos were in agreement on four main points. First, that Japan's success is substantially due to its management practices, especially those which deal with personnel. Second, that elements of the Japanese approach can be applied in the West (i.e. the United States); the most successful American firms already operate in a Japanese way. Third, that the adoption of a Japanese approach offers a solution to America's decline because the root cause of this is its management. And finally, that while the Japanese system cannot be applied in its entirety in the West it can be adapted to the different cultural and social conditions which prevail in America with positive consequences for organizational performance.

A dangerous folly?

The belief that America needed to learn the lessons of Japanese management spread rapidly in the early 1980s. Ouchi's *Theory Z* was especially popular (Keys and Miller, 1984). But not everyone was convinced.

In a pungent review of *Theory Z*, Gibney (1981) questioned the factual basis of Ouchi's claims. 'Ouchi,' he wrote, 'has given us a chrome-plated collection of hasty generalisations, slogan-type writing, and dimestore business sociology, based on what one might call a modified dart-board technique of research.' Bruce-Briggs (1982) was, if anything, even more dismissive. Calling *Theory Z* 'downright silly' and a 'dangerous folly', he argued that the key to Japan's success was not its management but its labour force, which was culturally conditioned to be submissive and pliant. 'It is expected to work hard, work right, and not block productivity improvements. American labour is told what to do but does not do it reliably; that is the difference.' The learn from Japan boom, he concluded, was an example of 'crisis exploitation' in which Japanese management was used as an exotic brand label for an old ideological package promising utopia at the workplace via participation and harmony.

A more analytical critique was offered by Sullivan (1983). This focused on three main aspects of Ouchi's thesis: its factual basis, its theoretical interpretation and its 'humanistic' implications. Sullivan stated that the association between Theory Z practices and productivity had never been tested by a specific research programme. This association therefore needed closer examination. In addition, he noted that industrial clans were not pervasive in Japan. Specialized career-paths, autocracy and authoritarianism, and resentment against the Japanese firm's paternalism had all been identified in case studies. Similarly, the claim that participative decision-making fostered trust and intimacy were questionable. Decision-making often took the form of a top-down process which aimed to make clear to employees what was being done rather than one in which consensus on proposed changes was sought. Furthermore, Hofstede's (1980a) cross-cultural study of national values had indicated that the type of organization that would fit best with Japan's culture was the bureaucracy, 'in which rigid rules and hierarchical relationships control employee behaviour, the power of superiors is high, and the tolerance for ambiguity is low'.

Apart from these factual inadequacies, Sullivan challenged Ouchi on theoretical grounds. *Theory Z* claimed that features such as lifetime employment, non-specialized career-paths, and consensus decision-making fostered intimacy and involvement which resulted in high trust, satisfaction and productivity. By contrast, Sullivan proposed an Anti-Theory Z. Lifetime employment and non-specialized careers produced managers of minimal competence. To offset the effects of this, it was necessary to involve subordinates in decisions and diffuse responsibility. By doing this, incompetent managers were protected and their status in the bureaucratic hierarchy was preserved. The firm's capacity to function productively was thus maintained, but at the expense of intimacy, involvement and trust rather than because of it.

Finally, Sullivan argued that far from being a humanistic theory, in which an organization is seen as a means to the satisfaction of individual human needs, Theory Z advocated conformity to overriding corporate values and procedures. As such it proposed a return to a medieval view of the proper relationship between man and society.

Sullivan's overall conclusion was that the validity of Theory Z was questionable. Both it and his own Anti-Theory Z required testing empirically. But Sethi *et al.* (1984) went further. In their view Theory Z was simply unworkable in the United States.

In *The False Promise of the Japanese Miracle* (1984), Sethi and his colleagues set out to explore what they called 'this current misguided attempt at a myopic imitation of the Japanese management system by businesses in the United States and other industrialised countries of the western world'. Their argument centred upon the relationship between national management systems and the wider social, political and economic contexts in which they are situated.

The Japanese management system was, they argued, deeply rooted in Japan's culture and traditions. In particular, collective responsibility and group loyalty were central values originating in part from the traditions of the Japanese household, the major organizational unit of Japan's pre-industrial past. Japanese industry had also benefited from the protective policies of the government, which was closely linked with business institutions by such means as the exchange of senior personnel between business and the government bureaucracy, business financing of political candidates, and the influence of the *zakai*, an 'inner circle' of big business leaders. In consequence, business interests had taken priority at considerable cost to other groups in Japanese society. These costs included systematic discrimination against women by their exclusion from the life-time employment system, the denial of economic mobility and freedom of expression for those within it, and the neglect of the physical environment and consumer interests. Such costs, they noted, were seldom mentioned by western celebrants of the Japanese way.

Sethi *et al.* did not deny that the Japanese system could be adapted to western conditions. They argued, however, that to do so might require changes in the host environment that were either unlikely to be achieved (such as the adoption of a highly interventionist role by the United States' government) or which were of questionable acceptability given western values (such as the suppression of individualism). 'Theory Z,' they declared, 'will not work in the United States because it is inconsistent with American cultural norms and values.' Japanese management was, in effect, alien to the American Way of Life and therefore could not, and should not, be adopted there.

Two important issues are highlighted by these contributions. One concerns the degree to which the Japanese management system is dependent upon a particular set of environmental factors for its success. This raises the question of whether particular practices can work in the same ways in different countries irrespective of substantial differences in context. The other is the matter of values. As Sethi *et al.* made clear, any management system is likely to distribute costs and benefits to various groups and interests in a specific way. To adopt a different system might mean adopting not only its benefits but also its costs. If the Japanese system is highly productive, is this necessarily at the cost of individual freedom, equality of opportunity, and so on? Or can one have the best of both worlds?

Japanese management in practice

A basic assumption of many of the protagonists in the debate has been that there is an identifiable set of practices that can be referred to as the Japanese management system. Although most observers agree that these practices are characteristic only of large firms, some commentators have questioned even this. Buckley and Mirza (1985), for example, suggested that the system 'is in fact found (if at all) only in larger, better-known companies'. Wide variations in organizational culture have also been noted among Japanese firms in Japan (Smith and Misumi, 1989). Also evidence drawn from case studies of firms may be atypical. Woronoff (1983), for example, has implied that Pascale and Athos's analysis of Matsushita Electric gives a misleading impression of Japanese management because it is a highly unusual firm in the Japanese context. So although it is perfectly legitimate to discuss management systems as models, it must be remembered that these are abstractions from reality. The claim that a 'unique' set of management practices are responsible for a nation's economic success is more problematic if the organizations concerned vary widely in the practices they adopt.

Japanese management in Japan

The best-known advocates of learning from Japan tended to assume that Japan's employment and personnel practices and the Japanese management style were the primary causes of the success of large firms, and hence of national success. This is a key claim. For unless it is so, it is difficult to see the point in trying to emulate these elements of the Japanese system.

Explaining national economic success, or failure, is no easy matter. Large-scale complex historical processes are difficult to study, and however much evidence is produced in favour of one explanation or another, it is never possible to re-run history to see which is right. The best that can be expected is a plausible story that corresponds with the available evidence. Many factors have been adduced to explain Britain's successful emergence as the world's first industrial nation and its subsequent post-war decline. In the same way there have been a variety of attempts to explain the Japanese 'miracle' (Hirschmeier and Yui, 1981; Morishima, 1982; Tsuru, 1993).

The least that can be said about this is that it seems extremely unlikely that Japanese management has been more than one factor among many. Other factors which may have contributed to Japan's post-war economic growth include political continuity (a single party in government for almost the entire period), low military spending (releasing funds for investment in industry), protectionist trading policies, and even national pride and a desire for 'economic revenge' following military defeat. Would the economy have fared as well if these conditions had not prevailed?

It has also been pointed out that although Japan's economy has been successful, its industry has not been uniformly so (Buckley and Mirza, 1985; Kono, 1984; Tsurumi, 1981). Japan's superiority in manufacturing has been displayed chiefly in the mass-production and high-technology industries. This could mean that firms in less successful industries have not applied the employment and personnel practices of Japanese management in the way that those in successful industries have. But an alternative and more plausible possibility is that these practices are less important to success than has been assumed. Abegglen and Stalk (1984) have shown that Japanese firms' superior labour productivity is especially evident where successful production requires the integration of many operations. When this is not so, the advantage is much less apparent. A more potent factor accounting for success in Japanese industry might therefore be the Japanese approach to the organization of manufacturing operations. To explore this possibility we must follow the Japanese abroad.

Japanese management in the West

Can the Japanese management system be transferred to western societies? Reasoned argument can only take us so far towards answering this question. What we really need is evidence that will show us what happens when Japanese management practices are utilized in western countries. Ideally, evidence of this kind would enable us to deal with two major questions:

1   To what extent do firms in the West, whether Japanese-owned or western-owned, adopt Japanese management practices? Do the Japanese take their management system with them when they operate abroad? Have large western firms adopted Japanese management practices?
2   Do firms which use Japanese management practices in the West (whether Japanese-owned or western-owned) perform more successfully than those which do not? Does the use of such practices in a western environment promote productivity?

These questions have been examined in a number of studies. The resulting evidence comes in two forms: that on the practices of Japanese-owned subsidiaries operating in the West, and that on the practices of western firms that have adopted Japanese-type practices in their home country.

Japanese firms in the West

Given the peculiarities of the Japanese management system when seen from a western point of view, it is perhaps not surprising to find that the Japanese have seldom tried to replicate it in full in their western establishments. The applications of the Japanese system abroad has generally been selective.

A study of thirty Japanese subsidiaries operating in Brazil (Ueki, 1982) found that only certain Japanese practices had been transferred. The extent of this transfer was related to the degree of Japanese control of the firms. The wholly Japanese owned subsidiaries used more of the practices than those which were joint ventures. They also returned a better performance, a finding which suggests that Japanese management may indeed be more effective even outside Japan. It is notable, however, that certain practices were not transferred. These included suggestion schemes, expectations of lifelong service and devotion to the firm, and collective responsibility.

A similar impression is given by studies of Japanese firms in the United States. Pascale and Maguire (1980) compared a number of Japanese-owned units in the United States with similar units operating in Japan, as well as with comparable US-owned units in America. Supervisory practices and worker attitudes and behaviour in the Japanese and American units located in the United States were quite similar to each other, but the Japanese units in America differed considerably from those in Japan.

A large-scale survey of Japanese firms in America (JETRO, 1981), covering 238 Japanese manufacturing firms, showed that the application of the traditional Japanese management system was patchy. For example, although many of the firms surveyed had adopted a 'permanent employment' policy, few used the seniority payment system or bonuses. Quality circles were not much in evidence, spiritual slogans were not in use and job-rotation was proving difficult to implement.

White and Trevor (1983) studied six Japanese firms in Britain, three banks and three manufacturing firms. They reported considerable variations in the 'Japaneseness' of these firms. Similarly, a comparative study of two Japanese and two non-Japanese television manufacturers operating in England showed that the Japanese firms differed from each other in their organizational cultures. Even so, both the Japanese firms generally outperformed their non-Japanese counterparts, especially in productivity and quality (Takamiya and Thurley, 1985).

A comprehensive overview of the experience of Japanese subsidiaries overseas has been provided by Negandhi *et al.* (1985). This review was based on comparative studies of over 400 Japanese, American and European firms located in many different countries, both in North and South America, Europe and Asia.

These authors pointed to the inherent difficulty of establishing the Japanese system on foreign soil: 'Japanese management practices mirror

Japanese language, culture and environment to such an extent that it is almost impossible to adopt the type of management and employment systems practised at the headquarters in foreign subsidiaries.' Although Japanese firms abroad did transfer some home-based practices, such as job security and corporate welfare provisions, they departed in many ways from the accepted model of Japanese management. The managers of Japanese overseas subsidiaries tended to use autocratic, rather than consensus, styles of decision-making; displayed a low level of confidence in employees' abilities; expressed low trust in non-Japanese managers; restricted promotion for non-Japanese managers, keeping them out of the higher levels of the organization; had difficulty in managing relationships with trades unions, avoiding them when possible; and tended to fall foul of equal employment opportunities legislation especially as regards women. However, the performance of Japanese companies still exceeded that of non-Japanese firms.

There seems little doubt that the Japanese themselves have not, and perhaps cannot, implement the full Japanese management system in the West. Yet a striking conclusion to be drawn from these studies is that even when the system is only partially implemented, Japanese firms still perform more successfully. This raises a crucial question: which parts of the system are consistently transferred to other countries?

Several elements seem to be important. The studies of both White and Trevor (1983) and Takamiya and Thurley (1985) suggested that 'what best accounts for the superior performance of the Japanese firms is their meticulous attention to production management, their superior co-ordination of different organizational functions, and the management of their relations with trade unions' (Smith and Misumi, 1989). Similarly, Negandhi *et al.* (1985) identify the smooth handling of relations with host country governments and 'competence in both production management and engineering'. In short, the 'secret' of Japanese firms' success may be as much to do with their approach to the management of external relations and to the organization of the production system as it is to do with their employment and personnel practices.

The experience of western firms

Advocates of learning from Japan based part of their argument on the belief that successful western firms were already managed in a Japanese manner. This seemed to them to support their contention that Japanese management, or at least Japanese-style management, could work in the West.

That there are some similarities in the management practices of large western and Japanese firms is not seriously at issue. In a study that pre-dated the onset of the Japanese management controversy, Dore (1973) noted some resemblances as well as differences in the workings of two electrical goods manufacturers, English Electric, in Britain, and Hitachi, in Japan. The British firm, for example, did not practise lifetime employment as Hitachi did. However, it did operate a policy of labour retention with redundancy used only as a last resort in hard times. The Japanese firm was different, but this was partly a matter of degree.

To what extent, then, have western firms followed the Japanese way? Given that the Japanese themselves have been selective in their application of Japanese management overseas, it seems highly probable that western firms will have been no less so. The evidence indicates exactly that.

Drawing on a survey of 1,158 American corporations conducted in 1982, Sethi *et al.* (1984) commented that there had been a slow take-up of Japanese management practices and that this had consisted mainly of quality circle programmes at shopfloor level. They noted, however, that market pressures were likely to drive firms increasingly in search of improvements in productivity and that the Japanese example might well be taken more seriously in the future. Oliver and Wilkinson's (1988) study of manufacturing firms in Britain shows that this has indeed happened.

These authors conducted a postal survey of large British and American-owned manufacturing companies active in Britain in 1986. Although less than 20 per cent of the 375 firms approached responded, information derived from the 66 participating companies together with case study materials provide what is probably the best picture of the extent of the use of Japanese management in British industry.

This study showed that the use of Japanese production methods and practices was widespread. Between 60 and 85 per cent of the firms reported that they were using such methods as team or group working, flexible work practices, quality circles, statistical process control, and total quality control. About a third were using the just-in-time system, but almost as many said they were in the process of implementing it or were planning to do so. Moreover, the timing of the introduction of these practices is significant. Although a few companies had introduced some of the practices prior to the Japan boom of the 1980s, a 'massive surge' had taken place after 1982. This may, then, indicate a genuine effort on the part of many firms to learn from Japan.

A similar picture emerges from the data on employment and personnel practices. Eighty-nine per cent of the firms were using comprehensive in-company communications schemes. At least 80 per cent had employee involvement programmes and single-status facilities. Nearly three-quarters provided 'staff' benefits to all categories of employee, and two-thirds said that they offered high job security to core workers. Over half the firms also reported that they employed a significant minority of the workforce on a 'temporary' basis. However, the pattern of the timing of the introduction of these practices differed from that observed for the manufacturing methods. The dates of adoption were more spread out. Although there did appear to have been a surge of applications of employee involvement schemes and temporary-worker policies after 1982, this was less notice-able or absent in the case of the other practices. High job security for core employees, for example, had been introduced by over half the firms before 1978: as we have seen, Dore (1973) had noted the practice in operation at English Electric in the early 1970s.

Further analysis suggested that there was a lack of synchronization in the introduction of the manufacturing and personnel practices. Not only had they tended to be introduced at different times, but also the firms tended to have developed either the manufacturing methods or the personnel practices but rarely both. Only ten of the sixty-six firms made extensive use of both Japanese manufacturing methods and Japanese personnel systems. Most companies seemed to be in possession of a Japanese horse or a Japanese cart, but not both. As one might expect, they frequently encountered significant problems in getting them to work effectively together.

These authors also argue that it is the nature of the production system that is at the heart of the explanation of the success of large Japanese manufacturing firms. Superior competitiveness arises from a capacity to produce high-quality goods at a relatively low price. The Japanese achieve this by organizing production on a 'total quality' basis using just-in-time techniques as the main element. However, if this production system is to work effectively it must be supported by an appropriate set of organiza-tional arrangements, and these must be congruent with the wider societal environment. Thus 'Japanese success with JIT (Just-In-Time) and total quality control may be seen as a consequence of an effective fit between their productions systems and their strategies for dealing with personnel, supplier relations, and so on, the whole system being supported by an appropriate set of social, political and economic conditions'.

Oliver and Wilkinson conclude that there is 'strong evidence' that many British manufacturing firms are adopting Japanese practices. Their success in doing so is, however, limited. This, they suggest, is because the effec-tiveness of Japanese methods depends not on the workings of any single practice but on the operation of the whole system. British firms have seldom achieved a good 'fit' between their production and personnel systems, whereas the Japanese have done so when operating both in Japan and in Britain. In the latter case this seems to be because Japanese firms starting up in Britain have not only been able to install highly efficient production systems but have also taken care to select employees who are willing to adopt the work practices and attitudes that are required to make the produc-tion system work well. In addition, Japanese firms have benefited from the long-term outlook of Japanese financial institutions which has aided the development of their marketing and investment strategies. British firms, setting out to introduce change to well-established organizations, have been less able to achieve the requisite fit and have been hampered by the short-termism of the City.

In America, Japanese practice remains highly influential and companies continue to be urged to learn from Japan (Liker *et al.* 1999). As in Britain, the Japanese approach to production management has been particularly important. Although many firms have yet to pay much attention to the Japanese example, others have taken it to heart. In the auto industry, for example, the Toyota production system has become a benchmark against which many American firms measure themselves (Womack and Jones, 1996). Indeed, the major US auto manufacturing companies are publicly committed to the adoption of the Toyota production system or something like it.

In general, Japanese practices have been applied in American industry with considerable success but not without adaptation to take account of local conditions. Moreover, the transfer of these practices has been far from easy. Summarizing the current situation, Liker *et al.* (1999) comment that: 'It is remarkable that, with all the hurdles facing transfer, the empirical evidence presented here and elsewhere strongly indicates that key aspects of JMSs [Japanese Management Systems] are indeed transferable and that they work well in the US environment.'

Japanese management: converging or still exceptional?

Convergence means becoming more similar. To the extent that elements of the Japanese system have been transferred successfully to countries like the US and Britain, then it can be said that some convergence has taken place. But the Japanese management system has itself been changing over the last decade. In which direction is it moving – closer to the West or perhaps further away?

Dunphy (1987) conducted an extensive review of the issue and found little evidence to support the contention that Japanese firms in Japan were converging with western practice. A few years later, Woronoff (1993) reported important changes taking place in the Japanese management system in response to the country's economic difficulties. In general he saw these developments as evolutionary rather than revolutionary, very much in keeping with Japan's culture and traditions. An important study by Berggren and Nomura (1997) yielded similar conclusions. Personnel practices were undergoing change but not to the extent of threatening the fundamental character of the management system. Thus they noted that 'in spite of the many initiatives to modify the post-war Japanese compensation and employment system, at company level as well as the level of employer and union organization, it is difficult to identify any broad trend towards convergence with Anglo-Saxon practices.'

Mroczkowski and Hanaoka (1998) have also reported significant changes in Japanese personnel practices but they reach an opposite conclusion: these practices are progressively being westernized albeit only slowly in some cases. Among the most significant changes they report are a move away from seniority-based pay in favour of merit systems based on formal appraisals, a decline in union membership and a declining commitment to traditional assumptions about loyalty to the firm in favour of more individualistic identification with one's profession. According to the Japanese corporate HRM managers, academics and consultants surveyed by Mroczkowski and Hanaoka, Japanese employees are 'rapidly adopting western-style attitudes to work'. Based on the forecasts of these experts, the end of Japanese management is nigh:

> The phase of particularism or 'Golden Age of Japanese Management' ends with the burst of the bubble economy in 1990 and ushers in a period of transition toward a universalist mode of pursuing global best practices. The forecast predicts that this phase will be completed around the year 2010 – when Japan 'joins the world' in terms of employment systems and HRM practices.

What shape the Japanese system will take in the future is, then, clearly open to debate. In any event, it seems likely that Japan's approach to management will continue to attract both scholarly and managerial interest, for although the Japanese management craze may be over (Davis *et al.* 1987) the issues it has raised are likely to be with us for some time to come.

Commentary

The emergence of Japan in the 1980s as America's leading industrial competitor seems to have induced a kind of 'moral panic' in business circles with the Japanese cast in the role of 'folk devils' (Cohen, 1987). The tacit assumption that America had the best management system in the world was now visibly in question, and from an American perspective this seemed shocking. Moreover, if Japanese management was indeed potent but could not be transferred to 'western' (i.e. American) firms, then the future for American business seemed bleak.

The problem of learning from Japan proved, however, to be complex, and it has raised difficult questions of fact and value. In some areas of the dispute evidence has been hard to come by whilst in others there have been sharply divergent interpretations of the data. A case in point is the impact of the Japanese system on Japanese employees. Should the Japanese worker be regarded as a secure, committed, satisfied employee embraced by a humanistic organizational culture which fosters pride of work and company loyalty as Ouchi's *Theory Z* proposes? Or is he better seen as a cheerless robot tied to a life of unending toil by an authoritarian management system and a punitive set of social values that stifle individuality and elevate conformity as a supreme end, a view characterized by Harper (1988) as Theory F = Fear? The Toyota Production System, for example, has been portrayed both as a fulfilling work environment (Womack *et al.,* 1990) and as a sweatshop (Morris *et al.,* 1993). Such questions cannot be answered by evidence alone because even facts must be interpreted. At this point cultural assumptions and values are likely to enter the debate so raising questions about what the facts mean.

Can the Japanese management system be transferred to the West? Increasingly it looks as if it can, if only in part. The evidence to date suggests that both the advocates and the critics of learning from Japan have grasped some part of the truth. It has been tacitly agreed on all sides that the Japanese 'must be doing something right' (Trevor, 1983). The question has been, what? The advocates pointed to the importance of an integrated set of employment and personnel practices which induce commitment, however grudgingly, to the firm. But the significance of such eye-catching features as lifetime employment, consensus decision-making and so on, when taken by themselves, seem to have been overestimated. Early interest in Japanese management focused heavily on these exotic aspects of the Japanese way, leaving the 'hard' skills relatively neglected (Nonaka and Johansson, 1985; Schonberger, 1982). Subsequent research strongly suggests that the Japanese approach to the organization of production is a vital element of the overall system. Similarly, the critics' view that Japanese management can only work effectively if the wider social environment is supportive of its practices has a strong plausibility. Japanese personnel practices do not appear to be transferable wholesale to a western environment. But, as Oliver and Wilkinson's (1988) and Liker *et al.*'s (1999) studies have shown, some Japanese practices have been implemented in the West with considerable success.

However, the Japanese management system should not be conceptualized as if it is constituted only by practices within firms. Japan's system of 'alliance capitalism' (Gerlach, 1992) comprises mutually supportive networks of industrial and financial firms and linkages with government which play a significant role in the economy's functioning. Berggren and Nomura (1997) argue that Japan's system is adjusting to new circumstances but that 'its basic model of corporate governance, competition and employment remains largely intact.' So even if the personnel practices employed by large Japanese firms are converging with those of the West, Japan's overall management system looks likely to retain its distinctive character.

What of the question of global convergence? Are there signs of the world's national management systems drawing closer together or do they appear to be as distinct as ever?

In the case of Japan and America, it seems that their management systems are indeed converging. On the one hand, there has been a significant adoption of Japanese production methods in America. On the other, Japan's personnel practices appear to be moving in a western direction. These two management systems can therefore be seen to be drawing closer together. This does not necessarily mean that they bear any close resemblance to each other, even less that one day American and Japanese ways of managing will be indistinguishable. That must surely be a remote prospect.

Evidence for a more general convergence between, for example, eastern and western countries is more difficult to come by. Recently, the emphasis of the management and culture debate has been on the importance of cultural differences for organizing and managing rather than upon similarities (Hickson and Pugh, 2001). Bartholomew and Adler (1996) conducted a survey of articles published between 1985 and 1990 which dealt with international aspects of organizational behaviour and HRM. Nearly all of the articles concluded that national cultural differences do make a difference to organizational structures and functioning.

As global communications and global corporations distribute the fruits of advanced industrialism to a widening circle of countries, perhaps it is only a matter of time before we all become members of a single global culture. Where Coca-Cola and McDonald's lead, must not management and organization soon follow? There may be doubts about the extent of global convergence of management to date, but what will tomorrow bring? That is an issue we will take up in our final chapter.

Questions for discussion

1   To what extent do national cultural differences influence the structure and functioning of organizations?
2   Which aspects of management are culture-bound and which are culture-free?
3   How did Japan become one of the world's largest economies?
4   What similarities and differences are there between western and eastern ways of organizing and managing?
5   Is a global culture emerging and, if so, is this a positive development?

Further reading

Adler, N.J. (1997) *International Dimensions of Organizational Behaviour*, Cincinnati: South-Western College Publishing.

Berggren, C. and Nomura, M. (1997) *The Resilience of Corporate Japan: New Competitive Strategies and Personnel Practices*, London: Paul Chapman.

Hickson, D.J. and Pugh, D.S. (2001) *Management Worldwide: Distinctive Styles Amid Globalization*, London: Penguin.

Hofstede, G. (1980) Leadership, Management and Organization: Do American Theories Apply Abroad? *Organizational Dynamics*, Summer, pp. 42–63.

Mroczkowski, T. and Hanaoka, M. (1998) The End of Japanese Management: How Soon? *Human Resource Planning*, 21 (3), pp. 20–30.

10 The future of management
Business as unusual?

the most powerful – and life enhancing – force on earth: globalization.

Peters (2000)

Preoccupation with the 'global' has become one of the emblematic features of our time . . . On the one hand, ambitious extrapolations are made, often from a small number of cases, to paint a scenario of unstoppable global forces leading to an ultimately homogenized world in which local differences will be virtually eradicated. On the other hand, there are those who argue that, really, nothing has changed very much; that the globalization story *is* little more than hype.

Dicken (1998)

Plus ça change, plus c'est la même chose.

Karr (1849)

If there is one theme that has dominated management thinking in the last few decades it must be that of change. The business world, we are constantly reminded, is changing fast and in unpredictable ways, so that both organizations and the managers and other employees who staff them must change too if they are not to be left behind. Successful organizations have been seen as those which are capable of 'riding the waves of change' (Morgan, 1989), and managers have been exhorted 'to learn to love change' (Peters, 1987). It seems truer now than it ever was that you have to run twice as fast just to stay where you are.

Yet it is not simply a matter of more rapid change but of the direction and destination of change. The French have a saying to the effect that 'the more things change, the more they remain the same'. Is it, then, simply a case of going faster along a well-trodden path towards a familiar end-point? Or have we perhaps entered a genuinely new, twenty-first century era in which organizations and management are being fundamentally transformed? Could we be on the verge of something called a post-modern world, or even of a post-managerial age?

The controversy in brief

This controversy focuses on alternative assessments of the current and future state of the world's economy and society, on the new forms of organization accompanying those assessments, and on the implications of changes in the business environment and in forms of organization for the practice of management.

Since we are concerned in this chapter with the future, we are dealing with a topic that is bound to be controversial. In his examination of what makes classic social theories classic, Davis (1986) noted that their authors were often struggling to make sense of the major social changes that were taking place around them as they wrote. Because these changes were ongoing and novel their character and significance could not be seen clearly at the time. Unlike the historian trying to make sense of a fixed and stable past, these writers were dealing with newly emerging processes and structures, and it was their genius which enabled them to grasp and give a coherent account of them before they became fully apparent. But each writer tended to see or to emphasize a particular aspect of their changing world and so produced different images of the future.

What many of today's social observers and analysts detect is a fundamental qualitative transformation of the societal framework within which business operates. Increasingly commentators writing from such varied points of view as sociology, economics, geography, political science, organizational analysis and management theory have proposed that the world has entered a global, post-modern era which is characterized by novel forms of organization and new approaches to management. But the labels used to describe this transformation process and the state to which it is leading us are many and varied. Some refer to the process as 'globalization', some as 'post-modernization', some as 'post-industrialization'. At the level of the business environment terms such as the 'new economy', 'knowledge economy', 'network society' and 'post-industrial society' abound. At the level of organizations, descriptors of newly emerging organizational forms include the 'virtual organization', 'post-bureaucratic organization', 'boundaryless organization', 'network organization', 'meta-organization', 'learning organization', 'shamrock organization', 'modular corporation' and 'cyberspace corporation' amongst others.

But whatever the point of view, there is a widespread sense that something deeply significant is going on. Just what that is, how it is to be explained and how managers might respond to it are, however, questions that remain open to argument. So, for example, some dissenting voices have been raised which refute the claim that we are witnessing a major break with the past. What these critics see is not so much novelty as continuity with existing systems and trends.

To deal with this diversity of ideas, we will proceed as follows. First we will introduce two key and related depictions of the changing state of the world: post-modernity and globalization. Then we will examine some responses to contemporary conditions in terms of the analyses and prescriptions offered by management theorists to management practitioners. Finally, we will review some of the evidence of the changes which are claimed to be taking place before giving a commentary on the future-of-management controversy.

What condition are we in?

In his influential book *The Postmodern Condition* (1979), the French writer, Jean-François Lyotard, drew attention to a new state of the world in the late twentieth century, one in which old certainties were disappearing. In so doing he reflected a broader sense among social observers that something fundamental was changing in modern society. Two major expressions of this theme are to be found in the post-modernity thesis and the globalization thesis.

From here to post-modernity

As a way of understanding history and of organizing accounts of it, historians typically divide the past into periods, eras or epochs (Thomas, 1999). Traditionally, history has been divided into the ancient, medieval and modern periods. In this periodization scheme the present phase of history is the modern: we live today in the modern world. Recently, however, an alternative framework has been proposed by some historians which divides history into the pre-modern, modern and post-modern eras. In this scheme the modern era is depicted as having been superseded by the post-modern era: we are living not in the modern but the post-modern world. Just as the modern world is very different from the medieval, so the post-modern world is claimed to constitute a distinct break from the recent past. For some sociologists at least, 'post-modernity bespeaks social and cultural transformation of a profound kind' (Lyon, 2000).

To understand this post-modernity thesis, we need to identify the key features of the modern era so that we can see the base from which transition to a new social and economic order may be taking place. Following Brown's (1995) account, we can locate the beginning of the modern era some time after the fifteenth century. The period that followed was one of major social, cultural, political, economic and technological change in the West. The key developments include the following:

The emergence of the nation-state

From the mid-sixteenth century the pre-modern feudal political order, based on a rigid set of relations between strata (aristocracy, landowners, peasants) gave way to the emergence of sovereign states, organized according to bounded geographical territories over which governments claimed autonomy and within which there developed a sense of nationhood.

The growth of science

Prior to the Enlightenment of the eighteenth century, knowledge in the West largely rested on religious authority. As a reaction against tradition and dogmatism, the scientific frame of mind emphasized the primacy of reason and rationality as the basis of knowledge; empiricism, the idea that knowledge is derived from observation and sense experience; scientific method and experiment as the means of identifying causal relations; general, universal laws as the determinants of all phenomena; scepticism towards all knowledge claims; and secularism, the idea that knowledge should be sought objectively without regard to superstition, religious authority or traditional beliefs.

Economic and technological development

By the mid-nineteenth century, population increases, rising standards of living, improvements in transport and communications, advances in agricultural efficiency, the easing of protectionism and the pursuit of *laissez-faire* economics, technological innovations, and the emergence of the factory system, produced the modern economy dominated by manufacturing and commerce. In the modern era, work tends to be organized on 'Fordist' lines in which economies of scale are achieved through mass production of standardized products for protected national markets; machinery is dedicated and task-specific, producing standardized parts for line assembly by a semi-skilled labour force performing tightly controlled, routinized tasks; hierarchical, bureaucratic forms of organization are used, with functional and divisional structures subject to centralized control; and mass marketing techniques are deployed to stimulate mass consumption of standardized products.

The rise of the West

The exploration and colonization of the non-European world helped to fuel industrialism, encouraged the emergence of new organizations (joint-stock companies, trading houses, merchant banks) and complex administrative institutions, and became associated with the belief in the supremacy of western culture and society and its inevitable and desirable extension throughout the world.

The secularization and democratization of society

Political absolutism was displaced in favour of more egalitarian and proto-democratic governmental and judicial institutions, and the dominance of religious authority was weakened in favour of secular authority in most spheres of life. The rise of the scientific and rational frame of mind was accompanied by the devaluation of other ways of knowing.

Commitment to progress

Brown suggests that if modernity had to be summarized in a single word 'that word would probably be progress'. The idea that humanity has advanced in the past, is advancing now, and will continue to advance in future has become largely taken for granted in the western world. It may therefore come as something of a surprise to realize that this familiar notion is a relatively recent idea. Prior to the eighteenth century the past was seen as a golden age, superior both to the present and to any likely future.

The transition from modernity to post-modernity entails significant shifts in all of these aspects of modernity. So it is proposed that we are experiencing the following:

The decline of the nation-state

Nation-states are claimed to be losing their significance as key political actors in the face of supra-national political and economic organizations (UN, EU, WTO, ASEAN, MERCOSUR, etc.). Paradoxically, the spread of global institutions and a global ethos occurs alongside growing localism and regionalism.

The decline of science

Unquestioning acceptance of scientific authority is being replaced by scepticism about many scientific claims, in part because of growing doubts about the beneficial effects of scientific knowledge and fears of its destructive consequences.

The rise of the service economy

Heavy manufacturing industries, large manual workforces and mass markets decline as knowledge-based industries, professionalized workforces and segmented markets rise. Within manufacturing, 'Fordist' methods are superseded by 'flexible specialization' involving extensive use of computer controlled and integrated manufacturing systems; smaller, more adaptable workforces, which are multi-skilled, team-orientated, and supplemented by part-time and short-contract labour; flatter organization structures with less emphasis on hierarchy and greater emphasis on autonomy and competition; more complex external relations via joint ventures, strategic alliances, and vertical disintegration; and the global dispersion of labour-intensive production to low-cost countries alongside the concentration of specialized production in new 'industrial districts'.

Displacement of the West

Western political, economic and cultural dominance is balanced by the emergence of strong eastern economies, such as Japan, and as non-western countries assert their cultural and political independence.

Displacement of rationality

There is renewed interest in alternative belief systems, a questioning of the dominance of the scientific frame of mind and a reassertion of the importance of emotion, intuition and religious belief.

Scepticism about progress

In the light of environmental degradation, technological catastrophes, social instability and the sense that humanity may have entered a cul-de-sac, optimism about progress is being replaced by doubt, nostalgia and outright pessimism.

The onset of post-modernity is also associated with a number of general, abstract processes which affect a wide range of individuals and institutions. These rather strange and perplexing tendencies are briefly summarized in Box 10.1. Two of them, fragmentation and de-differentiation, are of particular interest here.

Box 10.1 Some features of post-modernity

Fragmentation: the breaking up of established structures into fragments.

De-differentiation: the blurring or dissolution of established boundaries.

Hyper-reality: confusion and mixing of the real with artificial/virtual realities.

Chronology: interest in the past and its imitation alongside/instead of the future.

Pastiche: the playful mixing of styles of decoration, dress, expression, etc.

Anti-foundationalism: rejection of all basics, absolutes, fundamentals, universals, etc.

Pluralism: all of the above happening simultaneously!

Source: Adapted from S. Brown, *Postmodern Marketing,* London: Routledge, 1995.

Fragmentation refers to the breaking up, or down, of established structures into multiple elements. This process can be seen at work in many spheres: in politics, with the disintegration of the USSR in the early 1990s, the growth of regionalism in the UK and of separatist movements elsewhere; in economics, with the transition from mass to niche markets and the proliferation of products and distribution channels; in organizations, with de-mergers, buy-outs, decentralization and disacquisitions; and in personal life, with serial marriages, portfolio careers and even individualized rather than shared family mealtimes.

De-differentiation, on the other hand, refers to the blurring or dissolution of established boundaries. Unlike fragmentation, where previously unified entities become disaggregated, de-differentiation brings together elements that were previously separate, sometimes in bizarre and unexpected combinations. Politics and marketing become intertwined during election campaigns as candidates and party policies are 'sold' to the voters, education merges with entertainment to spawn infotainment, news and advertising mix in the form of the advertorial, and so on. In business organizations, grocery retailers move into financial services, petrol stations market groceries, networks, partnerships and alliances become prevalent among firms, functional silos are dissolved, teams become self-managing, and customers become involved in the production process.

These two processes of fragmentation and de-differentiation can be treated as indicators of a transition from modernity to post-modernity. Some of their manifestations are purely local, but others, such as the breaking up of previously unified countries and the unification of previously separate ones, are examples of fragmentation and de-differentiation taking place at the global level. Post-modern trends seem then to be related to a second process, that of globalization.

From internationalization to globalization

Globalization has been defined in a variety of ways, but a common thread in these definitions is that it refers to a process or a series of processes whereby the world's societies are becoming increasingly interlinked and interdependent. McLuhan's concept of the 'global village', in which geographically and culturally distant peoples would be brought together through electronic media into a worldwide community, was an early and influential expression of this idea (Carpenter and McLuhan, 1960). Through access to the same TV news broadcasts, for example, people around the world would come to share a common news environment. The topic of globalization did not enter the management literature until the early 1980s, but it became a major theme in management discourse in the 1990s and looks very likely to remain one.

Proponents of the globalization thesis emphasize different aspects of the global integration process, but generally this is seen to affect both economic, political and cultural relationships. Globalization is to be understood as a broad phenomenon not solely confined to economic affairs. All three types of linkage between states have, of course, a lengthy history: *international* relations are not new. However, it is the extensiveness and character of current developments that has encouraged the wide acceptance of the view that a new *global* condition prevails.

Dicken (1998), for example, states that 'the most significant development in the world economy during the past few decades has been the *increasing internationalization – and, arguably, the increasing globalization – of economic activities*' (emphasis in original). Until recently, he argues, the extension of economic activities beyond national boundaries largely took the form of trade in goods produced within a national unit. These trading relationships involved relatively few commodities exchanged between a limited number of nationally based firms. Today, however, trading relationships have been extended to cover a vast range of goods and services. More importantly, they have been supplemented by production relationships which require the functional integration of production processes across national borders. A given product may be assembled from parts manufactured in many disparate locations and be processed at many others en route to final assembly.

This new global division of labour, exemplified by the automobile, electronics and textile industries, is being extended to more and more industries and more and more countries. The older world pattern of core manufacturing countries trading with peripheral suppliers of food and raw materials has now been replaced by a new and more complex situation in which production is fragmented and geographically dispersed, cutting across national boundaries. Moreover, these trends in the organization of manufacturing have had their counterpart in financial and business services. The international financial system is dominated by the financial centres in London, Tokyo and New York, while services such as advertising, accounting and consultancy are now organized by giant, global companies operating on a worldwide scale.

Two elements are typically regarded as central to the globalization process, the transnational corporation (TNC) and new information and communication technologies (ICT). The TNC is an important channel for the distribution of products, production processes, and managerial techniques around the world. These corporations also promote the homogenization of consumer tastes via their global marketing activities. The new information technologies facilitate management and co-ordination within TNCs, and play an increasingly significant role in the marketing process. More generally ICT has accelerated the diffusion of cultural elements (symbols, images, languages, styles) around the globe via broadcast media and the Internet.

The TNC can be seen as a development from its predecessor, the multinational corporation (MNC). Some theorists of organizational design and of corporate strategy see the TNC and the MNC as types of international company which have different structures and orientations. The TNC is a distinct species of organization which is designed to cope effectively with global rather than simply international conditions.

Although these theorists do not necessarily agree on what specifically distinguishes these forms from each other, one view is that an MNC can be seen as an international firm that operates as a multidomestic business. That is, it consists of a set of relatively self-contained, nationally based units which are only loosely co-ordinated by the MNC's headquarters. The firm can thus be seen as a collection of essentially domestic businesses, each attuned to the country in which it is located. TNCs, by contrast, are international businesses that are run as integrated networks with strong co-ordination and a global outlook (Leontiades, 2001). Such firms attempt to combine local specialization with globally derived economies and synergies. Incidentally, a multinational company which is in the process of being restructured to achieve these ends is said to be undergoing 'globalization'. The term can thus refer both to the process whereby a firm structures itself in order to act as a successful player in global markets and to the broad process of economic, political and cultural integration that affects the world as a whole.

The spread and development of information and communication technologies is a second key element in the globalization process. Dramatic technical developments have rapidly expanded the scope of global communications and massively reduced their cost. In 1970 it cost $150,000 to transmit one trillion bits of information, $5,257 to provide one megabit of storage, and $7,601 to provide one MHz of processing power, but by 1999 these costs had fallen to less than 20 cents in each case (*Economist*, 2000). Fibre-optic cables are now capable of carrying many more channels than their metallic predecessors, communications satellites have linked previously isolated parts of the world, and the Internet (*inter*national *net*work) has brought millions of people into real-time contact relatively cheaply – as many as 700 million people were expected to be online by 2001 (Giddens, 2001). Although access to technologies such as telephones, televisions, and personal computers is unevenly distributed across the globe, it seems likely that availability and usage will continue to increase.

TNCs have been both the promoters and beneficiaries of these new information technologies. Thus telecommunications companies have themselves been in the forefront of globalization. But whatever the industry, new information and communication technologies have helped international firms transform themselves into global players. These technologies have also spawned a new breed of company, the Internet company or dot.com firm which, insofar as it aspires to reach a global market, may also be considered as an important element of the globalized economy.

Post-modernity and globalization

The term 'post-modernity' is not much used by management writers, even though the ideas associated with it overlap significantly with those of the much more favoured word, 'globalization'. Lyon (2000), for example, defines post-modernity as 'a concept used to describe contemporary social conditions in which communication and information technologies and consumerism have become predominant'. As we have seen, one of the features associated with post-modernity is the break up of established units into multiple fragments. Another is the dissolution of boundaries between previously distinct entities. Globalization can be seen to entail both these features. Globally dispersed information technology brings previously separated parts of the world together, dissolving previous boundaries. At the same time these technologies, together with flexible manufacturing methods and the 'global reach' of the TNC, enable mass markets to be fragmented into niches and individualized tastes to be catered for. De-differentiation and fragmentation occur simultaneously; paradoxically, globalization also produces localization.

Both the post-modernity and globalization theses imply a fundamental destabilization of previous boundaries. The maps with which we have been familiar have become fluid and therefore unreliable as a guide to the future. From the point of view of management, post-modernity and globalization are closely intertwined phenomena with significant implications for the future of organizations and those who run them. If a new, post-modern, global era is dawning, perhaps some new, post-modern, global organizations are emerging too.

The new organizers

As the new millennium approached, a growing number of influential management texts appeared which pointed to the imminent emergence of new organizational forms. Recognizing the changed business landscape that was being brought into being by a globalizing world, the authors of these texts saw the need for new types of organization designed to flourish under the new conditions. These 'new organizers' typically claimed to have glimpsed the future of business, organization and management in the twenty-first century.

The global environment and new organizations

The term 'globalization' seems to have first entered the management literature when Levitt's article on the globalization of markets appeared in the *Harvard Business Review* in the early 1980s (Levitt, 1983). In this paper, Levitt argued that companies were facing a new commercial reality, 'the emergence of global markets for standardized products on a previously unimagined scale of magnitude'. Driven by worldwide communications, consumer tastes had been homogenized. Thus, he declared, 'the globalization of markets is at hand.' This, Levitt argued, implied the end of the multinational corporation and the rise of the global corporation. The MNC varied its products and operations from country to country, so adopting a 'multidomestic' structure. The global corporation, however, treated the whole world as a single market. Companies such as Coca-Cola, McDonald's, Pepsi-Cola, and Sony were already adapting to the new global realities, as others would have to do if they were to survive in the global marketplace.

The management consultant, Kenichi Ohmae, wrote an influential series of articles on the globalization of business which appeared in the *Harvard Business Review* in 1989. The following year Ohmae, who was the managing director of McKinsey's in Japan, published a book-length version of his views, *The Borderless World* (1990). There he describes some of the significant changes that have been taking place in the global business environment and points out their implications for the management of international businesses. As the title of his book suggests, his argument is that for business purposes geographical boundaries have largely disappeared. Under the influence of modern information technologies, people have become 'global consumers' who are interested in what is produced but who are largely unconcerned with where it is produced. New products are now launched in many countries simultaneously, English is becoming the world's language, and a global marketplace has emerged. Moreover, companies themselves tend to use very similar production technologies so that exchange of personnel and ideas is relatively unproblematic. 'When information flows with relative freedom,' wrote Ohmae, 'the old geographic barriers become irrelevant.' The borderless world looks good for business except where bureaucrats intervene with their obstructive barriers and regulations.

A more scholarly contribution came from two business school academics, Bartlett and Ghoshal (1989). They reviewed three traditional solutions to the problem of how businesses can be organized in order to serve overseas markets: the multinational solution, the global solution and the international solution. The multinational solution involves treating various national markets separately with little co-ordination in the firm's approach to them. The global solution treats the world as a single market (as Levitt had proposed). The international solution involves a strong, innovative parent company supplying weak, dependent overseas subsidiaries. But Bartlett and Ghoshal argue that none of these solutions are viable since none can effectively respond to the three strategic imperatives of efficiency, responsiveness to market changes, and ability to diffuse innovations across the world. Since these imperatives must be satisfied under global conditions, a new solution is required, the transnational solution.

This solution is to be understood not so much as a new type of organization structure but as 'a broad organizational concept or philosophy, manifested in organizational capability and management mentality'. The transnational solution differs from previous approaches to managing across borders in its emphasis on the interdependence of business units and its recognition of the need to develop management processes capable of responding simultaneously to the resulting complexity. The firm must be both locally adapted as well as globally orientated and that requires managers to change the way they think about international business, to adopt a new paradigm. The message seems to have been well received for Bartlett and Ghoshal's work has been highly influential in the business world.

Davidow and Malone (1992) aimed to provide 'a single cohesive vision of the corporation in the twenty-first century'. Like Bartlett and Ghoshal they also identified the need for a new organizational form. For them, however, this need arises because of the emergence of a new type of product, the virtual product, which can be produced very quickly and customized according to the consumer's preferences. This type of product, they claim, requires a new type of organization to produce it, 'a "virtual corporation" [which] will have little in common with what existed before'. Instances of this corporation will have no single structure but will display certain key characteristics:

> To the outside observer, it will appear almost edgeless, with permeable and continuously changing interfaces between company, supplier and customers. From inside the firm the view will be no less amorphous, with traditional offices, departments and operating divisions constantly reforming according to need. Job responsibilities will regularly shift, as will lines of authority – even the very definition of employee will change, as some customers and suppliers begin to spend more time in the company than will some of the firm's own workers.

For Davidow and Malone, the need for a new organizational form arises largely from developments in technology. Globalization receives little attention in their discussion. Ashkenas and his colleagues (1995), however, argue that it is the globalization of the economy together with information technologies that has changed the nature of the competitive game. Whereas in the past factors such as organizational size, clarity of roles, specialization and control have been important, now it is speed, flexibility, integration and innovation that count.

To meet these demands requires 'a shift from rigid to permeable organizational structures and processes'. Boundaries inside the organization and outside it are to become much more fluid and penetrable, but they will not disappear completely for that would produce chaos. Internally, this weakening of boundaries applies vertically, between levels and ranks, and horizontally, between functions and disciplines. Externally, it applies to boundaries between the organization and its suppliers, customers and regulators, and to geographical boundaries between nations, cultures and markets. These shifts, they say, bring 'the dawning of the *boundary-less organization* of the twenty-first century' – even though, as the authors make clear, such an organization will still in fact have boundaries! Presumably it is the spirit rather than the letter of the idea that counts.

New managers and management processes

It seems reasonable to assume that new types of organization are likely to require new ways of managing and possibly even new types of manager. According to Ohmae (1990) managers need to respond to the borderless world not only by changing their organizations and strategies but, perhaps more importantly, their outlook or 'mentality'. They need to become 'equidistant managers'. Typically, international companies tend to have a 'home-and-overseas' outlook in which the home market dominates. Equidistant managers, however, do not think in this way but see the corporate centre as placed at an equal distance from its customers wherever they are geographically located. They also adopt subtle and flexible product strategies: sometimes product standardization is appropriate but sometimes it is not.

In the case of the virtual corporation, Davidow and Malone (1992) propose that while managers will continue to have to satisfy organizational stakeholders, the way they manage will have to change. Workers will be empowered so that they can react rapidly to customers' demands. This will change the directing role of management to one of facilitation and support. In addition, new information technologies will enable top management to acquire operational information without having to rely on middle managers, many of whom will disappear from the organization. The resulting structure will be flatter with fewer layers and much wider spans of control.

How will managers fare in this new organization? 'Stripped of many of the traditional perquisites of power and authority (often including even their titles), coping with an expanded and nearly impossible span of control after having lost many of their peers, working with a fluid group of employees . . . it seems reasonable to ask: what will motivate these men and women?' What indeed! That, Davidow and Malone propose, is a key question which can only be answered by visionary leadership.

Finally, Ashkenas *et al.* (1995) point to the need for 'global super-managers' to run global corporations. These managers will be truly international in capability and orientation, being multilingual and equipped with a multicultural outlook. A more detailed specification of the attributes of such 'transnationally competent' managers has been provided by Adler and Bartholomew (1992) as shown in Table 10.1. Is this the personnel specification of the international manager of the future?

Table 10.1 The attributes of transnationally competent managers

Traditional international managers	Transnationally competent managers
Focus on a single foreign country and on managing relationships between headquarters and that country	Understand worldwide business environment from a global perspective
Become an expert on one culture	Learn about many cultures
Work with and coach people in each foreign culture separately or sequentially	Work with and learn from people from many cultures simultaneously
Integrate foreigners into the headquarters' national organizational culture	Create a culturally synergistic organizational environment
Adapt to living in a foreign culture	Adapt to living in many foreign cultures
Use cross-cultural interaction skills primarily on foreign assignments	Use cross-cultural interaction skills on a daily basis throughout one's career
Interact within clearly defined hierarchies of structural and cultural dominance	Interact with foreign colleagues as equals
Expatriation or inpatriation primarily to get the job done	Transpatriation for career and organization development

Source: Adapted from N.J. Adler and S. Bartholomew (1992) Managing Globally Competent People, *Academy of Management Executive*, 6 (3), pp. 52–65.

Business as unusual?

Questioning post-modernity and globalization

Critiques of the post-modernity thesis have been grouped by Lyon (2000) into three variants: those which see globalization rather than post-modernity as the distinguishing characteristic of the new age (Albrow, 1996); those which deny that there has ever been a fully modern era and therefore argue that it is not really possible to speak coherently of a post-modern one (Latour, 1993); and those which propose that current developments are best understood as an extension of existing trends rather than as a distinct switch into something new (Giddens, 1990, 1991). These critiques tend to focus on the issue of whether current conditions do or do not constitute a major break from the past so justifying the attribution of a new label denoting a different era, type of society or type of organization. In addition, a number of Marxist writers have been deeply critical of the closely related discourse of post-modernism (Callinicos, 1989; Thompson, 1993).

Responses to the globalization thesis can be organized around the categories suggested by Held *et al.* (1999), those of sceptics, hyperglobalizers and transformationalists. Sceptics tend to argue that claims about globalization are much exaggerated. Economic interconnectedness between nations is not, they argue, new. Indeed greater degrees of connection can be identified in the past (Glyn and Sutcliffe, 1992; Hirst and Thompson, 1996). Moreover, to speak of a global economy is a misnomer for mostly this involves only what Ohmae (1990) called the Triad countries of North America, Europe and the Asia–Pacific region: vast areas of the world are tacitly excluded from economic participation. Some sceptics, such as Sklair (1995), also argue that globalization is not, as some of its apologists would claim, a mechanism for spreading wealth more evenly around the world. The border between the haves and the have-nots is not disappearing but is being redrawn on a global scale with the emergence of a transnational capitalist class. The claim that the world is becoming borderless and that nation-states have become economically irrelevant is also rejected. Sceptics argue that states continue to be vital players within the world economy (Hu, 1996).

Hyperglobalizers, by contrast, see globalization as both real and a dominant force in the contemporary world and one which is radically diminishing the influence of states in favour of markets. Many management gurus subscribe to this view. The future points to the emergence of global governance, a global culture, a global citizenry and, of course, to the rise of global corporations run by global supermanagers.

Transformationalists take an arguably more balanced position than either the sceptics or the hyperglobalizers. Recognizing continuities with the past, they also believe that a distinct transformation is under way: long-established processes of connectedness have accelerated and spread more widely in recent decades than they have hitherto. Thus Giddens (1991) accepts that profound changes are taking place in the modern world, but he is reluctant to accept that these amount to a break into a different kind of society. Rather, he uses such terms as 'late' or 'high' modernity to describe the contemporary situation. Globalization is a product of tendencies arising within modernity. Even so, he argues that the globalized era really is a genuine novelty. Similarly Waters's (2001) view is that globalization is a relatively recent process which has accelerated and has now produced a distinct condition.

New organizational forms

The transnational corporation

As we have seen, the transnational corporation has been widely regarded as a key driver of globalization and as an important institution of post-modernity. Its capacity to spread both cultural and material products around the world, seemingly with little regard for national boundaries, renders the TNC a potent globalizing force. Indeed, these giant corporations have been seen as threats to the continuing viability of the nation-state as the key political unit of modern times. As Hu (1996) has put it:

> The discourse of globalization draws much of its strength from the mental picture of the global, stateless corporation with its suggestive power. In this imagery, the corporate entity has no loyalty towards its home nation, thus undermining the nation-state politically; its operations cross national borders and are driven solely by pure economic rationality at a global level, economically undermining the nation-state and its economic policies. The global firm also works hand-in-hand with global telecommunications to promote the advent of the global village and the global standardization of tastes, thus undermining the nation-state culturally. In this vision the 'stateless' corporation is both the symbol and driver of globalization.

But how realistic is this image? Hu evaluated the world's leading international companies against six criteria in order to assess the extent to which they could be considered as transnational or global firms. These criteria were the geographical spread and scope of operations, extent of international ownership, extent of international control, international profile of staff, legal nationality and tax domicile. His results showed that the bulk of the operations of most international firms are located in their home country rather than being spread across numerous ones. He also found that most international firms are owned and controlled by home country individuals and institutions and are led by home country nationals. Legally the firms have no international existence, for each part of the corporation has legal corporate status only within the country in which it is located. Similarly, each constituent company within an international firm is taxed separately by the government of the country in which it is located. Hu concludes that apart from a few bi-national firms, such as Shell and Unilever, few if any international companies currently operating can be considered to be genuinely 'global' corporations.

Turner and Henry (1996) set out in search specifically of the transnational corporation as defined by Bartlett and Ghoshal. Their study of leading companies in mature, technology-intensive industries reached much the same conclusion as Hu had reached using his own criteria for 'global' corporations: it was difficult to find anything but a few examples of transnational companies in practice. Instead of the firms sharing a structure that was recognizably similar and worthy of the label 'transnational', there was considerable variety in ways they were organized. Turner and Henry conclude that 'for most international companies the transnational model is more of an aspiration than a reality'.

A recent major survey of workplace practices in Britain concluded that in general, companies in the UK still seem to adopt traditional control-oriented methods of management (Cully *et al.*, 1999). Even so, there probably has been a significant shift since about the 1980s within many of the largest international firms towards more open, flexible organizational structures, with flatter hierarchies, greater use of teamworking, greater 'empowerment' of employees, and more change-oriented corporate cultures. But whether such changes denote a new kind of organization is debatable.

Watson (2002) has suggested that many of the elements which are held to comprise these novel 'twenty-first-century' organizations bear a close resemblance to the 'organismic' type of structure identified by Burns and Stalker (1961) decades ago. Two broad forms of organization structure represent alternative fundamental approaches to organizing: mechanistic structures work best under stable conditions whereas organismic structures are well-suited to dealing with uncertainty and change. The new organizers' proposals for coping with a changed world therefore do not seem so novel after all:

> The labelling of more flexible forms of bureaucratic structure and culture as 'postmodern' or 'post-bureaucratic' is unhelpful. It is unrealistic to suggest that there is something new occurring to work organizations at the level of the basic organizing principle. There is no postmodern or post-bureaucratic organizational form available to us that is *essentially* different from the modernist bureaucratic organization.
>
> (Watson, 2002)

As so often happens when oversimplified models are compared with the messiness and complexity of the real world, the models look somewhat threadbare. Perhaps they are running ahead of reality which will, in time, catch up with them. Or it may be that the perspicacious corporate chief executives of companies that operate in many different countries are much more sophisticated and subtle managers, much better at improvisation, than some of the models allow.

Virtual organizations

What, though, of the more exotic notion of the 'virtual organization'? Groth's (1999) extensive exploration of the implications of information and communication technologies for the future of organizational design concludes that most applications of these technologies are likely to take the form of modifications and extensions of existing organizational designs. New information and communication technologies can be applied within existing forms of organization without fundamentally altering their basic character. A centralized organization, for example, may obtain information by means of electronic systems instead of through hierarchies of managers without affecting its centralized character. However, that still leaves open the possibility that entirely new forms will emerge, such as the virtual organization and what Groth calls the meta-organization and the organized cloud.

Unfortunately, the term 'virtual organization' has been used in a variety of ways, some of which amount to little more than the renaming of existing conventional forms. The description of the 'virtual corporation' given by Davidow and Malone, for example, sounds rather like Ashkenas *et al.*'s (1995) 'boundaryless organization' which in turn bears a family resemblance to Burns and Stalker's 'organismic' organization! It seems more helpful to follow both Groth (1999) and van Dijk (1999) who see the defining feature of a virtual organization as its heavy if not exclusive reliance on ICT. In a virtual organization members relate to each other primarily by means of electronic media with little or no face-to-face contact, and their work is largely unconstrained by physical conditions, place or time. A growing number of organizations are making extensive use of ICT, but few of them can be considered to be virtual organizations because they continue to rest heavily on traditional structures. In these organizations ICT is used as an adjunct to traditional systems rather than as the organization's major means of operating.

The virtual organization does seem technically feasible, but both Groth and van Dijk believe that it may well prove impossible to sustain in practice because of its impersonality and volatility. Its members lack the opportunity for face-to-face bonding and managing interpersonal relationships may become problematic. An organization with so few boundaries or borders seems unlikely to be able to hold together for very long. In other words, the virtual organization might turn out to be unworkable as a socio-technical system (Pasmore, 1988).

The meta-organization and the organized cloud may be more enduring. The meta-organization consists of a set of formally distinct firms which are extensively and strongly co-ordinated by means of unified computer-based systems. Although fragmented in terms of ownership, management structures and finances, they are interlinked into a single co-ordinated system through ICT. Groth cites the manufacturing system centred on Nissan's Sunderland factory as an example meta-organization.

The organized cloud, on the other hand, can be described as 'a cloud of stars, held together by the gravity of their common database' (Groth, 1999). A set of travel agents all using a common computerized booking system is one example. An electronic financial trading system is another. In both cases participants' behaviour is co-ordinated entirely by the computer system without any other form of contact between them. Indeed, they do not even know of each other's existence as individuals. However, this configuration lacks certain features normally associated with an organization, such as shared goals and a central authority. Organized clouds are organized but not managed, self-regulating rather than controlled. They may be considered to be at the limits of what we have come to understand as an organization. Interestingly, Groth considers that they could 'well emerge as one of the defining features of future societies'.

New managers and management processes

If there are doubts about the emergence of the new organizations, what of the new managers and new management processes that are needed to run them?

In 1990 the *Harvard Business Review* conducted a world leadership survey which drew responses from nearly 12,000 readers of similar management magazines in twenty-five countries (Kanter, 1991). From this it was concluded that although change was widespread in corporations regardless of country or culture, 'the idea of a corporate global village where a common culture of management unifies the practice of business around the world is more dream than reality'. One divisive factor was attitudes to globalization. Although most survey respondents were free-trade internationalists, there were still countries which defended protectionism and government support for domestic business. 'Economics', as Kanter put it, 'has not yet triumphed over politics' – as if it ever could or should!

A significant measure of a company's global management status is the national diversity of its top-most directors and senior managers. The transnational company is supposed to be polycentric and egalitarian, having no dominant national headquarters, with a mentality that is multicultural, seeking to achieve synergy from international differences among its managers. So far, at least, there seem to be few signs of these features in practice. Hu (1996) reports that far from there being a multinational mix of directors on the main boards of major American and Japanese MNCs, these directors are almost exclusively home country nationals. The boards of European multinationals are more diverse, but even there foreign members are frequently nationals of countries with cultures similar to those of the home country. Multinational polycentrism and cultural egalitarianism do not appear to be much in evidence.

Significant changes in the composition of company boards may take many years to realize (Thomas, 1991), but top managers' conceptions of the competitive game may be changing more rapidly. Leontiades (2001), noting the effects of improvements in information technologies on TNCs' operations, comments:

> The key difference between the new and the old approach to international business today is not one of organization structure or catering to a global market. It is much broader and more basic than that.

Improved information capability has changed management's view of the world and the position of their business within it. It has changed their view of international competition and the global threats and opportunities. In other words, it has changed management's perception of the way the game is played.

In short, managers' 'mentalities' may well be undergoing a significant transformation even though the organizations they head have not yet done so.

Hofstede (1999), on the other hand, argues that management processes are essentially unchanging; they have changed little in the past and will not change much in the future. This is because management is primarily concerned with people, whether employees, customers, clients or whatever, and human nature exhibits extreme stability throughout history. The same fundamental management problems recur at all times and in all places, and although there are differences in the ways in which these are solved, they are primarily a reflection of cultural variations among countries. Within countries management processes do not change much over time. Hence he concludes that 'management in the 21st century will not be basically different from management in the 20th'.

Commentary

Getting to grips with the future is never straightforward. Wild speculations and flights of fancy are as likely to catch attention as sober projections, forecasts and carefully built scenarios. The problem in today's world is knowing which of these is more likely to provide a meaningful guide to the future. Our difficulties are compounded when we are interested not in the fate of some small, familiar unit but in that of the entire world. It is easy to get carried away by grand predictive schemes and by what post-modernists call 'grand narratives' or overarching attempts to explain everything. When management writers go large, there is always the risk of lapsing into megalomania, magic and mysticism.

It is noticeable, for example, that a good deal of recent writing on the future of management and organization has drawn on a specious millennial logic which depicts the coming of a new century and a new millennium as in and of itself heralding change. So, for example, Daft (2001) writes of organizations coping 'with tremendous upheaval and struggle through the transition to a new century'. According to this logic the occurrence of the year 2000 (or 2001 if you are a millennial purist) is necessarily associated with the onset of a widespread process of organizational transition, which seems a strangely superstitious belief. It also ignores the culturally relative status of calendars: according to the Muslim calendar the year was not 2000 but 1420. In the Jewish calendar it was 5760. No sign of a new millennium nor even a new century there!

This insensitivity to cultural differences has been evident in the globalization debate in other ways. Global means worldwide but, as Waters (2001) indicates, 'globalization' can, for the moment at least, be more accurately described as a process of westernization, spreading western capitalism and western culture across the world. Frequently, however, this is not the way in which it has been portrayed. Instead there has been a tendency to mix technical analyses of international developments with the essentially political advocacy of free trade as if the latter were also a purely technical issue and an unquestionable good. It is not surprising then that critics of capitalism have frequently been hostile to the globalization thesis. Economics, like management itself, cannot be divorced from politics. Globalization must not be confused with globaldegook.

Is there anything really new about the changes which it is claimed are taking us towards a different future? It seems at least arguable that the inhabitants of Victorian Britain saw vastly more real change – wholly new industrial, transport and communications technologies, fundamental reconstructions of urban and rural landscapes and ways of life, and so on – than those who live in Los Angeles, Tokyo or London do today. Are we overestimating the significance of novelty or underestimating it?

It is probable that the information and communication technology revolution is only in its early stages. New technical developments have taken place very recently and very rapidly and these are likely to continue. Investment in developing information technologies continues and there is vast scope for further adoption of existing technologies. Even among developed countries, as few as 30 per cent of the population is online and e-commerce accounts for a tiny percentage of total sales. Only about one-third of US companies are using the Internet for procurement or sales, yet it is these business-to-business applications which are likely to be especially significant (*The Economist*, 2000). ICT enables companies to revolutionize their relationships with both suppliers and customers through the creation of electronic markets. These dramatically reduce transaction costs. In the automobile industry, for example, major companies such as Ford, Daimler–Chrysler and General Motors have collaborated to secure supplies via the web. Electronic technologies are also being adopted to secure the distribution of products to global customers. Leontiades (2001) suggests that the impact of ICT on organization is only just beginning and that it will be 'enormous'. Increasingly, internal functions will be contracted out to external suppliers so that 'it is possible to envisage global co-ordinating companies with little more than a small staff, managing the worldwide inflow of supplies and distribution of products through such means'. The bursting of the dot.com bubble at the start of the new millennium may thus signify not so much the beginning of the end as the end of the beginning of the impact of ICT on business.

It seems that different eras produce different dominant forms of organization – the pre-modern community, the modern bureaucracy, the

---

Box 10.2 **Possible attributes of the post-modern manager**

Modern manager	Post-modern manager
Specialist-generalist	Generalist-specialist
Local/national orientation	International/global orientation
Control focus	Facilitation focus
Action focus	Practical theorist
Qualified	Continuous development
Male attributes	Male–female attributes
Reactive	Proactive
Authoritarian	Participative
Functional outlook	Process outlook
Knower/believer	Sceptic/learner

---

post-modern network – each of which offers an alternative solution to the problem of organizing co-operative production. If the pre-modern community produced the paternalistic or charismatic leader and the modern bureaucracy gave birth to the modern manager, what sorts of skills and competencies might be needed of the manager in a globalized, post-modern world (Box 10.2)?

Will management continue to be recognizable in the form in which it came to be known during the twentieth century, or are we entering a new and as yet uncharted post-managerial age? The fact is, of course, that none of the ideas we have examined in this chapter may withstand the test of time. When it comes to the future, we just don't know.

Will controversies in management continue to arise as the twenty-first century progresses? Without a doubt! That is one prediction that really does seem future-proof.

Questions for discussion

1 In what ways are developments in information and communication technologies changing the way organizations are structured and managed?
2 What are the prospects for the spread of virtual organizations?
3 Is globalization a myth?
4 To what extent are we living in a post-modern world?
5 What features would you expect organizations and management to display in a post-managerial age?

Further reading

Brown, S. (1995) *Postmodern Marketing*, London: Routledge.
Dicken, P. (1998) *Global Shift*, London: Paul Chapman.
Leontiades, J.C. (2001) *Managing the Global Enterprise: Competing in the Information Age*, Harlow: Pearson.
van Dijk, J. (1999) *The Network Society: Social Aspects of New Media*, London: Sage.

Bibliography

Abegglen, J.C. and Stalk, G. (1984) *Kaisha: The Japanese Corporation*, New York: Basic Books.

Abrahamson, E. (1991) Managerial Fads and Fashions: The Diffusion and Rejection of Innovations, *Academy of Management Review*, 16 (3), pp. 586–612.

Ackoff, R. (1979) The Future of Operational Research is Past, *Journal of the Operational Research Society*, 30, pp. 93–104.

Ackoff, R. (1993) The Art and Science of Mess Management, in C. Mabey and B. Mayon-White (eds) *Managing Change*, London: Paul Chapman, pp. 47–54.

Acton Society Trust (1956) *Management Succession: The Recruitment, Selection, Training and Promotion of Managers*, London: Acton Society Trust.

Adler, N.J. (1997) *International Dimensions of Organizational Behaviour*, Cincinnati: South-Western College Publishing.

Adler, N.J. and Bartholomew, S. (1992) Managing Globally Competent People, *Academy of Management Executive*, 6 (3), pp. 52–65.

Adler, N.J. and Izraeli, D.N. (eds) (1988) *Women in Management Worldwide*, Armonk, NY: M.E. Sharpe.

Albrow, M. (1996) *The Global Age*, Cambridge: Polity Press.

Allen, M.P., Panian, S.K. and Lotz, R.E. (1979) Managerial Succession and Organizational Performance: A Recalcitrant Problem Revisited, *Administrative Science Quarterly*, 24, pp. 167–80.

Alvesson, M. and Billing, Y.D. (1997) *Understanding Gender and Organizations*, London: Sage.

Anderson, N. and Shackleton, V. (1986) Recruitment and Selection: A Review of Developments in the 1980s, *Personnel Review*, 15, pp. 19–26.

Anderson, N. and Shackleton, V. (1993) *Successful Selection Interviewing*, Oxford: Blackwell.

Anderson, R.J., Hughes, J.A. and Sharrock, W.W. (1985) *The Sociology Game: An Introduction to Sociological Reasoning*, London: Longman.

Anderson, R.J., Hughes, J.A. and Sharrock, W.W. (eds) (1987) *Classic Disputes in Sociology*, London: Allen and Unwin.

Andreski, S. (1974) *Sociology as Sorcery*, Harmondsworth: Penguin.

Antal, A.B. and Izraeli, D.N. (1993) A Global Comparison of Women in Management: Women Managers in Their Homelands and as Expatriates, in E.A. Fagenson (ed.) *Women in Management: Trends, Issues and Challenges in Managerial Diversity*, Thousand Oaks, CA: Sage, pp. 52–96.

Ashkenas, R., Ulrich, D., Jick, T. and Kerr, S. (1995) *The Boundaryless Organization*, San Francisco: Jossey-Bass.

Bacharach, S. and Lawler, E.J. (1980) *Power and Politics in Organizations*, San Francisco: Jossey-Bass.

Bailey, C. (1975) Neutrality and Rationality in Teaching, in D. Bridges and P. Scrimshaw (eds) *Values and Authority in Schools*, London: Hodder and Stoughton, pp. 121–34.

Barlow, G. (1989) Deficiencies and the Perpetuation of Power: Latent Functions in Management Appraisal, *Journal of Management Studies*, 26, pp. 499–517.

Bartholomew, S. and Adler, N.J. (1996) Building Networks and Crossing Borders: The Dynamics of Knowledge Generation in a Transnational World, in P. Joynt and M. Warner (eds) *Managing Across Cultures: Issues and Perspectives*, London: Thomson, pp. 7–32.

Bartlett, C.A. and Ghoshal, S. (1989) *Managing Across Borders: The Transnational Solution*, Boston, MA: Harvard Business School Press.

Bass, B.M. (1990) *Bass and Stogdill's Handbook of Leadership: Theory, Research and Managerial Applications*, New York: Free Press.

Beals, R.L. and Hoijer, H. (1971) *An Introduction to Anthropology*, New York: Macmillan.

Beatty, R.P. and Zajac, E.J. (1987) CEO Change and Firm Performance in Large Corporations: Succession Effects and Manager Effects, *Strategic Management Journal*, 8, pp. 305–17.

Benn, S.I. and Mortimer, G.W. (1976) *Rationality and the Social Sciences*, London: Routledge and Kegan Paul.

Berger, P. (1967) *The Sacred Canopy*, New York: Doubleday.

Berger, P. and Luckmann, T. (1963) Sociology of Religion and Sociology of Knowledge, *Sociology and Social Research*, 47, pp. 417–27.

Berger, P. and Luckmann, T. (1967) *The Social Construction of Reality*, Harmondsworth: Penguin.

Berggren, C. and Nomura, M. (1997) *The Resilience of Corporate Japan: New Competitive Strategies and Personnel Practices*, London: Paul Chapman.

Billing, Y.D. and Alvesson, M. (1994) *Gender, Managers and Organizations*, Berlin: de Gruyter.

Bonis, J. (1972) Organization and Environment, *International Studies of Management and Organization*, Fall, pp. 314–43.

Bottomore, T. and Rubel, M. (1963) *Karl Marx: Selected Writings in Sociology and Social Philosophy*, Harmondsworth: Penguin.

Bowles, M. (1989) Myth, Meaning and Work Organization, *Organization Studies*, 10 (3), pp. 405–21.

Bowles, M. (1997) The Myth of Management: Direction and Failure in Contemporary Organizations, *Human Relations*, 50 (7), pp. 779–803.

Bowman, G.W. (1964) What Helps or Harms Promotability?, *Harvard Business Review*, 42, pp. 6–26, 184–96.

Boyatzis, R.E. (1982) *The Competent Manager*, New York: Wiley.

Braverman, H. (1974) *Labor and Monopoly Capital*, New York: Monthly Review Press.

Breasted, J.H. (1909) *A History of Egypt*, London: Hodder and Stoughton.

Breeze, J.D. (1985) Harvest from the Archives: The Search for Fayol and Carlioz, *Journal of Management*, 11, pp. 43–54.

Brodie, M.B. (1967) *Fayol on Administration*, London: Lyon, Grant & Green.

Brookfield, S. (1987) *Developing Critical Thinkers*, Milton Keynes: Open University Press.

Brown, A. (1998) *Organizational Culture*, London: Pitman.

Brown, M.C. (1982) Administrative Succession and Organizational Performance: The Succession Effect, *Administrative Science Quarterly*, 27, pp. 1–16.

Brown, S. (1995) *Postmodern Marketing*, London: Routledge.

Browne, K. (1995) Sex and Temperament in Modern Society: A Darwinian View of the Glass Ceiling and the Gender Gap, *Arizona Law Review*, 37, pp. 971–1106.

Browne, K. (1998a) An Evolutionary Account of Women's Workplace Status, *Managerial and Decision Economics*, 19, pp. 427–40.

Browne, K. (1998b) *Divided Labours: An Evolutionary View of Women at Work*, London: Weidenfeld and Nicolson.

Brubaker, R. (1984) *The Limits of Rationality: An Essay on the Social and Moral Thought of Max Weber*, London: George Allen and Unwin.

Bruce-Briggs, B. (1982) The Dangerous Folly Called Theory Z, *Fortune*, May 17, pp. 41–4.

Bryman, A. (1986) *Leadership and Organizations*, London: Routledge and Kegan Paul.

Buchanan, D.A. and Huczynski, A.A. (1985) *Organizational Behaviour: An Introductory Text*, Englewood Cliffs, New Jersey: Prentice-Hall.

Buckley, P.J. and Mirza, H. (1985) The Wit and Wisdom of Japanese Management, *Management International Review*, 25, pp. 16–32.

Burgoyne, J.G. and Stuart, R. (1976) The Nature, Use and Acquisition of Managerial Skills and Other Attributes, *Personnel Review*, 5, pp. 19–29.

Burns, T. (1955) The Reference of Conduct in Small Groups, *Human Relations*, 8, pp. 467–86.

Burns, T. and Stalker, G.M. (1961) *The Management of Innovation*, London: Tavistock.

Burrell, G. and Morgan, G. (1979) *Sociological Paradigms and Organizational Analysis*, Aldershot: Gower.

Callinicos, A. (1989) *Against Postmodernism: A Marxist Critique*, Cambridge: Polity Press.

Carlson, S. (1951) *Executive Behaviour: A Study of the Work Load and Working Methods of Managing Directors*, Stockholm: Strombergs.

Carlyle, T. (1841) *On Heroes, Hero Worship and the Heroic in History*, Chicago and New York: Belford, Clarke and Co.

Carpenter, E. and McLuhan, M. (1960) *Explorations in Communication*, London: Cape.

Carr, W. and Kemmis, S. (1986) *Becoming Critical: Education, Knowledge and Action Research*, London: Falmer Press.

Carroll, D.T. (1983) A Disappointing Search for Excellence, *Harvard Business Review*, November–December, pp. 78–88.

Carroll, S.J. and Gillen, D.J. (1987) Are the Classical Management Functions Useful in Describing Managerial Work?, *Academy of Management Review*, 12, pp. 38–51.

Casti, J.L. (1992) *Searching for Certainty*, London: Scribners.

Chalmers, A.F. (1996) *What Is This Thing Called Science? An Assessment of the Nature and Status of Science and Its Methods*, Milton Keynes: Open University Press.

Child, J. (1969) *British Management Thought*, London: George Allen and Unwin.

Child, J. (1974) What Determines Organization Performance? The Universals vs. the It-All-Depends, *Organizational Dynamics*, Summer, pp. 2–18.

Child, J. (1977, 1984) *Organization: A Guide to Problems and Practice*, London: Harper and Row.

Child, J. (1981) Culture, Contingency and Capitalism in the Cross-national Study of Organizations, in L.L. Cummings and B.M. Staw (eds) *Research in Organizational Behaviour*, Vol. 3, Greenwich, CT: JAI Press, pp. 303–56.

Chorafas, D.N. (1988) *Membership of the Board of Directors: The Job Top Executives Want No More*, Basingstoke: Macmillan.

Clark, D.G. (1966) *The Industrial Manager: His Background and Career Pattern*, London: Business Publications.

Clark, R.C. (1979) *The Japanese Company*, New Haven, CT: Yale University Press.

Clegg, S. and Dunkerley, D. (1980) *Organization, Class and Control*, London: Routledge and Kegan Paul.

Clements, R.V. (1958) *Managers: A Study of Their Careers in Industry*, London: George Allen and Unwin.

Cleverley, G. (1971) *Managers and Magic*, London: Longman.

Coates, C.H. and Pellegrin, R.J. (1957–58) Executives and Supervisors: Informal Factors in Differential Bureaucratic Promotion, *Administrative Science Quarterly*, 2, pp. 200–15.

Cohen, M.D., March, J.G. and Olsen, J.P. (1972), A Garbage Can Model of Organizational Choice, *Administrative Science Quarterly*, 17, pp. 1–25.

Cohen, S. (1987) *Folk Devils and Moral Panics*, Oxford: Basil Blackwell.

Collingwood, H. (2001) Management Theory – or Theology? *Harvard Business Review*, 79 (8), pp. 24, 26.

Collins, D. (2000) *Management Fads and Buzzwords*, London: Routledge.

Collins, R.K. (1982) *Sociological Insight: An Introduction to Non-obvious Sociology*, New York: Oxford University Press.

Collinson, D.L. (1988) *Barriers to Fair Selection: A Multi-Sector Study of Recruitment Practices*, London: HMSO.

Collinson, D.L. (1990) *Managing to Discriminate*, London: Routledge.

Connell, R.W. (1995) *Masculinities*, Cambridge: Polity Press.

Constable, J. and McCormick, R. (1987) *The Making of British Managers*, London: BIM/CBI.

Cooper, A. (1989) Theorizing Gender, in I. Reid and E. Stratta (eds) *Sex Differences in Britain*, Aldershot: Gower, pp. 13–44.

Copeman, G.H. (1955) *Leaders of British Industry*, London: Gee and Co.

Covey, S.R. (1989) *The Seven Habits of Highly Effective People: Powerful Lessons in Personal Change*, New York: Simon and Schuster.

Crompton, R. (1997) *Women and Work in Modern Britain*, Oxford: Oxford University Press.

Cuff, E.C. and Payne, G.C.F. (eds) (1979) *Perspectives in Sociology*, London: George Allen and Unwin.

Cuff, E.C., Sharrock, W.W. and Francis, D.W. (1998) *Perspectives in Sociology*, London: Routledge.

Cully, M., Woodland, S., O'Reilly, A. and Dix, G. (1999) *Britain at Work: As Depicted by the 1998 Workplace Employee Relations Survey*, London: Routledge.

Cyert, R.M. and March, J.G. (1963) *A Behavioural Theory of the Firm*, Englewood Cliffs, New Jersey: Prentice-Hall.

Daft, R.L. (2001) *Organization Theory and Design*, Cincinnati, OH: South-Western.

Dahl, R.A. (1957) The Concept of Power, *Behavioral Science*, 2, pp. 201–5.

Daily, C.M., Certo, S.T. and Dalton, D.R. (1999) A Decade of Corporate Women: Some Progress in the Boardroom, *None* in the Executive Suite, *Strategic Management Journal*, 20, pp. 93–9.

Dalton, M. (1951) Informal Factors in Career Achievement, *American Journal of Sociology*, 56, pp. 407–15.

Dalton, M. (1959) *Men Who Manage*, New York: Wiley.

Danieli, A. and Thomas, A.B. (1999) What About the Workers? Studying the Work of Management Teachers and Their Orientations to Management Education, *Management Learning*, 30 (4), pp. 449–71.

Davidow, W.H. and Malone, M.S. (1992) *The Virtual Corporation: Structuring and Revitalizing the Corporation for the 21st Century*, New York: HarperCollins.

Davis, J., Kerr, S. and Von Glinow, M.A. (1987) Is the Japanese Management Craze Over? *International Journal of Management*, 4, pp. 486–95.

Davis, M.S. (1986) 'That's Classic!' The Phenomenology and Rhetoric of Successful Social Theories, *Philosophy of Social Science*, 16, pp. 285–301.

Davis, R. (1951) *The Fundamentals of Top Management*, New York: Harper and Row.

Davis, W. (1987) *The Innovators: The Essential Guide to Business Thinkers, Achievers and Entrepreneurs*, London: Ebury Press.

Dearden, R.F. (1981) Controversial Issues and the Curriculum, *Journal of Curriculum Studies*, 13, pp. 37–44.

Dennis, N., Henriques, F. and Slaughter, C. (1969) *Coal is Our Life*, London: Tavistock.

Dicken, P. (1998) *Global Shift*, London: Paul Chapman.

Dore, R.P. (1973) *British Factory, Japanese Factory*, London: Allen and Unwin.

Dore, R.P. (1984) The 'Learn from Japan' Boom, *Speaking of Japan*, 5, pp. 16–24.

Drucker, P.F. (1955) *The Practice of Management*, London: Heinemann.

Drucker, P.F. (1971) What Can We Learn from Japanese Management? *Harvard Business Review*, 49, pp. 110–22.

Dunphy, D.C. (1987) Convergence/divergence: A Temporal Review of the Japanese Enterprise and its Management, *Academy of Management Review*, 12, pp. 445–59.

Economist, The (1997) Instant Coffee as Management Theory, January 25, p. 83.

Economist, The (2000) The New Economy, September 23, pp. 5–52.

Eden, C. and Huxham, C. (1996) Action Research for Management Research, *British Journal of Management*, 7, pp. 75–86.

Edwards, R. (1979) *Contested Terrain*, London: Heinemann.

Eitzen, D.S. and Yetman, N.R. (1972), Managerial Change, Longevity and Organizational Effectiveness, *Administrative Science Quarterly*, 17, pp. 110–16.

Eldridge, J., Cressey, P. and MacInnes, J. (1991) *Industrial Sociology and Economic Crisis*, Hemel Hempstead: Harvester Wheatsheaf.

Farnham, A. (1996) In Search of Suckers, *Fortune*, 134 (7), pp. 78–84.

Fausto-Sterling, A. (1992) *Myths of Gender: Biological Theories About Men and Women*, New York: Basic Books.

Fayol, H. (1916) Administration, industrielle et générale, *Bulletin of the Societé de l'Industrie Minérale*.

Fayol, H. (1949) *General and Industrial Management*, trans. Constance Storrs, London: Pitman.

Federal Glass Ceiling Commission (1995) *Good for Business: Making Full Use of the Nation's Human Capital: Fact Finding Report of the Federal Glass Ceiling Commission*, Washington, DC: Government Printing Office.

Ferguson, K.E. (1984) *The Feminist Case Against Bureaucracy*, Philadelphia, PA: Temple University Press.

Ferris, G.R. and King, T.R. (1991) Politics in Human Resources Decisions: A Walk on the Dark Side, *Organizational Dynamics*, 20, pp. 59–73.

Filley, A.C., House, R.J. and Kerr, S. (1976) *Managerial Process and Organizational Behavior*, Glenview, IL: Scott Foresman.

Fincham, R. (1996) Management as Magic: Reengineering and the Search for Business Salvation, paper presented at the Fourteenth International Labour Process Conference, Lancashire Business School.

Fincham, R. and Rhodes, P. (1999) *Principles of Organizational Behaviour*, Oxford: Oxford University Press.

Florence, P.S. (1961) *The Logic of British and American Industry*, London: Routledge and Kegan Paul.

Frank, T. (2000) *One Market Under God*, New York: Doubleday.

Freedley, E.T. (1853) *A Practical Treatise on Business*, London: Thomas Bosworth.

Freeman, J. (1986) Data Quality and the Development of Organizational Social Science, *Administrative Science Quarterly*, 31, pp. 298–303.

Friedman, A.L. (1977) *Industry and Labour*, London: Macmillan.

Galbraith, J.K. (1967) *The New Industrial State*, Boston: Houghton Mifflin.

Gamson, W.A. and Scotch, N.A. (1964) Scapegoating in Baseball, *American Journal of Sociology*, 70, pp. 69–72.

Gardner, P. (1984) Another Look at Controversial Issues and the Curriculum, *Journal of Curriculum Studies*, 16, pp. 379–85.

Gerlach, M. (1992) *Alliance Capitalism: The Social Organization of Japanese Business*, Berkeley, CA: University of California Press.

Gibney, F.B. (1981) Now It's Time to Imitate the Japanese, *Pacific Basin Quarterly*, 6, pp. 17–18.

Giddens, A. (1974) Elites in the British Class Structure, in P. Stanworth and A. Giddens (eds) *Elites and Power in British Society*, London: Cambridge University Press, pp. 1–21.

Giddens, A. (1989) *Sociology*, Cambridge: Polity Press.

Giddens, A. (1990) *The Consequences of Modernity*, Cambridge: Polity Press.

Giddens, A. (1991) *Modernity and Self-identity*, Cambridge: Polity Press.

Giddens, A. (2001) *Sociology*, Cambridge: Polity Press.

Gill, D. (1980a) *Selecting Managers: How British Industry Recruits*, London: IPM/BIM.

Gill, D. (1980b) How British Industry Selects its Managers, *Personnel Management*, September, pp. 49–52.

Gimpl, M.L. and Dakin, S.R. (1984) Management and Magic, *California Management Review*, 27, pp. 125–36.

Gioia, D.A. and Longenecker, C.O. (1994) Delving into the Dark Side: The Politics of Executive Appraisal, *Organizational Dynamics*, 22 (3), pp. 47–58.

Glyn, A. and Sutcliffe, B. (1992) Global but Leaderless? The New Capitalist Order, in R. Miliband and L. Panitch (eds) *New World Order: The Socialist Register*, London: Merlin Press, pp. 76–95.

Goffee, R. and Jones, G. (2000) Why Should Anyone Be Led by You? *Harvard Business Review*, September–October, pp. 63–70.

Goldberg, S. (1974) *The Inevitability of Patriarchy*, New York: Morrow.

Goldberg, S. (1993) *Why Men Rule: A Theory of Male Dominance*, Chicago: Open Court.

Goldsmith, W. and Clutterbuck, D. (1984) *The Winning Streak*, London: Weidenfeld and Nicolson.

Gordon, G.E. and Rosen, N. (1981) Critical Factors in Leadership Succession, *Organizational Behaviour and Human Performance*, 27, pp. 227–54.

Gowler, D. and Legge, K. (1986) Personnel and Paradigms: Four Perspectives on the Future, *Industrial Relations Journal*, 17, pp. 225–35.

Gray, J. (1993) *Men Are from Mars, Women Are from Venus*, New York: Harper Collins.

Grint, K. (1997) *Fuzzy Management: Contemporary Ideas and Practices*, London: Oxford University Press.

Grint, K. (2000) *The Arts of Leadership*, Oxford: Oxford University Press.

Groth, L. (1999) *Future Organizational Design: The Scope for the IT-based Enterprise*, Chichester: John Wiley.

Grusky, O. (1960) Administrative Succession in Formal Organizations, *Social Forces*, 39, pp. 105–15.

Grusky, O. (1963) Managerial Succession, *American Journal of Sociology*, 69, pp. 72–6.

Guest, D. and Mackenzie, K. (1996) Don't Write Off the Traditional Career, *People Management*, February, pp. 22–5.

Hague, D.C. (1971) *Managerial Economics*, London: Longman.

Hakim, C. (2000) *Research Design: Successful Designs for Social and Economic Research*, London: Routledge.

Hales, C.P. (1986) What Do Managers Do? A Critical Review of the Evidence, *Journal of Management Studies*, 23, pp. 88–115.

Hales, C.P. (1999) Why Do Managers Do What They Do? Reconciling Evidence and Theory in Accounts of Managerial Work, *British Journal of Management*, 10, pp. 335–50.

Hall, R.H. (1977, 1987) *Organizations: Structures, Processes and Outcomes*, Englewood Cliffs, New Jersey: Prentice-Hall.

Hall, R.H. (2002) *Organizations: Structures, Processes and Outcomes*, Upper Saddle River, NJ: Prentice-Hall.

Hammer, M. (1990) Reengineering Work: Don't Automate, Obliterate, *Harvard Business Review*, 67 (4), pp. 104–12.

Handal, G. and Lauvas, P. (1987) *Promoting Reflective Teaching: Supervision in Action*, Milton Keynes: Open University Press.

Handy, C.B. (1987) *The Making of Managers: A Report on Management Education, Training and Development in the USA, West Germany, France, Japan and the UK*, London: NEDO.

Handy, C.B. (1993) *Understanding Organizations*, Harmondsworth: Penguin.

Hannan, M.T. and Freeman, J. (1984) Structural Inertia and Organizational Change, *American Sociological Review*, 49, pp. 149–64.

Harper, S.C. (1988) Now That the Dust Has Settled: Learning from Japanese Management, *Business Horizons*, July–August, pp. 43–51.

Harvey, B., Smith, S. and Wilkinson, B. (1984) *Managers and Corporate Social Policy: Private Solutions to Public Problems*, London: Macmillan.

Hayes, R.H. (1981) Why Japanese Factories Work, *Harvard Business Review*, 59, pp. 56–66.

Hearn, J. and Parkin, W. (1988) Women, Men and Leadership: A Critical Review of Assumptions, Practices, and Change in the Industrialized Nations, in N.J. Adler and D.N. Izraeli (eds) *Women in Management Worldwide*, Armonk, NY: M.E. Sharpe, pp. 17–40.

Held, D., McGrew, A., Goldblatt, D. and Perraton, J. (eds) (1999) *Global Transformation*, Cambridge: Polity Press.

Heller, R. (1967) Britain's Top Directors, *Management Today*, March, pp. 62–5.

Heller, R. (1970) Britain's Boardroom Anatomy, *Management Today*, September, pp. 83–5.

Heller, R. (1973) The State of British Boardrooms, *Management Today*, May, pp. 81–3.

Hersey, P. and Blanchard, K.H. (1977) *Management of Organizational Behaviour: Utilizing Human Resources*, Englewood Cliffs, New Jersey: Prentice-Hall.

Hickson, D.J. and Pugh, D.S. (2001) *Management Worldwide: Distinctive Styles Amid Globalization*, London: Penguin.

Hirschmeier, J. and Yui, T. (1981) *The Development of Japanese Business*, London: Allen and Unwin.

Hirst, P. and Thompson, G. (1996) *Globalization in Question*, Cambridge: Polity Press.

Hofstede, G. (1980a) *Culture's Consequences: International Differences in Work-Related Values*, Beverly Hills, CA: Sage.

Hofstede, G. (1980b) Motivation, Leadership and Organization: Do American Theories Apply Abroad? *Organizational Dynamics*, Summer, pp. 42–63.

Hofstede, G. (1999) Problems Remain but Theories Will Change: The Universal and the Specific in 21st-century Global Management, *Organizational Dynamics*, 28 (1), pp. 34–44.

Hofstede, G. and Bond, M. (1988) The Confucius Connection: from Cultural Roots to Economic Growth, *Organizational Dynamics*, 16 (4), pp. 4–21.

Holmes, R. (1985) *Firing Line*, London: Jonathan Cape.

Holton, V. (1995) Women on the Boards of Britain's Top 200 Companies, *Women in Management Review*, 10 (3), pp. 16–20.

Holton, V., Rabbetts, J. and Scrivener, S. (1995) Women on the Boards of Britain's Top 200 Companies: a Progress Report, *The Occupational Psychologist*, 24, pp. 3–17.

Hu, Y-S. (1996) Globalization and Corporate Nationality, in M. Warner (ed) *International Encyclopedia of Business and Management*, London: Routledge, pp. 1664–72.

Huczynski, A.A. (1993) *Management Gurus: What Makes Them and How to Become One*, London: Routledge.

Hudson, L. (1972) *The Cult of the Fact*, London: Jonathan Cape.

Hughes, J. and Steiner, R. (2001) Public Schools Lose Hold on Industry, *Sunday Times*, December 16, p. 7.

Hult, M. and Lennung, S. (1980) Towards a Definition of Action Research: A Note and Bibliography, *Journal of Management Studies*, 17, pp. 241–50.

Hunt, J. (1979) *Managing People at Work*, London: McGraw-Hill.

Institute of Management/Remuneration Economics (1998) *National Management Salary Survey*, London: Institute of Management/Remuneration Economics.

International Labour Organization (2000) *Yearbook of Labour Statistics*, Geneva: ILO.

Izraeli, D. (1977) 'Settling-In': An Interactionist Perspective on the Entry of the New Manager, *Pacific Sociological Review*, 20, pp. 135–59.

Jackall, R. (1989) *Moral Mazes: The World of Corporate Managers*, New York: Oxford University Press.

Jackson, B. (2001) *Management Gurus and Management Fashions: A Dramatistic Inquiry*, London: Routledge.

Jackson, N. and Carter, P. (2000) *Rethinking Organizational Behaviour*, Harlow: Pearson.

Jacobs, D. and Singell, L. (1993) Leadership and Organizational Performance: Isolating Links Between Managers and Collective Success, *Social Science Research*, 22, pp. 165–89.

Jacobs, R. (1989) *Assessing Management Competencies*, Berkhamstead: Ashridge Management Research Group.

James, T.G.H. (1985) *Pharaoh's People: Scenes from Life in Imperial Egypt*, Oxford: Oxford University Press.

Jamieson, I. (1980) *Capitalism and Culture: A Comparative Analysis of British and American Manufacturing Organizations,* Aldershot: Gower.

Japan External Trade Organization (JETRO) (1981) *The Actual Conditions of the Japanese Company in the United States*, Tokyo: JETRO.

Kahn, H. (1970) *The Emerging Japanese Superstate*, Harmondsworth: Penguin.

Kakabadse, A. (1983) *The Politics of Management*, Aldershot: Gower.

Kanter, R.M. (1977) *Men and Women of the Corporation*, New York: Basic Books.

Kanter, R.M. (1991) Transcending Business Boundaries: 12,000 World Managers View Change, *Harvard Business Review*, 69 (3), pp. 151–64.

Kanter, R.M. (1995) *World Class: Thriving Locally in the Global Economy*, New York: Simon and Schuster.

Karr, A. (1849) *Les Guepes*, January, vi.

Kassem, M.S. (1978) Tolstoy on Organization, *Management International Review*, 18, pp. 7–14.

Katz, D. and Kahn, R.L. (1978) *The Social Psychology of Organizations*, New York: John Wiley.

Keegan, J. (1976) *The Face of Battle*, London: Jonathan Cape.

Kemmis, S. (1981) Research Approaches and Methods: Action Research, in D. Anderson and C. Blackers (eds) *Transition from School: An Exploration of Research and Policy*, Canberra: Australian National University Press.

Kerr, C., Dunlop, J.T., Harbison, F.H. and Myers, C.A. (1960) *Industrialism and Industrial Man*, Cambridge, MA: Harvard University Press.

Kets de Vries, M. (1996) Leaders Who Make a Difference, *European Management Journal*, 14 (5), pp. 486–93.

Keys, J.B. and Miller, T.R. (1984) The Japanese Management Theory Jungle, *Academy of Management Review*, 9, pp. 342–53.

Kingston, N. (1971) *Selecting Managers: A Survey of Current Practice in 200 Companies*, London: BIM.

Klein, L. (1976) *A Social Scientist in Industry*, London: Gower.

Klein, L. and Eason, K. (1991) *Putting Social Science to Work: The Ground Between Theory and Use Explored Through Case Studies in Organizations*, Cambridge: Cambridge University Press.

Knights, D. and Raffo, C. (1990) Milkround Professionalism in Personnel Recruitment: Myth or Reality? *Personnel Review*, 19, pp. 28–37.

Knights, D. and Willmott, H. (2002) *Organizational Analysis: A Critical Text*, London: Thomson.

Kono, T. (1984) *Strategy and Structure of Japanese Enterprises*, London: Macmillan.

Koontz, H. (1961) The Management Theory Jungle, *Journal of the Academy of Management*, 4, pp. 174–88.

Koontz, H. (1980) The Management Theory Jungle Revisited, *Academy of Management Review*, 5, pp. 175–87.

Koontz, H. and O'Donnell, C. (1974) *Essentials of Management*, New York: McGraw-Hill.

Kotter, J.P. (1982a) General Managers are not Generalists, *Organizational Dynamics*, Spring, pp. 5–19.

Kotter, J.P. (1982b) *The General Managers*, New York: Free Press.

Kuhn, T.S. (1962) *The Structure of Scientific Revolutions*, Chicago: University of Chicago Press.

Kumar, K. (1978) *Prophecy and Progress: The Sociology of Industrial and Post-Industrial Society*, Harmondsworth: Penguin.

Latour, B. (1993) *We Never Were Modern*, New York: Harvester Wheatsheaf.

Lawler, E.E. (1985) Challenging Traditional Research Assumptions, in E.E. Lawler and Associates, *Doing Research That Is Useful for Theory and Practice*, San Francisco: Jossey-Bass, pp. 1–17.

Lawrence, P. (1986) *Invitation to Management*, Oxford: Basil Blackwell.

Lawrence, P. (1996) *Management in the USA*, London: Sage.

Lawrence, P.R. and Lorsch, J.W. (1967), *Organization and Environment*, Cambridge, MA: Harvard Business School.

Lee, R.A. (1985a) The Theory and Practice of Promotion Processes: Part One, *Leadership and Organization Development Journal*, 6 (2), pp. 3–21.

Lee, R.A. (1985b) The Theory and Practice of Promotion Processes: Part Two, *Leadership and Organization Development Journal*, 6 (4), pp. 17–21.

Lee, R.A. and Piper, J. (1988) Dimensions of Promotion Culture in Midland Bank, *Personnel Review*, 17, pp. 17–24.

Leggatt, T. (1978) Managers in Industry: Their Backgrounds and Education, *Sociological Review*, 26, pp. 807–25.

Leontiades, J.C. (2001) *Managing the Global Enterprise: Competing in the Information Age*, Harlow: Pearson.

Levitt, T. (1983) The Globalization of Markets, *Harvard Business Review,* 83 (3), pp. 92–102.

Lewin, K. (1946) Action Research and Minority Problems, *Journal of Social Issues*, 2, pp. 34–46.

Lieberson, S. and O'Connor, J.F. (1972) Leadership and Organizational Performance: A Study of Large Corporations, *American Sociological Review*, 37, pp. 117–30.

Liker, J.K., Fruin, W.M. and Adler, P.S. (eds) (1999) *Remade in America: Transplanting and Transforming Japanese Management Systems*, New York: Oxford University Press.

Littler, C.R. and Salaman, G. (1984) *Class at Work: The Design, Allocation and Control of Jobs*, London: Batsford.

Loewe, M. (1968) *Everyday Life in Early Imperial China*, London: Batsford.

Lupton, T. (1966) *Management and the Social Sciences*, London: Lyon, Grant & Green.

Lupton, T. (1971, 1983) *Management and the Social Sciences*, Harmondsworth: Penguin.

Lupton, T. (1984) The Functions and Organization of University Business Schools, in A. Kakabadse and S. Mukhi (eds) *The Future of Management Education*, Aldershot: Gower, pp. 203–17.

Lussato, B. (1976) *A Critical Introduction to Organization Theory*, London: Macmillan.

Luthans, F. (1977) *Organizational Behaviour*, Tokyo: McGraw-Hill Kogakusha.

Luthans, F. (1988) Successful vs. Effective Real Managers, *Academy of Management Executive*, 2 (2), pp. 127–32.

Luthans, F., Hodgetts, R.M. and Rosenkrantz, S.A. (1988) *Real Managers*, Cambridge, MA: Ballinger.

Lyon, D. (2000) Post-modernity, in G. Browning, A. Halcli and F. Webster (eds) *Understanding Contemporary Society*, London: Sage, pp. 221–35.

Lyotard, J.-F. (1979) *The Postmodern Condition: A Report on Knowledge*, trans. G. Bennington and B. Massumi, Manchester: Manchester University Press.

Mahoney, T.A., Jerdee, T.H. and Carroll, S.J. (1963) *Development of Managerial Performance: A Research Approach*, Cincinnati: South-Western.

Makridakis, S. (1996) Forecasting: Its Role and Value for Planning and Strategy, *International Journal of Forecasting*, 12, pp. 513–37.

Malinowski, B. (1982) *'Magic, Science and Religion'; and Other Essays*, London: Souvenir Press.

March, J.G. and Simon, H.A. (1958) *Organizations*, New York: John Wiley.

Margetts, J. (ed) (1991) *Who's Who in Industry*, London: Fulcrum.

Marshall, J. (1984) *Women Managers:Travellers in a Male World*, Chichester: Wiley.

Marshall, S.L.A. (1947) *Men Against Fire*, New York: William Morrow.

Martin, J. and Siehl, C. (1983) Organizational Culture and Counterculture: An Uneasy Symbiosis, *Organizational Dynamics*, Autumn, pp. 52–64.

Marwick, A. (1981) *The Nature of History*, London: Macmillan.

Marx, K. (1867) *Capital*, Vol. 1, Hamburg.

Massie, J.L. (1965) Management Theory, in J.G. March (ed.) *Handbook of Organizations*, Chicago: Rand-McNally, pp. 387–422.

McGivering, I.C., Matthews, D.G.J. and Scott, W.H. (1960) *Management in Britain: A General Characterization*, Liverpool: Liverpool University Press.

Meehan, E.J. (1969) *Value Judgment and Social Science*, Homewood, IL: Dorsey Press.

Meindl, J.R. and Ehrlich, S.B. (1987) The Romance of Leadership and the Evaluation of Organizational Performance, *Academy of Management Journal*, 30, pp. 91–109.

Meyer, J.W. and Rowan, B. (1977) Institutionalised Organizations: Formal Structure as Myth and Ceremony, *American Journal of Sociology*, 83, pp. 340–63.

Micklethwait, J. and Wooldridge, A. (1997) *The Witch Doctors: What the Management Gurus Are Saying, Why It Matters and How to Make Sense of It*, London: Mandarin.

Miller, T.R. and Vaughan, B.J. (2001) Messages from the Management Past: Classic Writers and Contemporary Problems, *SAM Advanced Management Journal*, 66 (1), pp. 4–11, 20.

Mills, C.W. (1956) *The Power Elite*, Oxford: Oxford University Press.

Mills, C.W. (1970) *The Sociological Imagination*, Harmondsworth: Penguin.

Miner, J.B. (1975) The Uncertain Future of the Leadership Concept: An Overview, in J.G. Hunt and L.L. Larsen (eds) *Leadership Frontiers*, Kent, OH: Comparative Administration Research Institute, Kent State University, pp. 197–208.

Mintzberg, H. (1973) *The Nature of Managerial Work*, New York: Harper and Row.

Mintzberg, H. (1975) The Manager's Job: Folklore and Fact, *Harvard Business Review*, 53, pp. 49–61.

Mintzberg, H. (1983) *Power In and Around Organizations*, Englewood Cliffs, New Jersey: Prentice-Hall.

Mintzberg, H. (1994) Rounding Out the Manager's Job, *Sloan Management Review*, 36 (1), pp. 11–26.

Mooney, J.D. and Reiley, A.C. (1939) *The Principles of Organization*, New York: Harper and Row.

Moore, S. (2001) *The Mail on Sunday*, 1 July, p. 31.

Morgan, G. (1989) *Riding the Waves of Change: Developing Managerial Competencies for a Turbulent World*, Oxford: Jossey-Bass.

Morgan, G. (1997) *Images of Organization*, Beverly Hills, CA: Sage.

Morishima, M. (1982) *Why Has Japan 'Succeeded'?* Cambridge: Cambridge University Press.

Morris, J., Munday, M. and Wilkinson, B. (1993) *Working for the Japanese: The Economic and Social Consequences of Japanese Investment in Wales,* London: Athlone Press.

Mouzelis, N. (1967) *Organization and Bureaucracy*, London: Routledge and Kegan Paul.

Mroczkowski, T. and Hanaoka, M. (1998) The End of Japanese Management: How Soon? *Human Resource Planning*, 21 (3), pp. 20–30.

Murray, V. and Gandz, J. (1980) Games Executives Play: Politics at Work, *Business Horizons*, December, pp. 11–23.

National Industrial Conference Board (1954), *Company Organization Charts*, New York: NICB.

Negandhi, A.R., Eshghi, G.S. and Yuen, E.C. (1985) The Management Practices of Japanese Subsidiaries Overseas, *California Management Review*, 27, pp. 93–105.

Newell, H. and Dopson, S. (1996) Muddle in the Middle: Organizational Restructuring and Middle Management Careers, *Personnel Review*, 25 (4), pp. 4–20.

Nicholson, N. (1996) Career Systems in Crisis: Change and Opportunity in the Information Age, *Academy of Management Executive*, 10 (4), pp. 40–51.

Nicholson, N. (1998) How Hardwired is Human Behaviour? *Harvard Business Review*, July–August, pp, 135–47.

Nicholson, N. (2000) *Managing the Human Animal*, London: Texere.

Nonaka, I. and Johansson, J.K. (1985) Japanese Management: What About the 'Hard' Skills? *Academy of Management Review*, 10, pp. 181–91.

Numagami, T. (1998) The Infeasibility of Invariant Laws in Management Studies: A Reflective Dialogue in Defence of Case Studies, *Organization Science*, 9 (1), pp. 2–15.

Offe, C. (1976) *Industry and Inequality*, London: Edward Arnold.

Ohmae, K. (1990) *The Borderless World: Power and Strategy in the Interlinked Economy*, London: Collins.

Olins, R. and Steiner, R. (1997) Who Runs British Business? *Sunday Times*, October 12, pp. 8–9.

Oliver, N. and Wilkinson, B. (1988) *The Japanization of British Industry*, Oxford: Basil Blackwell.

Osterman, P. (ed.) (1996) *Broken Ladders: Managerial Careers in the New Economy*, New York: Oxford University Press.

Ouchi, W.G. (1981) *Theory Z: How American Business Can Meet the Japanese Challenge*, Reading, MA: Addison-Wesley.

Pahl, J.M. and Pahl, R.E. (1971) *Managers and Their Wives: A Study of Career and Family Relationships in the Middle Class*, Harmondsworth: Penguin.

Pahl, R.E. and Winkler, J.T. (1974) The Economic Elite: Theory and Practice, in P. Stanworth and A. Giddens (eds) *Elites and Power in British Society*, London: Cambridge University Press, pp. 102–22.

Parker, S.R., Brown, R.K., Child, J. and Smith, M.A. (1977) *The Sociology of Industry*, London: George Allen and Unwin.

Pascale, R.T. and Athos, A.G. (1981) *The Art of Japanese Management: Applications for American Executives*, New York: Simon and Schuster.

Pascale, R.T. and McGuire, M.A. (1980) Comparison of Selected Work Factors in Japan and the United States, *Human Relations*, 33, pp. 433–55.

Pasmore, W.A. (1988) *Designing Effective Organizations: the Sociotechnical Systems Perspective*, New York: John Wiley.

Pateman, C. (1988) *The Sexual Contract*, Cambridge: Polity Press.

Pease, A. and Pease, B. (2001) *Why Men Don't Listen and Women Can't Read Maps*, New York: Orion.

Peters, M. and Robinson, V. (1984) The Origins and Status of Action Research, *Journal of Applied Behavioral Science*, 20, pp. 113–24.

Peters, T.J. (1987) *Thriving on Chaos: Handbook for a Management Revolution*, London: Guild.

Peters, T.J. (2000) Endorsement of J. Micklethwait and A. Wooldridge, *A Future Perfect: The Challenge and Hidden Promise of Globalisation*, London: Random House.

Peters, T.J. and Waterman, R.H. (1982) *In Search of Excellence: Lessons from America's Best Run Companies*, New York: Harper and Row.

Pettigrew, A. (1985), *The Awakening Giant: Continuity and Changes in ICI*, Oxford: Basil Blackwell.

Pfeffer, J. (1977) The Ambiguity of Leadership, *Academy of Management Review*, 2, pp. 104–12.

Pfeffer, J. (1981) *Power in Organizations*, Boston, MA: Pitman.

Pfeffer, J. and Salancik, G.R. (1978) *The External Control of Organizations: A Resource Dependence Perspective*, New York: Harper and Row.

Phelan, P. and Reynolds, P. (1996) *Argument and Evidence: Critical Analysis for the Social Sciences*, London: Routledge.

Phillips, D.J. (1971) *Knowledge from What? Theories and Methods in Social Research*, Chicago: Rand-McNally.

Pollard, S.J. (1965) *The Genesis of Modern Management*, London: Edward Arnold.

Pollard, S.J. (1982) *The Wasting of the British Economy*, London: Croom Helm.

Powell, R.M. (1963) Elements of Executive Promotion, *California Management Review*, 6, pp. 83–90.

Punch, M. (1981) *Management and Control of Organizations: Occupational Deviance, Responsibility and Accountability,* Leiden/Antwerp: H.E. Steinfert Kroese.

Quaid, M. (1993) Job Evaluation as an Institutional Myth, *Journal of Management Studies*, 30 (2), pp. 239–60.

Quinn, R.E. (1988) *Beyond Rational Management: Mastering the Paradoxes and Competing Demands of High Performance*, San Francisco: Jossey-Bass.

Quinn, R.P., Kahn, R.L., Tabor, J.M. and Gordon, L.K. (1968) *The Chosen Few: A Study of Discrimination in Executive Selection*, Ann Arbor, Michigan: Institute for Social Research, University of Michigan.

Quinn, R.P., Tabor, J.M. and Gordon, L.K. (1968) *The Decision to Discriminate: A Study of Executive Selection*, Ann Arbor, Michigan: Institute for Social Research, University of Michigan.

Rahim, A. (1981) Organizational Behavior Courses for Graduate Students in Business Administration: Views from the Tower and Battlefield, *Psychological Reports*, 49, pp. 583–92.

Rapoport, R. (1970) Three Dilemmas in Action Research, *Human Relations*, 23, pp. 488–513.

Raube, S.A. (1954) Principles of Good Organization, reprinted in M.D. Richards and W.A. Nielander (eds) (1969) *Readings in Management*, Cincinnati, OH: South-Western Publishing, pp. 689–700.

Reed, M.I. (1989) *The Sociology of Management*, Hemel Hempstead: Harvester Wheatsheaf.

Reischauer, E.O. and Craig, A.M. (1979) *Japan: Tradition and Transformation*, Sydney: Allen and Unwin.

Richards, M.D. and Nielander, W.A. (1969), *Readings in Management*, Cincinnati, OH: South-Western Publishing.

Robertson, I.T. and Cooper, C.L. (1983) *Human Behaviour in Organizations*, Estover, Plymouth: Macdonald and Evans.

Robertson, I.T. and Makin, P.J. (1986) Management Selection in Britain: A Survey and Critique, *Journal of Occupational Psychology*, 59, pp. 45–57.

Rose, H. and Rose, S. (eds) (2000) *Alas Poor Darwin: Arguments Against Evolutionary Psychology*, London: Jonathan Cape.

Rose, M. (1988), *Industrial Behaviour*, Harmondsworth: Penguin.

Rose, S., Lewontin, R.C. and Kamin, L.J. (1990) *Not in Our Genes: Biology, Ideology and Human Nature*, London: Penguin.

Rosener, J.B. (1990) Ways Women Lead, *Harvard Business Review*, November–December, pp. 119–25.

Salaman, G. (1981) *Class and the Corporation*, Glasgow: Fontana.

Salaman, G. and Thompson, K. (1978) Class Culture and the Persistence of an Elite: The Case of Army Officer Selection, *Sociological Review*, 26, pp. 283–304.

Salancik, G.R. and Pfeffer, J. (1977) Constraints on Administrator Discretion: The Limited Influence of Mayors on City Budgets, *Urban Affairs Quarterly*, 12, pp. 475–97.

Samuelson, B.A., Galbraith, C.S. and McGuire, J.W. (1985) Organizational Performance and Top-Management Turnover, *Organization Studies*, 6, pp. 275–91.

Saunders, J. and Wong, V. (1985) In Search of Excellence in the UK, *Journal of Marketing Management*, 1, pp. 119–37.

Savoie, A., Cournoyer, L.G. and Nadeau, D. (1996) The Influence of the Manager on the Economic Effectiveness of His Financial Institution, *Le Travail humain*, 59 (2), pp. 155–72.

Sayer, A. (1992), *Method in Social Science: A Realist Approach*, London: Routledge.

Sayles, L.R. (1989), *Leadership: Managing in Real Organizations*, New York: McGraw-Hill.

Schon, D. (1983) *The Reflective Practitioner*, London: Temple Smith.

Schonberger, R.J. (1982) The Transfer of Japanese Manufacturing Management Approaches to US Industry, *Academy of Management Review*, 7, pp. 477–87.

Schumacher, E.F. (1995) *A Guide for the Perplexed*, London: Vintage.

Schwenk, C.R. (1990) Illusions of Management Control? Effects of Self-Serving Attributions on Resource Commitments and Confidence in Management, *Human Relations*, 4, pp. 333–47.

Scott, J. and Rochester, A. (1984) *What Is a Manager?* London: Sphere/BIM.

Seear, N. and Pearn, M. (1983) Selection Within the Law, in B. Ungerson (ed.) *Recruitment Handbook*, London: Gower, pp. 331–46.

Senge, P.M. (1990) *The Fifth Discipline: The Art and Practice of the Learning Organization*, New York: Doubleday.

Sethi, S.P., Namiki, N. and Swanson, C.L. (1984) *The False Promise of the Japanese Miracle: Illusions and Realities of the Japanese System*, Marshfield, MA: Pitman.

Sexton, P.C. (1967) *The American School: A Sociological Analysis*, Englewood Cliffs, New Jersey: Prentice-Hall.

Shakespeare, T. and Erickson, M. (2000) Different Strokes: Beyond Biological Determinism and Social Constructionism, in H. Rose and S. Rose (eds) *Alas Poor Darwin: Arguments Against Evolutionary Psychology*, London: Jonathan Cape, pp. 190–205.

Sheldon, O. (1923) *The Philosophy of Management*, London: Pitman.

Shipman, M. (1972, 1988, 1997) *The Limitations of Social Research*, London: Longman.

Shipman, M. (1976) *The Organization and Impact of Social Research*, London: Routledge and Kegan Paul.

Simon, H.A. (1947) *Administrative Behaviour*, New York: Macmillan.

Sisson, K. and Storey, J. (2000) *The Realities of Human Resource Management: Managing the Employment Relationship*, Buckingham: Open University Press.

Sklair, l. (1995) *Sociology of the Global System*, London: Harvester.

Smith, J.E., Carson, K.P. and Alexander, R.A. (1984) Leadership: It Can make A Difference, *Academy of Management Journal*, 27, pp. 765–76.

Smith, P.B. and Misumi, J. (1989) Japanese Management: A Sun Rising in the West?, in C.L. Cooper and I.T. Robertson (eds) *International Review of Industrial and Organizational Psychology*, Chichester: John Wiley, pp. 330–71.

Sneath, F., Thakur, M. and Medjuck, B. (1976) *Testing People at Work*, London: IPM.

Soeters, J.L. (1986) Excellent Companies as Social Movements, *Journal of Management Studies*, 23, pp. 299–312.

Stephenson, T. (1985) *Management: A Political Activity*, Basingstoke: Macmillan.

Stewart, R. (1967) *Managers and Their Jobs*, Maidenhead: McGraw-Hill.

Stewart, R. (1976) *Contrasts in Management*, Maidenhead: McGraw-Hill.

Stewart, R. (1982) *Choices for the Manager*, Englewood Cliffs, New Jersey: Prentice-Hall.

Stewart, R. (1983) Managerial Behaviour: How Research Has Changed the Traditional Picture, in M.J. Earl (ed.) *Perspectives on Management*, London: Oxford University Press, pp. 82–9.

Stogdill, R.M. (1974) *Handbook of Leadership: A Survey of Theory and Research*, New York: Free Press.

Sullivan, J.J. (1983) A Critique of Theory Z, *Academy of Management Review*, 8, pp. 132–42.

Takamiya, S. and Thurley, K. (1985) *Japan's Emerging Multinationals: An International Comparison of Policies and Practices*, Tokyo: Tokyo University Press.

Thomas, A.B. (1978) The British Business Elite: The Case of the Retail Sector, *Sociological Review*, 26, pp. 305–26.

Thomas, A.B. (1980) Management and Education: Rationalisation and Reproduction in British Business, *International Studies of Management and Organization*, Spring/Summer, pp. 71–109.

Thomas, A.B. (1983) Managerial Careers and the Problem of Control, *Social Science Information*, 22, pp. 1–25.

Thomas, A.B. (1988) Does Leadership Make a Difference to Organizational Performance? *Administrative Science Quarterly*, 33, pp. 388–400.

Thomas, A.B. (1989) One Minute Management Education: A Sign of the Times? *Management Education and Development*, 20 (1), pp. 23–38.

Thomas, A.B. (1991) Leadership and Change in British Retailing 1955–1984, *The Service Industries Journal*, 11, pp. 381–92.

Thomas, A.B. (1996) Working in Space: Skylab, in A.B. Thomas (ed.) *The Organizational Behaviour Casebook: Cases and Concepts in Organizational Behaviour*, London: Thomson, pp. 214–26.

Thomas, A.B. (1997) The Coming Crisis of Western Management Education, *Systems Practice*, 10 (6), pp. 681–701.

Thomas, A.B. (1999) Organizing the Past: A History and its (De)Construction, *Studies in Cultures, Organizations and Societies*, 5, pp. 151–77.

Thomas, A.B. (2001) Women at the Top in British Retailing: A Longitudinal Analysis, *The Service Industries Journal*, 21 (3), pp. 1–12.

Thomas, A.B. (2003) *Research Skills for Management Studies*, London: Routledge.

Thomas, A.B. and Anthony, P.D. (1996) Can Management Education Be Educational? in R. French and C. Grey (eds) *Rethinking Management Education*, London: Sage, pp. 17–35.

Thompson, I. (1986) *Religion*, London: Longman.

Thompson, J.D. (1956) On Building an Administrative Science, *Administrative Science Quarterly*, 1, pp. 102–11.

Thompson, P. (1993) Postmodernism: Fatal Distraction, in J. Hassard and M. Parker (eds) *Postmodernism and Organizations*, London: Sage, pp. 183–203.

Thompson, P. and McHugh, D. (2002) *Work Organizations: A Critical Introduction*, Basingstoke: Palgrave.

Thomson, A. (1996) *Critical Reasoning: A Practical Introduction*, London: Routledge.

Thorngate, W. (1976) Possible Limits on a Science of Social Behaviour, in L.H. Strickland, F.E. Aboud and K.J. Gergen (eds) *Social Psychology in Transition*, New York: Plenum, pp. 121–30.

Thouless, R.H. (1953) *Straight and Crooked Thinking*, London: Pan.

Tjosvold, D. (1985) Implications of Controversy Research for Management, *Journal of Management*, 11, pp. 21–37.

Tolstoy, L.N. (1957), *War and Peace*, 2 vols, trans. Rosemary Edmonds, Harmondsworth: Penguin, first published 1869.

Tranfield, D. and Starkey, K. (1998) The Nature, Social Organization and Promotion of Management Research: Towards Policy, *British Journal of Management*, 9, pp. 341–53.

Trevor, M. (1983) Does Japanese Management Work in Britain? *Journal of General Management*, 8, pp. 28–43.

Tsuru, S. (1993) *Japan's Capitalism: Creative Defeat and Beyond*, Cambridge: Cambridge University Press.

Tsurumi, Y. (1981) Productivity: The Japanese Approach, *Pacific Basin Quarterly*, 6, pp. 7–11.

Turner, I. and Henry, I. (1996) In Search of the Transnational: A Study of Structural Choice in International Companies, in P. Joynt and M. Warner (eds) *Managing Across Cultures: Issues and Perspectives*, London: Thomson, pp. 310–25.

Turner, S.P. and Turner, J.H. (1990) *The Impossible Science: An Institutional Analysis of American Sociology*, London: Sage.

Udwadia, F.E. (1986) Management Situations and the Engineering Mindset, *Technological Forecasting and Social Change*, 29, pp. 387–97.

Ueki, H. (1982) *Transfer of Management Skill*, Tokyo: Bushindo.

Urwick, L.F. (1933) Organization as a Technical Problem, reprinted in L. Gulick and L.F. Urwick (eds) (1937) *Papers on the Science of Administration*, New York: Columbia University Press, pp. 49–88.

Urwick, L.F. (1943) *The Elements of Administration*, London: Pitman.

Useem, M. and Karabel, J. (1986) Pathways to Top Corporate Management, *American Sociological Review*, 51, pp. 184–200.

van Dijk, J. (1999) *The Network Society: Social Aspects of New Media*, London: Sage.

Vickers, G. (1970) *Freedom in a Rocking Boat: Changing Values in an Unstable Society*, London: Allen Lane.

Vogel, E. (1980) *Japan as Number One: Lessons for America*, Cambridge, MA: Harvard University Press.

Wajcman, J. (1998) *Managing Like a Man: Women and Men in Corporate Management*, University Park, PA: Pennsylvania State University Press.

Warmington, A. (1980) Action Research: Its Methods and its Implications, *Journal of Applied Systems Analysis*, 7, pp. 23–39.

Waters, M. (2001) *Globalization*, London: Routledge.

Watson, T.J. (1986) *Management, Organization and Employment Strategy*, London: Routledge and Kegan Paul.

Watson, T.J. (1990) *Sociology, Work and Industry*, London: Routledge.

Watson, T.J. (2001) *In Search of Management*, London: Thomson.

Watson, T.J. (2002) *Organizing and Managing Work: Organizational, Managerial and Strategic Behaviour in Theory and Practice*, Harlow: Pearson.

Weber, M. (1946) *From Max Weber: Essays in Sociology*, in H.H. Gerth and C.W. Mills (eds) New York: Oxford University Press.

Weiner, N. (1978) Situational and Leadership Influences on Organization Performance, *Proceedings of the Academy of Management*, pp. 230–34.

Weiner, N. and Mahoney, T.A. (1981) A Model of Corporate Performance as a Function of Environmental, Organizational and Leadership Influences, *Academy of Management Journal*, 24, pp. 453–70.

Welch, J. (1998) Women 'Not Programmed to Succeed in the Workplace', *People Management*, November 12, p. 21.

Wellington, J.J. (ed.) (1986) *Controversial Issues in the Curriculum*, Oxford: Basil Blackwell.

Westergaard, J. and Resler, H. (1975) *Class in a Capitalist Society*, London: Heinemann.

Wheatley, M. (1992) *The Future of Middle Management*, Corby: BIM.

White, M. and Trevor, M. (1983) *Under Japanese Management: The Experience of British Workers*, London: Heinemann.

Wiener, M.J. (1981) *English Culture and the Decline of the Industrial Spirit*, London: Cambridge University Press.

Willmott, H.C. (1984) Images and Ideals of Managerial Work: A Critical Examination of Conceptual and Empirical Accounts, *Journal of Management Studies*, 21, pp. 349–68.

Wilson, E.O. (1975) *Sociobiology: The New Synthesis*, Cambridge, MA: Harvard University Press.

Wilson, D.C. (1998) Foreword to Tranfield and Starkey, *British Journal of Management*, 9, p. 341.

Wilson, W. (1887) The Study of Administration, *Political Science Quarterly*, 2, pp. 197–222.

Womack, J.P., Jones, D.T. and Ross, D. (1990) *The Machine That Changed the World*, New York: Rawson Associates, Macmillan.

Womack, J.P. and Jones, D.T. (1996) *Lean Thinking*, New York: Simon and Schuster.

Wood, S. (1986) Personnel Management and Recruitment, *Personnel Review*, 15, pp. 3–11.

Woodward, J. (1958) *Management and Technology*, London: HMSO.

World Bank (2001) *World Development Indicators 2001*, Washington, DC: World Bank.

Woronoff, J. (1983) *Japan's Wasted Workers*, Totowa, New Jersey: Allenheld, Osmun.

Woronoff, J. (1993) Japan Ends Its Life Sentence, *Asian Business*, December, pp. 46–7.

Yukl, G. (1989) Managerial Leadership: A Review of Theory and Research, *Journal of Management*, 15, pp. 251–89.

Zaleznik, A. (1970) Power and Politics in Organizational Life, *Harvard Business Review*, May–June, pp. 47–60.

Author Index

Subject Index